THE SIEGFRIED LINE

The Stackpole Military History Series

**THE AMERICAN
CIVIL WAR**
Cavalry Raids of the Civil War
Ghost, Thunderbolt, and
   Wizard
Pickett's Charge
Witness to Gettysburg

WORLD WAR I
Doughboy War

WORLD WAR II
After D-Day
Armor Battles of the Waffen-
   SS, 1943–45
Armoured Guardsmen
Army of the West
Australian Commandos
The B-24 in China
Backwater War
The Battle of Sicily
Battle of the Bulge, Vol. 1
Battle of the Bulge, Vol. 2
Beyond the Beachhead
Beyond Stalingrad
The Brandenburger
   Commandos
The Brigade
Bringing the Thunder
The Canadian Army and the
   Normandy Campaign
Coast Watching in
   World War II
Colossal Cracks
A Dangerous Assignment
D-Day Deception
D-Day to Berlin
Destination Normandy
Dive Bomber!
A Drop Too Many
Eagles of the Third Reich
Eastern Front Combat
Exit Rommel
Fist from the Sky
Flying American Combat
   Aircraft of World War II
Forging the Thunderbolt
Fortress France
The German Defeat in the
   East, 1944–45
German Order of Battle, Vol. 1
German Order of Battle, Vol. 2
German Order of Battle, Vol. 3
The Germans in Normandy

Germany's Panzer Arm in
   World War II
GI Ingenuity
Goodwood
The Great Ships
Grenadiers
Hitler's Nemesis
Infantry Aces
Iron Arm
Iron Knights
Kampfgruppe Peiper at the
   Battle of the Bulge
The Key to the Bulge
Kursk
Luftwaffe Aces
Luftwaffe Fighter Ace
Massacre at Tobruk
Mechanized Juggernaut or
   Military Anachronism?
Messerschmitts over Sicily
Michael Wittmann, Vol. 1
Michael Wittmann, Vol. 2
Mountain Warriors
The Nazi Rocketeers
No Holding Back
On the Canal
Operation Mercury
Packs On!
Panzer Aces
Panzer Aces II
Panzer Commanders of the
   Western Front
Panzer Gunner
The Panzer Legions
Panzers in Normandy
Panzers in Winter
The Path to Blitzkrieg
Penalty Strike
Red Road from Stalingrad
Red Star under the Baltic
Retreat to the Reich
Rommel's Desert Commanders
Rommel's Desert War
Rommel's Lieutenants
The Savage Sky
The Siegfried Line
A Soldier in the Cockpit
Soviet Blitzkrieg
Stalin's Keys to Victory
Surviving Bataan and Beyond
T-34 in Action
Tank Tactics
Tigers in the Mud
Triumphant Fox

The 12th SS, Vol. 1
The 12th SS, Vol. 2
Twilight of the Gods
The War against Rommel's
   Supply Lines
War in the Aegean
Wolfpack Warriors
Zhukov at the Oder

**THE COLD WAR /
VIETNAM**
Cyclops in the Jungle
Expendable Warriors
Flying American Combat
   Aircraft: The Cold War
Here There Are Tigers
Land with No Sun
Phantom Reflections
Street without Joy
Through the Valley

**WARS OF THE
MIDDLE EAST**
Never-Ending Conflict

**GENERAL MILITARY
HISTORY**
Carriers in Combat
Cavalry from Hoof to Track
Desert Battles
Guerrilla Warfare
Ranger Dawn
Sieges

THE SIEGFRIED LINE

The German Defense of the West Wall,
September–December 1944

Samuel W. Mitcham, Jr.

STACKPOLE
BOOKS

Published by
STACKPOLE BOOKS
5067 Ritter Road
Mechanicsburg, PA 17055
www.stackpolebooks.com

Cover design by Tracy Patterson

Printed in the United States of America

10 9 8 7 6 5 4 3 2 1

Library of Congress Cataloging-in-Publication Data

Mitcham, Samuel W.
  The Siegfried Line : German defense of the west wall, September–December 1944 / Samuel W. Mitcham, Jr.
      p. cm. — (Stackpole military history series)
  Includes bibliographical references and index.
  ISBN 978-0-8117-3602-2
  1. World War, 1939–1945—Campaigns—Germany. 2. Siegfried Line (Germany) 3. World War, 1939–1945—Campaigns—Western Front. I. Title.
    D757.9.S47M58 2009
    940.54'2134—dc22
                                    2008048377

Contents

CHAPTER 1

The Great Wall of Hitler

The original Siegfried Line (*Siegfriedstellung*) was a series of forts, bunkers, and defensive positions built along the German border with France as part of the Hindenburg Line during World War I. After the war, the Siegfried Line fell into disrepair. During the 1930s, Germany constructed a new defensive zone opposite France's Maginot Line using many of the old Siegfried positions. It extended farther north than the original, to a point north of the German-Dutch border where the Rhine turns west into the Netherlands, roughly twenty miles northeast of Eindhoven. The Germans, incidentally, never called this second position the Siegfried Line; to them, it was the West Wall (*Westwall*). Only the Allies referred to it by its Great War–era name. The British, in fact, wrote a popular song in 1939 about how they were going to hang their laundry on it.

✠

World War I ended on November 11, 1918, and Germany's Second Reich was replaced by the Weimar Republic. The peace terms forced on Germany by the Treaty of Versailles were harsh. Among other things, the German armed forces (*Reichswehr*) were limited to 115,000 men—100,000 in the army (*Reichsheer*) and 15,000 in the navy (*Reichsmarine*). The German military remained at roughly these levels until January 30, 1933, when Adolf Hitler and his Nazi Party (the *Nationalsozialistische Deutsche Arbeiterpartei*, or NSDAP) took power in Germany and established the Third Reich.[1]

Hitler rapidly established his dictatorship in 1933 and set about Nazifying every aspect of German life. In foreign affairs, he pursued a policy of "making Germany great again," to the approval of the vast majority of German citizens. On March 9, 1935, he officially established the German *Luftwaffe* (air force), which had been building up clandestinely since 1933. When the response of the former Allies was muted, Hitler renounced the Treaty of Versailles altogether on March 16 and announced that Germany was expanding its 100,000-man army (ten divisions) to 550,000 men (thirty-six divisions). Three of the new divisions were panzer units; under the terms of the treaty, Germany had not been allowed to have tanks.

On February 4, 1938, Hitler established his military organization for the next war. As Fuehrer, he was the supreme war lord. Under him was the High Command of the Armed Forces (*Oberkommando der Wehrmacht*, or OKW), which was headed by Hitler's notorious yes-man Gen. of Artillery Wilhelm Keitel.[2] Theoretically subordinate to OKW were the High Command of the Army (*Oberkommando des Heeres*, or OKH), the High Command of the Air Force (*Oberkommando der Luftwaffe*, or OKL), and the High Command of the Navy (*Oberkommando der Marine*, or OKM). However, the supreme commander of the *Luftwaffe*, Field Marshal (later *Reichsmarschall*) Hermann Goering pointedly refused to accept orders from Keitel, and OKM under Grand Adm. Erich Raeder (and later Karl Doenitz) also remained virtually independent of OKW. Even so, Germany was a traditional land power; whoever controlled the army controlled the German military, and whoever controlled the military controlled the Reich. Hitler sacked the last independent commander in chief of the army, Col. Gen. Baron Werner von Fritsch,[3] on trumped-up charges of homosexuality and, on February 4, 1938, replaced him with Gen. of Artillery Walter von Brauchitsch, a man who was willing to compromise. By purging the army of its top anti-Nazi generals—as well as some who merely were not members of the Nazi Party[4]—and replacing them with officers who were more sympathetic to the NSDAP, Brauchitsch essentially handed the army over to Hitler. In exchange, the Nazis paid off Brauchitsch's wife, who wanted a cash settlement in lieu of alimony; in turn, she agreed to divorce him quietly, rather than expose his infidelities publicly and create a messy scandal. Brauchitsch was promoted to colonel general that same day and married his fanatically pro-Nazi mistress shortly thereafter.[5] Meanwhile, the German military expansion continued.

Hitler had begun his *Blumenkriegen* ("Flower Wars") at dawn on March 7, 1936, when he reoccupied the Rhineland, which had been demilitarized under the terms of the Treaty of Versailles. The peaceful annexation of Austria (called the *Anschluss*) followed in March 1938. Hitler pushed the world to the brink of war, however, when he tried to force Czechoslovakia to hand over the predominately German Sudetenland in the summer and fall of 1938.

By the autumn of 1938, the Third Reich had forty-seven regular army divisions: thirty-four infantry, four motorized, three mountain, three light and only three panzer, with a fourth panzer and fourth light division in the process of being formed. Germany also had enough trained reservists to form eight new divisions very quickly. In addition, it had twenty-one *Landwehr* divisions, made up of men aged thirty-five to forty-five (many of them World War I veterans), but their usefulness was limited to holding static positions against less than all-out assaults.

To direct the campaign against Czechoslovakia, OKH mobilized ten army headquarters and one army group headquarters in August 1938. Seven armies were earmarked to overrun Czechoslovakia. Army Group 2 under Gen. of Infantry Wilhelm Adam was charged with the task of defending the Western Front against Prague's allies, France and Britain. Headquartered at Frankfurt am Main, this army group controlled three armies: the 7th, under Gen. of Infantry Baron Hans Seutter von Loetzen, in the south defending the eastern bank of the Rhine; the 1st, under Gen. of Artillery Ludwig Beck, defending the Rhineland between Karlsruhe and Trier; and the 5th, under Gen. of Infantry Curt Liebmann, in the north, opposite the Low Countries, screening Adam's right flank.[6]

Adam's force of three armies looked very impressive, but only on paper. An "army" is primarily a headquarters unit, not a self-contained combat formation; it is no stronger than the forces assigned to it.[7] General Adam had only five active-duty divisions—all of them marching infantry, not motorized or mechanized infantry. He also had four fairly good reserve infantry divisions and five marginal *Landwehr* divisions. But he faced several French armies with more than 100 divisions. Naturally, he made strengthening the West Wall, which had been largely neglected between 1919 and 1938, a top priority. During the Rhineland crisis of 1936, German labor battalions had worked feverishly on the fortifications, but when the crisis passed, the West Wall lost its priority and was again neglected.

All of this would soon change. On May 28, 1938, Hitler called a meeting at his chancellery. Present were Keitel; Goering; Brauchitsch; Beck, then chief of the General Staff; Raeder; Foreign Minister Joachim von Ribbentrop; and Konstantin von Neurath, the recently deposed foreign minister and now a minister without portfolio.[8] To the shock of most of those present, Hitler announced that it was his "unshakable will" to wipe Czechoslovakia off the map. He ordered that full military preparations—not just planning—for the invasion of Czechoslovakia be completed by October 1. He further ordered that the army plan for the mobilization of ninety-six divisions (a completely unrealistic idea) and that the construction of the West Wall be greatly accelerated. He placed Dr. Fritz Todt, the builder of Germany's highways, in charge of the construction. Soon dozens of Reich Labor Service battalions and tens of thousands of men were working on it, all under the general supervision of the army.[9] They could not fully reverse nineteen years of neglect.

On August 4, 1938, at the urging of General Beck, Brauchitsch called a conference of army and corps commanders in Berlin. Here General Adam told the generals that the West Wall was totally inadequate for its mission and was only partially manned. It could not hold out for long. Knowing that some of the pro-Nazi generals would relay Adam's words to Hitler, Brauchitsch carried a memorandum from General Beck to the Fuehrer the next day. Hitler's reaction was unprecedented. He invited all officers designated to be a chief of staff of an army in the Czechoslovakian invasion to a luncheon at the Berghof on August 10. This was a flagrant violation of protocol because the army commanders and other senior generals were not invited. Privately, Hitler said that he would take Czechoslovakia with one set of generals and fight his next campaign with another set.

After lunch, the dictator spoke for three hours. He told the officers that the French could not penetrate the West Wall. He was interrupted and contradicted by Gen. of Infantry Gustav von Wietersheim, the chief of staff of Army Group 2 and the senior officer present, who repeated Adam's assessment of the situation and his conclusion that the West Wall could not be held for three weeks against a major French attack. Hitler immediately flew into a rage and called the generals defeatists and scoundrels. When he regained a measure of control over himself, he assured Wietersheim that the West Wall could be held for *three years.* The officers were shocked and intimidated by Hitler's tantrum, and no one dared to question his invasion plans further. According to Erich von Manstein, who was present at the meeting, this was the last time Hitler permitted any questions or discussions from his military officers.[10]

Brauchitsch, naturally, immediately fell in line behind the Fuehrer. In view of Hitler's attitude, and with no support from his commander in chief, General Beck resigned as chief of the General Staff on August 18. Hitler accepted his resignation on August 21 and replaced him with Gen. of Artillery Franz Halder.[11] Adam then named Beck commander of his most important army (the 1st) in the center of his line.

The crisis continued to boil throughout August 1938. On August 26, Hitler began a personal inspection of the West Wall, accompanied by Dr. Todt; Konstantin Hierl, the head of the Reich Labor Service; Reichsfuehrer-SS Heinrich Himmler; Alfred Jodl, the chief of operations at OKW; and others. To Hitler's untrained eye, the progress was impressive, and the entire inspection was an exercise in unfounded optimism.

Wilhelm Adam did not join the party until August 27. By the twenty-ninth, he had had enough of Hitler's cronies, who heaped praise on the supposedly impenetrable fortifications. He abruptly told Hitler that he wished to speak to him in private. The entourage guffed and snickered, but Adam got his private audience with the Fuehrer. When he told the dictator that the West Wall could not be held against a major French offensive, Hitler flew into another rage. "The man who doesn't hold these fortifications is a scoundrel!" he screamed hysterically,[12] adding that the general in charge would have to be "a despicable fellow not to hold these fortifications for as long as it should be required."[13] He ended the meeting by telling Adam that his only regret was that he was Fuehrer and therefore could not be Supreme Commander of the Western Front.

Hitler was saved from his own rashness by the Munich accords. On September 29, 1938, British prime minister Neville Chamberlain, the champion of appeasement, and French premier Edouard Daladier signed an agreement with Hitler and Mussolini in which they sacrificed the Sudetenland in order to avoid war with the Third Reich. They did not realize it at the time, but they were also sacrificing all of

Czechoslovakia, for Hitler gobbled it up without firing a shot in March 1939. Meanwhile, General Adam retired on November 9, 1938, with the honorary rank of colonel general. He was also named honorary colonel of the 98th Mountain Infantry Regiment—a high tribute in the German Army in 1938. Ludwig Beck was also promoted to colonel general on the retired list effective November 1, 1938, and was named honorary colonel of the 5th Artillery Regiment. Neither would be employed during World War II.[14]

✠

As we have seen, the construction of the West Wall began in earnest in 1936 and went through several phases. The initial construction phase was called the Border Watch (*Grenzwacht*) program, during which only the most advanced positions—right along the French border—were constructed along the most obvious routes of potential enemy advances. The bunkers built at this time were small and exposed, with three embrasures (firing portals) situated at the front and small, round, armored "lookout" sections on the roof. The walls were only 20 inches thick, so they offered protection from bullets, shrapnel, and grenades but were vulnerable to even medium-range artillery. These bunkers were also uncomfortable—the soldiers did not have beds, for example, only hammocks.

In 1938, during the Sudetenland crisis, the Limes Program began. Some 3,500 pillboxes and hundreds of tank traps were built all along the border of western Germany during this phase, and they were more solidly constructed. Construction of bunkers (commonly called pillboxes) and tank traps was standardized because of the lack of raw materials, transport, workers, and, above all, time. Each bunker required 10,000 cubic feet of concrete to construct. The ceilings and walls were 5 feet thick, and the bunker had a central room that provided shelter for about a dozen men, as well as a combat section, which was constructed 19 inches higher. It included front and side embrasures for machine guns and several smaller embrasures for rifles, a safety oven, and a chimney covered with a thick grating to protect it against hand grenades. Each man had a sleeping space and a stool; only the commanding officer or NCO had a chair. The men had only about three square feet of living area apiece.

The tank traps consisted mainly of reinforced concrete obstacles called *Hoeckern* or "humps," which were also referred to as "dragon's teeth." They were generally arranged in four or five rows and increased in height from the first row to the last. When the terrain allowed it, steep ditches filled with water were dug instead of building the more expensive dragon's teeth. The Americans would later run into this type of obstacle, most famously near Geilenkirchen.

In 1939, the Organization Todt initiated the Aachen-Saar Program, in which construction of the West Wall focused on those geographical areas, though not exclusively. The bunkers built during this program featured double machine-gun casemates with concrete walls up to 11.5 feet thick. Most of these bunkers had no embrasures at the front, only on the sides. Even so, Adolf Hitler was proud of his accomplishments in the west. "I am the greatest builder of all time!" he crowed to his entourage of yes-men, who naturally concurred wholeheartedly.

After Hitler invaded Poland on September 1, 1939, the Geldern Program began, with the main construction taking place between Brueggen near Düsseldorf and Cleve near the Dutch border. The main positions built during this time were concrete dugouts.

By the time Hitler's generals were ready to invade France the following spring, the West Wall extended more than 390 miles, from Cleve to Weil am Rhein on the Swiss frontier. Although not impressive when compared to the French Maginot Line, it included more than 18,000 bunkers and tank traps. Construction on the Siegfried Line continued until May 10, 1940, when German panzers roared into the Low Countries. Ten days later, they reached the English Channel west of Abbeville, cutting off the main French and British armies north of Paris. The Dunkirk Pocket was eliminated on June 4, Paris fell on June 14, and France surrendered on June 21. Hitler and his men promptly forgot all about the West Wall, which quickly fell into disrepair. All of its weapons were removed and sent elsewhere, and its bunkers were either abandoned or used by local residents, mainly for storing farm equipment. The German Army and Fuehrer Headquarters lost all interest in it for the next four years.

CHAPTER 2

The Retreat

While the West Wall deteriorated, Hitler turned his attention to all points of the compass. In 1940, his *Luftwaffe* assaulted England, only to be checked in the Battle of Britain. Then, after ordering the Afrika Korps to Libya in February 1941, German troops overran the Balkans that spring and—against the advice of most of his generals—invaded Russia on June 22, 1941. Although the Germans won some spectacular victories on the Eastern Front, the Soviets ultimately stopped them within six miles of the Kremlin in December 1941. The two-front war—a major contributing factor to the German defeat in World War I—again became a reality.

In March 1942, Hitler was able to battle the Soviet Union to a stalemate following Stalin's winter offensive of 1941–42. Then the Germans drove to the Volga and into the Caucasus before being decisively defeated at Stalingrad the following winter.

After the remnants of the German 6th Army surrendered at Stalingrad on February 2, 1943, the *Wehrmacht* fell back on all active fronts. The German Navy was decisively defeated in the Battle of the North Atlantic in May 1943, just as Army Group Afrika surrendered in Tunisia. Allied invasions of Sicily and Italy followed, along with the Battle of Kursk, Hitler's last major offensive in the east. Of perhaps greater significance, the *Luftwaffe* was also decisively defeated in 1943–44, and Germany was forced to endure a rain of Allied bombs—and occasionally firestorms caused by incendiary bombs.

With their control of the air and sea, the Allies were able to launch their long-awaited invasion of western Europe on June 6, 1944. Field Marshal Erwin Rommel, the legendary "Desert Fox" and now commander in chief of Army Group B, was able to check—but not repulse—the great invasion. The Third Reich had lost its last, best chance to survive the war.

Hitler had entrusted the defense of the Western Front to OB West, the German abbreviation for *Oberbefehlshaber West*, a term that referred to the Supreme Commander of the Western Front or his headquarters. Since March 1942, the OB West had been Field Marshal Gerd von Rundstedt, a sixty-eight-year-old Prussian who had commanded army groups in Poland (1939), the west (1940), and Russia (1941).[1] Table 1 shows the order of battle of OB West on June 6, 1944, and the map on page 10 shows Normandy and the D-Day landings.

TABLE 1: ORDER OF BATTLE, OB WEST, JUNE 6, 1944

OB West: Field Marshal Gerd von Rundstedt

Army Group B: Field Marshal Erwin Rommel
　　　　Armed Force Netherlands: Gen. of Fliers Friedrich Christiansen
　　　　15th Army: Col. Gen. Hans von Salmuth
　　　　7th Army: Col. Gen. Friedrich Dollmann

Army Group G: Col. Gen. Johannes Blaskowitz
　　　　19th Army: Gen. of Infantry Georg Sodenstern[a]
　　　　1st Army: Gen. of Infantry Kurt von der Chevallerie

Panzer Group West[b]: Gen. of Panzer Troops Baron Leo Geyr von Schweppenburg

1st Parachute Army[c]: *Luftwaffe* Col. Gen. Kurt Student

---

a. Succeeded by Gen. of Infantry Friedrich Wiese on June 29, 1944.
b. Upgraded to 5th Panzer Army, August 5, 1944.
c. On June 6, the 1st Parachute Army was employed as a training command only.

There were heavy casualties from the beginning. On D-Day, the Allies lost more than 10,000 men, but they landed more than 156,000 men and more than 1,200 tanks.[2] Of the five Allied beachheads—Gold, Juno, Sword, Omaha, and Utah—only Omaha Beach was still in jeopardy when the sun set.

After June 6, some of the Allied bombers turned their attention back to the French rail and highway systems, which they had already

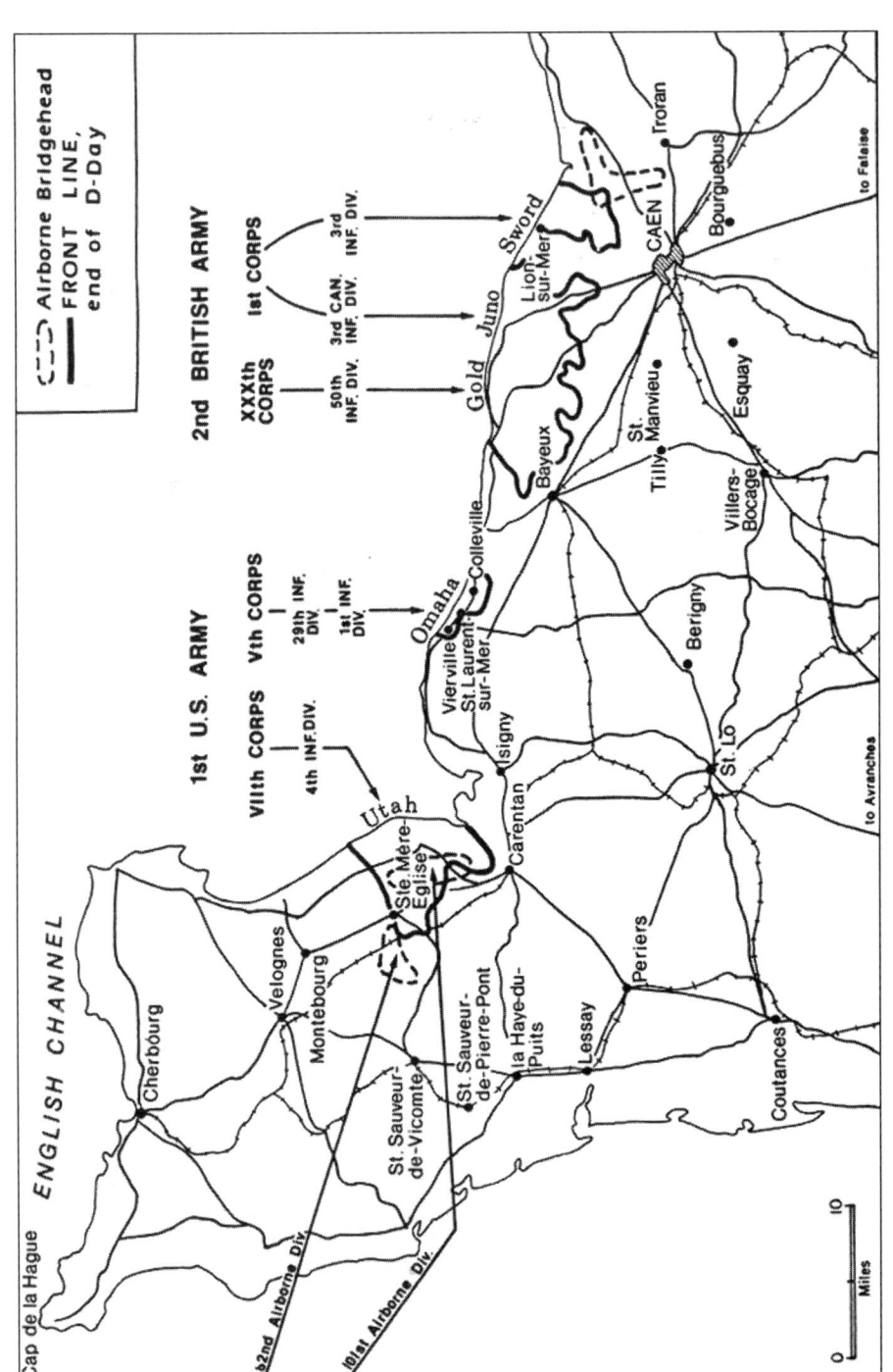

The Allied Invasion of Normandy

devastated. Before the Allied antirail offensive began in April 1944, the German transportation staff had been running more than 100 supply trains a day in France; this figure had been reduced to 20 by the end of May. All of the important highway bridges were also bombed. After D-Day, the French National Railway was operating at 10 percent of its normal capacity, and Normandy was, for all practical purposes, a strategic island.[3] Because of the Allied control of the air—augmented by the French Resistance, which cut railroads thousands of times in June 1944—Rommel was able to reinforce his front at only a fraction of the speed that Eisenhower did. By June 12, for example, the Allies had 326,000 soldiers in Normandy; Rommel may have had 120,000.[4] As a result, Army Group B was gradually crushed.

The strategic objective of the Allied landings was the French port of Cherbourg, defended by Lt. Gen. Wilhelm von Schlieben's battle group (*Kampfgruppe*), which controlled the battered 709th Infantry, 243rd Infantry, and 91st Air Landing Divisions, as well as the fresh 77th Infantry Division, 1261st Army Coastal Artillery Regiment, 100th Mortar Regiment, 456th and 457th Motorized Artillery Battalions, and miscellaneous units. Schlieben placed a brilliant young officer, Maj. Friedrich Wilhelm Kueppers, in charge of the artillery, despite his lack of seniority.

Lt. Gen. J. Lawton "Lightning Joe" Collins's U.S. VII Corps began an offensive to take the port on June 11.[5] Its objective was to cut across the Cotentin Peninsula from east to west, in order to isolate Cherbourg. It would then strike north to capture the former home base of the French Atlantic Fleet and destroy Schlieben's defenders.

Schlieben and his men fought well, but Collins finally broke the Germans' thin line on June 15 and drove west across the Cotentin. At 5:05 A.M. on June 18, the Americans severed the peninsula and isolated the bulk of the German 91st, 243rd, 709th, and 77th Divisions and part of the 265th Infantry Division in the Cherbourg *Landfront* north of the main German lines. Twenty-two hours later, Collins began his drive toward Cherbourg. Schlieben and Rear Adm. Walter Hennecke, the naval commander of Normandy, surrendered at 1:30 P.M. on June 26.[6] Maj. Gen. Robert Sattler, the commandant of the city, capitulated the next day, and the last pocket of resistance was overcome on July 1, almost two weeks behind Eisenhower's schedule.[7] Germany had lost an estimated 47,070 men killed, wounded, and captured, including six generals.[8] Collins had lost only 22,000 men.[9]

According to Allied plans, Cherbourg would be the solution to their supply problems, but it was not the prize Eisenhower and his generals hoped it would be. Col. Alvin G. Viney, the American engineer officer in charge of rehabilitating the harbor, reported: "The demolition of the port of Cherbourg is a master job, beyond a doubt the most complete, intensive, and best-planned demolition in history." The U.S. official history recorded that "the whole port was as nearly a wreck as demolitions could make it."[10] Three weeks would pass before the Americans could get the slightest use out of the place, which would remain essentially unusable until September. Even then, it operated at only a small fraction of its prewar capacity. Hitler was so delighted with the destruction of the harbor that he awarded Hennecke the Knight's Cross, even though he was in captivity.[11]

Meanwhile, attrition set in on the Western Front. By the first week of July, the Allied forces in Normandy totaled 929,000 men and outnumbered the Germans roughly three to one. Two weeks later, Army Group B had lost 113,079 men, of which only 10,078 had been replaced. The Allies had lost 117,000 men, but they had been more than fully replaced. Army Group B had also lost 150 Panzer Mark IVs (PzKw IVs), 85 Panthers, 15 Tigers, and 167 57-millimeter assault guns. Only 17 had been replaced.[12]

On July 2, an increasingly irrational Hitler cleaned house in the west. He sacked Rundstedt and replaced him with Field Marshal Guenther von Kluge.[13] He also fired Gen. of Panzer Troops Baron Leo Geyr von Schweppenburg, the commander of the 5th Panzer Army (formerly Panzer Group West), and Col. Gen. Friedrich Dollmann, the commander of the 7th Army.[14] (Fuehrer Headquarters was not aware that Dollmann had suffered a fatal heart attack a few hours before.) They were replaced by Gen. of Panzer Troops Heinrich Eberbach and SS Col. Gen. Paul Hausser, respectively. Rundstedt reacted with relief. "I thank God that I won't be in command during the coming catastrophe!" he exclaimed to Erwin Rommel. "I shall be next," the Desert Fox remarked.[15] He was, but not in the manner in which he expected. On July 17, his staff car was attacked by an Allied fighter-bomber. As the car hit a ditch and turned over, Rommel was thrown out onto the highway. He was taken to a nearby French religious hospital, where it was discovered that his skull had been badly fractured in four places, his left cheekbone destroyed, his left eye injured, his temple penerated, and his head full of numerous shell splinters and fragments. He was not expected to live.[16] Because he feared that Hitler might place Hausser in charge of Army Group B, Kluge named himself Rommel's successor, while simultaneously retaining control of OB West.

✠

From June 7 to July 24, the Allies launched several major offensives aimed at breaking the stalemate in Normandy, in addition to many probing operations and company- and battalion-size attacks almost daily. The decisive moment came on July 25 with Operation Cobra. Eisenhower and Lt. Gen. Omar Bradley, commander of the U.S. First Army, committed thousands of bombers and fighter-bombers (including the use of strategic bombers in a tactical role) against a single German unit, the Panzer Lehr Division. The Allies dropped twelve bombs for every German soldier in the target area. Lt. Gen. Fritz Bayerlein, the Panzer Lehr's commander, later estimated that at least 70 percent of his men were killed, wounded, driven crazy, or temporarily stunned by the bombardment.[17]

Eisenhower and Bradley had chosen "Lightning Joe" Collins to command the breakout forces that would attack after the aerial bombardment. Initially, Collins committed the U.S. 4th, 9th, and 30th Infantry Divisions, but they failed to achieve the expected breakthrough. Eisenhower and Bradley were greatly agitated and thought that the offensive had failed. Collins did not agree and, without consulting his superiors, committed his pursuit forces: the 1st Infantry, 2nd Armored, and 3rd Armored Divisions. It was a pivotal decision.

The senior German generals, most notably Kluge and Hausser, were slow to recognize the danger the air attacks posed, and when they did react, their countermeasures could not immediately be implemented because of the ubiquitous Allied fighter-bombers. As a result, the Americans achieved their decisive breakthrough, and the German left wing disintegrated.

Meanwhile, on August 1, the U.S. Third Army was officially activated under the command of Lt. Gen. George S. Patton, the grandson of one of the officers of the legendary Stonewall Jackson. He was soon off and running, pushing out of Normandy through the narrow Avranches corridor and into Brittany and the interior of France. In three days (August 1–3), he shoved seven divisions—100,000 men— beyond Kluge's left flank. This drive would end only when it reached the German border. The map on the next page shows Patton's drive across France and his conquest of Brittany. Table 2 shows the command structure of the Allied ground forces on August 1.

TABLE 2: ORDER OF BATTLE, ALLIED GROUND FORCES, AUGUST 1, 1944

Supreme Headquarters, Allied Expeditionary Force (SHAEF): Gen. Dwight Eisenhower[a]

U.S. 12th Army Group: Gen. Omar N. Bradley
    U.S. First Army: Lt. Gen. Courtney Hodges
    U.S. Third Army: Lt. Gen. George S. Patton

British 21st Army Group: Gen. Bernard Law Montgomery[b]
    British Second Army: Gen. Miles Dempsey
    Canadian First Army: Lt. Gen. Henry Crerar

a. Assumed command of active ground operations on September 1. Montgomery directed ground operations until then.
b. Promoted to field marshal, September 1, 1944.

Adolf Hitler thought he saw an opportunity in all of this. If Army Group B could counterattack and break through to the sea, it would sever Patton's supply line and cut off the U.S. Third Army. The goal of this operation, however, exceeded the capability of the battered German divisions by a wide margin. Every senior German commander in Normandy except Hausser opposed it. "It's madness, sheer madness!" SS Col. Gen. Sepp Dietrich shouted at Hitler's representative, Gen. of Artillery Walter Warlimont. "We shall run into a trap!"[18]

He was right. Nevertheless, on the orders of the Fuehrer, Gen. of Panzer Troops Baron Hans von Funck, the commander of the XXXXVII Panzer Corps, struck toward the sea with three panzer divisions. (A fourth division, the 116th Panzer, did not advance because

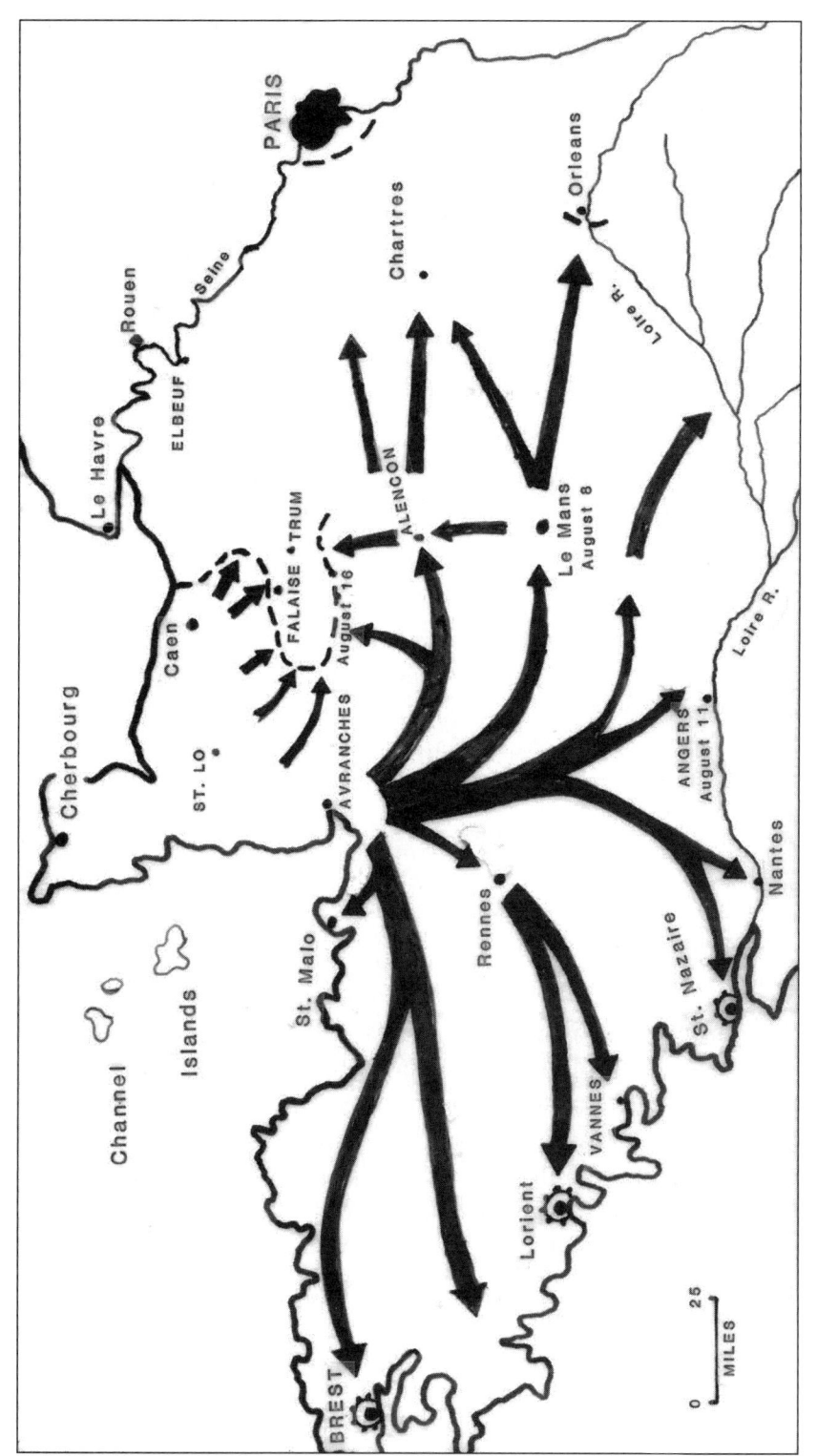

The Conquest of Brittany

its commander, Lt. Gen. Gerhard von Schwerin, decided to disobey orders and did not participate in the disaster.) The 2nd Panzer, 1st SS Panzer, and 2nd SS Panzer Divisions were slaughtered.

As soon as he realized that Army Group B was not going to retreat, Bradley, now commanding the 12th Army Group, devised a plan to destroy the 5th Panzer and 7th Armies in Normandy. He ordered Patton to drive deep into France, south and east of Army Group B, and then turn north, deep into the German rear. Meanwhile, he called on Montgomery's 21st Army Group to attack the German front south of Caen. According to Bradley's plan, the British and Americans would meet in the vicinity of Falaise, encircling the 7th Army and the bulk of the 5th Panzer Army. Although more German soldiers escaped or broke out than Bradley had hoped, the operation worked out more or less the way he had envisioned it. On August 19, the encirclement was complete. By August 24, it was all over. Of the 100,000 men encircled in the pocket, 10,000 were killed and 40,000 to 50,000 were captured or missing. Fewer than 50,000 escaped, and a high percentage of those were service troops. The seven panzer divisions in Normandy escaped with only sixty-two tanks and twenty-six guns among them. (In 1940, the average German tank division had more than 200 tanks.)

On July 20, Col. Count Claus von Stauffenberg, the one-eyed, one-armed chief of staff of the Replacement Army, attended a Fuehrer conference in Rastenberg, East Prussia, with a bomb in his briefcase. When it exploded, however, Hitler was only wounded. The subsequent Gestapo investigation revealed a widespread anti-Nazi conspiracy. Among those involved was the OB West, Field Marshal Guenther von Kluge. Hitler relieved him of his command on August 15 and ordered him to report to Berlin. Kluge knew what that meant. On the ride back on August 19, he ordered his driver to stop near Metz, where he asked to be left alone. Here he spread out a blanket and bit a cyanide capsule.

Kluge was replaced by Field Marshal Walter Model,[19] perhaps the most capable of the Nazi generals. He was a live-wire general—energetic, bold, fearless, arrogant, completely devoted to the Fatherland

and the Fuehrer, and brutal on his officers. Hard drinking and hard driving, he never showed fatigue and seemed to be everywhere at once. He was given only the most difficult and dangerous assignments, and he preferred it that way.

✠

August was a disastrous month for the Germans all the way around. Army Group Center was virtually destroyed on the Eastern Front and Army Group North was isolated in the Baltic region when the Red Army reached the Gulf of Riga. On the Western Front, Rennes fell on August 4 and the XXV Corps was cut off in Brittany on August 6, the same day the siege of Brest began. (It fell on September 19.) The Avranches counteroffensive was defeated on the seventh, and the U.S. 6th Army Group, which included the U.S. Seventh and Free French First Armies, invaded southern France on August 15, the same day that Hitler ordered Model to report to La Roche-Guyon to assume command of OB West and Army Group B.

The British began their drive on the Seine on August 16, Falaise and the minor port of St. Malo fell on the seventeenth, and the Americans established a bridgehead across the Seine on the twentieth. Hitler ordered Model to hold Paris, but when he could not provide the field marshal with his minimum requirements, he ordered it destroyed instead. The city's commandant, Gen. of Infantry Dietrich von Choltitz, would not do this; he surrendered the French capital on August 25, along with about 20,000 men. Model immediately filed court-martial charges against him. (The map on the next page shows the Allied drive to the Seine and the capture of Paris.)

Simultaneously, in southern France, Bordeaux and Cannes fell on August 24, and Marseilles and Toulon were liberated on the twenty-eighth. Meanwhile, the largely nonmotorized German 19th Army abandoned southwestern France, while the U.S. Seventh and French First Armies tried to cut its escape route by pushing the German 1st Army up the Rhone River Valley. The Americans and French captured Soisson on August 29, while the British Second Army captured Amiens and began crossing the Somme on August 31. They would capture Nice on September 1 and Lyon the following day. On the Eastern Front, the Soviet army reached the East Prussian border on

THE ALLIED DRIVE TO THE SEINE

Le Harve

Rouen

Rheims

Chateau-Thiery

PARIS

SEINE R.

Troyes

Sens

XX US

VII US

V US

XII US

Elbeuf

XIX US

XII BR

XXX BR

XV US

XXX BR

XV US

Chartres

XX US

FRONT AS OF AUGUST 26

LOIRE R.

Orleans

XII US

Caen

1 CAN ARMY

II CAN

XII BR

Falaise

V US

Alencon

3 US ARMY

FRONT ON AUGUST 13

2 BR ARMY

XXX BR

XIX US

Mortain

VII US

1 US ARMY

LeMans

Laval

0   10   20

MILES

August 17 and launched a major offensive into Romania on the twentieth. The Romanians promptly defected from the Axis camp, effectively trapping the rebuilt German 6th Army and much of the 8th—a total of sixteen German divisions. Romania officially surrendered to Stalin on August 23 and declared war on Berlin three days later. Slovakia revolted against Germany on August 30, while the Germans began withdrawing from the Aegean Islands in Greece and Bulgaria. Most importantly, that same day, the Russians occupied the Ploesti oil fields north of Bucharest, depriving the Third Reich of its most important source of oil. It seemed to most observers that the Third Reich would be finished within a matter of weeks, if not days.

Amidst these disasters, on August 24, on the very eve of the liberation of Paris and with Army Group B in disarray and in full retreat for the German border, Adolf Hitler issued his "Befehl über den Ausbau der deutschen Westallung" (Order for the Enlargement of the German Western Fortifications). It basically declared that the West Wall was open for business once more. New trench lines, antitank ditches, bunkers, and pillboxes were to be built—large enough to accommodate 1944-type weapons. The Fuehrer commanded that a million workers were to be provided for the construction, including men and women, Reich Labor Service, Hitler Youth, and Organization Todt members, as well as slave laborers and just about anyone else he could get his hands on. The Gauleiters (district Nazi Party leaders) and Kreisleiters (county party leaders) were to be in charge of the actual construction. The Allies were advancing so rapidly at this point, however, that it seemed to the informed military observers that the Allies would breach the line before Hitler's new construction program got off the ground.[20]

CHAPTER 3

The Retreat Ends

The forward elements of the British Second and U.S. First Armies reached the Belgian frontier on September 2, 1944, and pushed into the Low Countries without pause. Montgomery intended to capture the Belgian capital via airborne assault, but the tanks of Brian Horrock's XXX Corps were moving so rapidly that this was not necessary. Early on the morning of September 3, they crossed the Scheldt at Tournai, breaching the last natural barrier to Brussels. German resistance continued to be weak as Horrocks sent the British 11th Armoured Division on his left flank toward Antwerp and the Guards Armoured Division forward Brussels, which was seventy miles away. By late afternoon, the Guards were entering the Belgian capital. The next day, the 11th Armoured entered Antwerp. German command of the city rested with Maj. Gen. Count Christoph zu Stolberg-Stolberg's 136th Special Employment Division, but the speed of the British drive and an uprising by Belgian partisans had taken Stolberg by surprise.[1] Stolberg had 15,000 to 17,000 men at his disposal, but they were poorly armed and of little or no combat value. By the time the British neared the city, Stolberg himself had been isolated by the partisans. The Allies had moved so rapidly that the Germans did not even have time to blow up the port installations. The British captured the huge 1,000-acre harbor intact, along with six miles of wharves, quays, and dry docks. Not even the bridges or giant cranes had been damaged or destroyed. Six thousand prisoners had been captured; initially, they were locked up in the city zoo.

The news of the fall of Antwerp was met with consternation and shock at Fuehrer Headquarters in East Prussia. Its loss not only held out to the Allies the immediate possibility of solving their supply problems, but it also threatened to make the Albert Canal line from Antwerp to Maastricht useless and placed the 15th Army in imminent danger of being surrounded in the lowlands of Flanders. In two days, Montgomery had driven a seventy-five-mile wedge between the 15th and Dietrich's 5th Panzer Army, which was now retreating in the direction of Aachen. All Model had with which to cover the gap was the low-quality 719th Infantry Division, a two-regiment unit that had been on guard duty along the Dutch coast since it was formed in the summer of 1941; a "Normandy" division now at regimental strength; a brigade of Dutch SS; and a few garrison and security units from the Netherlands. Heinrich Himmler, who had been the commander in chief of the Home Army since the failure of the July 20 plot, could offer Model only one ad hoc convalescent division, the 176th Infantry, which was made up of soldiers who would not have been in the army four years ago.[2] The men of this unit were grouped into battalions according to their health problems. The "stomach battalion," for example, consisted of men who had ulcers and required special diets. There was also an ear battalion, a foot battalion, and an eye battalion. Not even the most optimistic Nazi believed they could stop, or even significantly delay, the British Second Army.

Adolf Hitler was in a bad mood after Antwerp fell, and he took his rage out on Hermann Goering, among others, threatening to end the *Luftwaffe*'s existence as a separate branch of the military. At this point, Goering came to the rescue of the army. To the complete surprise of General Guderian and the General Staff, he announced that he had six parachute regiments more or less ready for frontline duty and could raise two more from convalescent battalions, making a total combat force of 20,000 men. He could also send, he declared, as many as 10,000 from *Luftwaffe* air and ground crews whose training or operations had been suspended because of a lack of fuel. In addition, he pointed out, these were *Luftwaffe* personnel, thoroughly indoctrinated with the spirit of National Socialism; unlike army soldiers, they could be counted on to fight to the end.

When he heard this news, an excited Fuehrer forgot about allowing the army to absorb the *Luftwaffe*, just as Goering had calculated. Hitler immediately ordered Col. Gen. Kurt Student, the commander of the 1st Parachute Army, to move his headquarters—until then an administrative and training command—to the Netherlands and defend the canal line.[3] Model had planned to use this headquarters to direct a Führer-ordered counterattack against Patton's right flank and rear in the Nancy-Langres area; now the dictator transferred Dietrich's 5th Panzer Army Headquarters to eastern France for that purpose. Dietrich handed over his sector to Headquarters, 7th Army, which had been hastily rebuilt and was now under the command of Gen. of Panzer Troops Erich Brandenberger. It left at once for Nancy. Finally, Model ordered the 15th Army to withdraw the bulk of its troops to the banks of the Scheldt estuary, leaving behind garrisons at Boulogne, Dunkirk, Le Havre and Calais, with orders to deny the Channel ports to the Allies as long as possible. He also instructed Gen. of Infantry Gustav-Adolf von Zangen, the commander of the 15th Army, to counterattack to the northeast, but these orders were countermanded on September 6.

Meanwhile, Hitler reinstated Field Marshal Gerd von Rundstedt as OB West, although Model remained commander in chief of Army Group B. To Hitler, the aging Rundstedt had proven his political reliability as president of the Court of Honor that discharged the conspirators of July 20 from the *Wehrmacht* so that they could stand trial in Judge Roland Friesler's infamous People's Court.[4] Rundstedt's appointment as Supreme Commander in the west at this time, Hitler felt, would reassure the officer corps and help restore its morale. The situation Rundstedt inherited now, however, was much worse than it had been in July, when he told Keitel to "end the war, you fools!" In Model's estimation, OB West now had the equivalent of only twenty-five full-strength divisions but needed thirty-five to forty more to conduct an effective defense in the west. Since everyone knew that these were not available, he saw only one option: a retreat to the West Wall. Model had made this recommendation to Fuehrer Headquarters the day before he was superseded by Rundstedt.

Hitler, for once, was correct in separating the posts of OB West and commander in chief of Army Group B. Commanding an army group and the entire Western Front was too big a job for a single man. Kluge probably realized this when he assumed both positions on July 17, the day Rommel was critically wounded. He apparently took personal command of Army Group B only because he was afraid that Hitler would give the post to an SS general, Hausser, and he was probably right. (Kluge and Hausser had been cadets together at Gross Lichterfeldt, Imperial Germany's West Point, prior to World War I.

They had not liked each other then, and Kluge's low opinion of Hausser's abilities apparently dated from those days. Old grudges aside, Hausser had proven to be a poor army commander in Normandy.) In the eighteen days that he held both posts, Model had not shown that he could handle both jobs at the same time, although, in fairness to him, he inherited a battle already lost and, twice during this period, Model had informed Hitler of his inability to command both Army Group B and OB West.

Hitler summoned Rundstedt to the Wolf's Lair at the end of August and invited him to attend the daily situation conferences. According to Jodl's deputy, Gen. of Artillery Walter Warlimont, Hitler treated Rundstedt with "unwonted diffidence and respect," even though the aging field marshal sat through the sessions "motionless and monosyllabic." Rundstedt was kept in the dark about the reason for his presence in Rastenburg until the afternoon of September 4, when Hitler asked him to reassume command of the Western Front. Stiffly, with both hands on his marshal's baton, Rundstedt replied, "My Fuehrer, whatever you may command, I will do my duty to my last breath."[5] He left for the Western Front that same afternoon. The next day, even before the field marshal resumed his command, Hitler transferred his longtime chief of staff, Gen. of Infantry Guenther Blumentritt, to the staff of the LXXXVI Corps, where he was to undergo training as a corps commander, and replaced him with Lt. Gen. Siegfried Westphal, the former chief of staff of OB Southwest, who had just recovered from the nervous breakdown he had suffered in Italy that summer. Rundstedt protested the change, but to no avail. He and Westphal worked well together, however, and Westphal was certainly a better chief of staff than Blumentritt.

Model also received a new chief of staff on September 5, when Lt. Gen. Hans Speidel was arrested in connection with the assassination attempt of July 20. He was replaced by the less capable Gen. of Infantry Hans Krebs, who had been Model's chief of staff when he commanded the 9th Army on the Eastern Front. Model tried, unsucessfully, to protect Speidel.[6] Speidel spent the rest of the war in prison and escaped execution only because he was lucky.

The appointment of Rundstedt, on the other hand, was not a fortunate one. The aging Prussian field marshal took one look at his decimated and dispirited forces and decided that the war was lost. When he

WESTERN FRONT: September 5, 1944

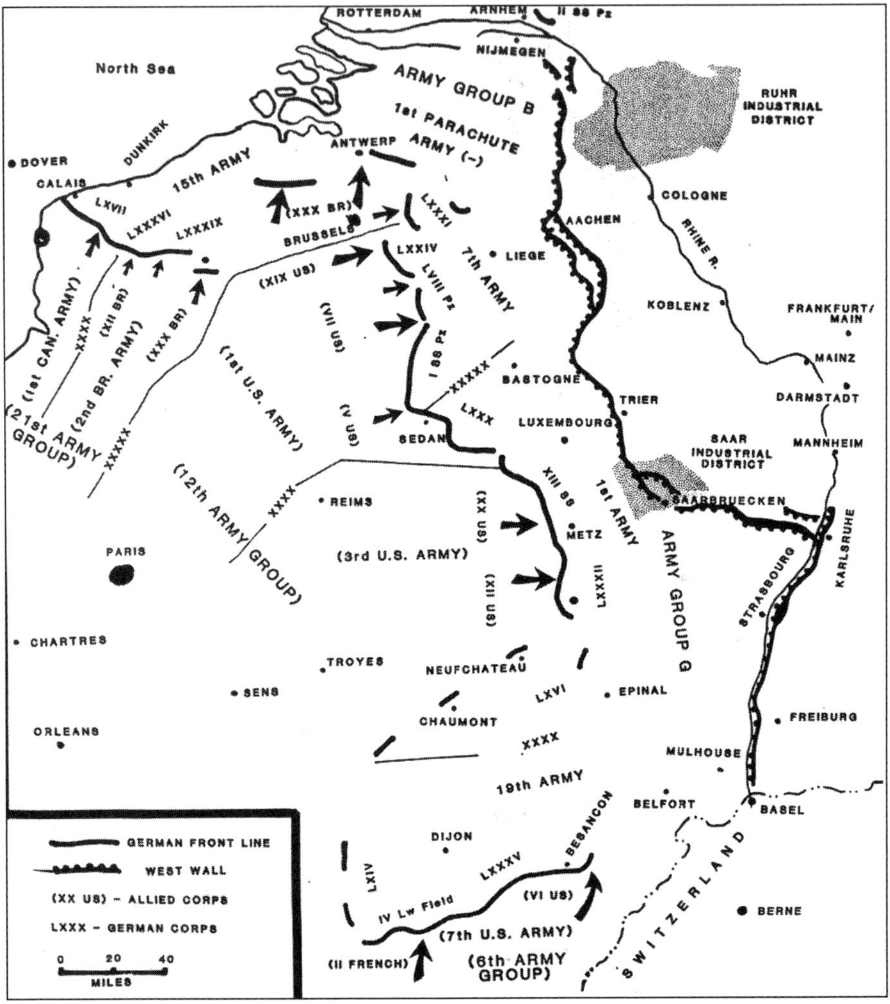

arrived at OB West, now headquartered at Aremberg, a small town near
Koblenz, on the afternoon of September 5, his operations officer, Lt.
Gen. Bodo Zimmermann, gave him an inventory of his divisions.[7] OB
West now had forty-eight infantry and fifteen panzer-type divisions, but
only fifteen of these were at anywhere near full strength. In all, OB
West's combat power was equivalent to only twenty-seven divisions.
Eisenhower had an estimated sixty divisions on the continent.[8] OB
West's condition on September 5 is illustrated in Table 3. The map
above shows the situation on the Western Front that same day.

TABLE 3: OB WEST'S CONDITION, SEPTEMBER 5, 1944

	Infantry Divisions	Panzer Divisions	Panzer Brigades
Completely Fit	13	3	2
Partially Fit	12	2	2
Totally Unfit	14	7	—
Dissolved	7	—	—
Rebuilding	9	—	—

On September 7, two days after he resumed command, Rundstedt informed Fuehrer Headquarters that the Allies were advancing with approximately 2,000 tanks (a very close estimate), but that he had only about 100 panzers fit for action. He estimated that he was outnumbered more than 2 to 1 in men, 2.5 to 1 in artillery, 20 to 1 in tanks, and 25 to 1 in airplanes. Furthermore, his soldiers were worn out and exhausted, and there were serious shortages in transport, gasoline, and ammunition. He asked all available tanks and assault guns to be rushed to the Western Front, but Hitler had nothing left to give him in the way of armor. During the month of July, the army had lost 1,969 tanks and assault guns, but German industry could provide only 1,256 replacements, and nearly all of these had been sent to the Eastern Front, where Army Group Center was being crushed. In August, the army received only 1,122 replacements, but lost twice that many.[9] To make matters worse, the situation in the east was no less catastrophic than that in the west, so OB West could not claim priority for new tanks and panzer units. "As far as I was concerned," Rundstedt said later, "the war ended in September."[10] He retired to his headquarters with his cigarettes and cognac and seldom reemerged, leaving the daily conduct of operations in the hands of his subordinates, his chief of staff, and OKW (i.e., Fuehrer Headquarters).

Hitler ordered Rundstedt to restore the line and "to fight for time so that the West Wall can be prepared for defense." He also ordered him to launch an attack from the Epinal area against the right flank of Patton's Third Army, regardless of losses.[11]

Meanwhile, in Belgium, General Student never had a chance to hold the sixty-mile-long Albert Canal line. It would take at least a week for most of his new regiments to reach the front, and the British had already breached the line by September 6. He was also given command of the *Wehrmacht* forces in the Netherlands, and given the British supply difficulties, Student felt that he might be able to establish a thin front near the Dutch-Belgian border.

Field Marshal Model, meanwhile, turned his attention to the rescue of the 15th Army, the strongest army left in Army Group B. It had been under the command of Gen. of Infantry Gustav-Adolf von Zangen since the anti-Nazi Gen. Hans von Salmuth had been relieved of his command on August 25.[12] The 15th had 90,000 men, 600 guns, 6,200 vehicles and 6,200 horses. It was no longer possible for it to escape solely by land. To make its getaway, 15th Army would have to cross the Scheldt estuary—a boat trip of three and a half miles from Breskens to Flushing on Walcheren Island. The trip would be thirteen miles for troops departing from Terneuzen. From Flushing, the troops would have to march over the narrow, open, unprotected causeway that connected Walcheren Island with South Beveland peninsula; then they would have to take a single road leading to the mainland, only fifteen miles north of Antwerp. All of this would have to be done in the flat, open terrain of the Netherlands and in the face of an enemy who had absolute control of both sea and air. Even if everything went perfectly, it would take at least three weeks to complete the evacuation. Undaunted, Zangen posted a strong rearguard to check the Canadian and British forces advancing in his rear and started the evacuation on September 6.

Elsewhere, the battered units from Normandy were still trying to escape the Montgomery's juggernaut, which, unlike much of Patton's Third Army, had not yet completely run out of gas.

On Montgomery's left flank, the Canadian First Army sealed off most of the escape routes of Zangen's 15th Army and besieged the ports of Le Havre, Dunkirk, Calais, and Boulogne. In his center,

Dempsey's British Second Army advanced north of Antwerp, across the Albert Canal and the Meuse. On his right flank, Hodges's U.S. First Army took Mons on September 3, and surrounded the remnants of several German divisions and three German corps headquarters: the LXXIV, under Gen. of Infantry Erich Straube; the LVIII Panzer, under Lt. Gen. Walter Krueger; and the I SS Panzer, under the command of SS-Obergruppenführer Georg Keppler. As the senior general, Straube assumed command of the encircled forces, which were much more interested in escaping than fighting.

Straube ordered his disorganized forces to break out. A great many did, but 25,000 were captured. The U.S. IX Tactical Air Command later claimed the destruction of 851 motorized vehicles, 50 armored vehicles, and 652 horse-drawn vehicles in the Mons pocket. All three corps commanders escaped, along with most of their staffs, but several divisions were smashed, including the 6th Parachute Division, which went into the battle with a combat strength of only two battalions. Its commander, Lt. Gen. Ruediger von Heyking, was among the prisoners.[13] Its sister division, the 3rd Parachute, was at less than regimental strength, but managed to escape, thanks to the leadership of its acting commander, Lt. Gen. Walter Wadehn. Lt. Gen. Joachim von Treschow of the 18th Luftwaffe Field Division also escaped, but only 300 men came out of the pocket with him. Most preferred to surrender to the Americans.[14]

The 18th Field was dissolved after Mons. Maj. Gen. Karl Wahle of the 47th Infantry Division and Lt. Gen. Paul Seyffardt of the 348th Infantry succeeded in escaping the pocket but were captured before they could reach the safety of the West Wall. The 47th Infantry had to be rebuilt as a Volksgrenadier division, and the remnants of Lt. Gen. Eugen-Felix Schwalbe's 344th Infantry Division, also at Mons, had to be taken out of the line. Later, it absorbed the remnants of the 91st Air Landing Division and elements of the 172nd Replacement Division, reemerging as the 344th Volksgrenadier Division. The 271st Infantry, mauled at Mons, was sent to Slovakia, where it abosrbed the 576th Volksgrenadier Division and was sent to the Eastern Front as the 271st Volksgrenadier Division.

Other German units were also pounded as they tried to reach the frontier. Kurt Meyer, who had spent years in the *Leibstandarte* (the 1st

SS Panzer Division), visited his old unit on August 20, and barely recognized it, so few men were left. He could not stop the tears from pouring down his cheeks. Indeed, Normandy was, in a very real sense, the graveyard of the Waffen-SS as an elite fighting force. A partial list of the key SS men killed or seriously wounded in Normandy is shown below:

- SS Capt. Wilhelm Beck, commander of the 2nd Company, 1st SS Panzer Regiment, and winner of the Knight's Cross on the Eastern Front; killed near Caen on June 10.
- Reserve Capt. Otto Toll, company commander in the 12th SS Panzer Engineer Battalion and winner of the Knight's Cross as a platoon leader in the Afrika Korps; killed on June 10;
- SS Maj. Gen. Fritz Witt, holder of the Knight's Cross with Oak Leaves and commander of the 12th SS Panzer Division; killed on June 12.
- SS Maj. Gen. Werner Ostendorff, commander of the 17th SS Panzer Grenadier Division "Goetz von Berlichingen"; seriously wounded on June 16 and unable to return to duty for months.
- SS Master Sgt. Alfred Guenther, Knight's Cross holder from the Eastern Front and platoon leader in the 1st SS Assault Gun Battalion; killed in action in June.
- SS Sgt. Emil Duerr, gun commander in the 4th (Heavy) Company, 26th SS Panzer Grenadier Regiment of the Hitler Youth Division; killed in action at St. Mauvieu on June 27 and awarded the Knight's Cross posthumously.
- SS Maj. Georg Heinrich Karl Karck, commander of the 2nd Battalion of the 2nd SS Panzer Grenadier Regiment of the *Leibstandarte Adolf Hitler*, killed in action on July 3.
- SS Maj. Gen. Heinz Lammerding, commander of the 2nd SS Panzer Division "Das Reich"; seriously wounded on July 26.
- SS Capt. Karl Keck, commander of the 15th (Engineer) Company of the 21st SS Panzer Grenadier Regiment, 10th SS Panzer Division "Frundsberg"; killed at Avenay, Normandy, and awarded the Knight's Cross posthumously.
- SS Lt. Col. Christian Tychsen, commander of the 2nd SS Panzer Division "Das Reich" and holder of the Oak Leaves; killed in action on July 28.

- SS Oberführer Sylvester Stadler, commander of the 9th SS Panzer Division "Hohenstaufen"; wounded on July 10, returned to duty on July 15, but more seriously wounded on July 31 and permanently replaced.
- SS Master Sgt. Adolf Rued, a member of the staff of the 3rd SS Panzer Grenadier Regiment "Deutschland" of the 2nd SS Panzer Division; killed in action on August 2 and awarded the Knight's Cross posthumously.
- SS PFC Hermann Alber of the 20th SS Panzer Grenadier Regiment, 9th SS Panzer Division "Hohenstaufen"; killed in the Battle of Hill 176 on August 2 and awarded the Knight's Cross posthumously.
- SS Maj. Ludwig Kepplinger, commander of the 17th SS Panzer Battalion, 17th SS Panzer Grenadier Division; killed by Maquis seven miles southeast of Laval on August 6.
- SS Lt. Helmut Wendorff, platoon leader in the 13th (Heavy) Company of the 1st SS Panzer Regiment LAH; killed in action southeast of Caen on August 6.
- SS Lt. Michael Wittmann of the 501st SS Heavy Panzer Battalion, perhaps the greatest tank ace of all time and a holder of the Knight's Cross with Oak Leaves and Swords; killed south of Caen on August 8.
- SS Capt. Karl Bastian, commander of the 2nd Battalion of the 21st SS Panzer Regiment of the 10th SS Panzer Division "Frundsberg"; killed in the Argentan-Falaise zone on August 10 and posthumously awarded the Knight's Cross.
- SS Maj. Karl-Heinz Prinz, commander, 2nd Battalion of the 12th SS Panzer Regiment; killed in action on August 14.
- SS Sgt. Hans Reiter, member of the staff company of the 21st SS Panzer Grenadier Regiment, 10th SS Panzer Division; killed in action at St. Clair and posthumously awarded the Knight's Cross.
- SS Maj. Hans Becker, commander of the 1st Battalion of the 2nd SS Panzer Grenadier Regiment in the *Leibstandarte Adolf Hitler*; killed in action on August 20.

- SS Reserve Technical Sgt. Josef Holte, platoon leader in the 9th SS Panzer Regiment; killed near Livarot on August 20 and posthumously awarded the Knight's Cross.
- SS Maj. Gen. Theodor "Teddy" Wisch, the commander of the 1st SS Panzer Division *Leibstandarte Adolf Hitler*; wounded so badly on August 20 that both of his legs had to be amputated.
- SS Maj. Heinrich Heimann of the 1st SS Assault Gun Battalion, 1st SS Panzer Division; killed in action west of Chambois on August 20.
- SS Col. Gen. Paul Hausser, commander of the 7th Army; struck in the face by shrapnel south of Falaise on August 20 and unable to return to duty until 1945.
- SS Lt. Josef Amberger, commander of the 8th Company, 1st SS Panzer Regiment; killed in action on August 21 and posthumously awarded the Knight's Cross.
- SS Col. Max Wünsche, commander of the 12th SS Panzer Regiment and holder of the Knight's Cross with Oak Leaves; severely wounded in the Falaise Pocket and captured on August 24.
- SS Lt. Col. Otto Meyer, commander of the 9th SS Panzer Regiment, 9th SS Panzer Division; killed in action northeast of Amiens on August 28 and posthumously awarded the Oak Leaves to the Knight's Cross.
- SS Lt. Col. Hans Waldmueller, commander of the 1st Battalion of the 25th SS Panzer Grenadier Regiment of the 12th SS Panzer Division; died of wounds on September 8.[15]

After Normandy, the Waffen-SS divisions had lost so many of their best leaders and veterans and Himmler and Gottlob Berger were filling their places with so many substandard replacements that they never performed at quite the same level again.

During the retreat through Belgium, casualties among the Waffen-SS units continued to mount, both in the upper and lower echelons. On September 2, SS Maj. Erich Olboeter, the commander of the 26th SS Panzer Grenadier Regiment of the Hitler Youth Division, was retreating through a Belgian village when his vehicle ran over a mine laid by a partisan. Both of his legs were blown off. He died later that night in the hospital at Charleville. A few days later, SS Capt. Heinz Schrott, another "old hare" (as German veterans called themselves) and a battalion commander in the 12th SS Panzer Division "Hitler Youth," was shot in the back and killed by a partisan.

On September 5, the remnants of the 12th SS Panzer Division tried to prevent the Americans from breaching the Meuse River line, but it no longer had the men to do so. The Americans crossed the river that night near Namur, only fifty-five miles from the German border. At first, Kurt "Panzer" Meyer, commander of the 12th, did not believe the news; his men had always held before. When it was confirmed, he ordered the division to retreat behind the Ourthe. Meyer himself went ahead of his unit with a small motorized detachment to make sure the Americans had not already captured the critical crossroads of Durnal. When he entered the village, however, he saw the people greeting the American vanguard. One of the Shermans spotted the SS general's column and blasted the first vehicle. "A few Volkswagen against a column of tanks is not very amusing," Meyer recalled later. Despite fleeing, Meyer was eventually captured by partisans and handed over to U.S. forces.[16] His division—or what was left of it—made its way behind the Meuse under the temporary command of SS Lt. Col. Hubert Meyer, the division's chief of operations (and no relation to Kurt).

The Allied pursuit, however, was slowing. On September 3, the U.S. 9th Infantry Division of Collins's VII Corps had crossed the Meuse just south of Dinant, expecting to meet no resistance. They were suddenly pounced on by elements of the tough 2nd SS Panzer Division and the remnants of the 12th SS Panzer Division, both operating under Keppler's I SS Panzer Corps. One American battalion was nearly surrounded and lost more than 200 men. The 9th Infantry was forced to cling to a small foothold on the east bank for a day and a half before it could be rescued by a task force from the U.S. 3rd Armored Division coming from the north. Even so, Dinant was not captured until the morning of September 7.

The Allied advance continued. The U.S. VII Corps took Liege on September 7. To the south, Bastogne was captured by Leonard Gerow's U.S. V Corps on the 8th, Luxembourg, the capital of the Grand Duchy by the same name, was occupied on the tenth, and Malmedy was in American hands by the eleventh. But resistance seemed to be stiffening. The American soldiers were now in the Ardennes, only a few miles from the German border, and there was a noticable chill in the air, not solely because of the changing season. A few days before, one American soldier wrote of a liberated town, "Once again cognac, champagne, and pretty girls." His tone was slightly bored; he had come to expect such things. Now, however, the attitude of the civilians had changed. "There were no more V-for-Victory signs, no more flowers, no more shouts of *Vive l'Amerique*," historian Martin Blumenson recalled. "Instead, a sullen border populace showed hatred, and occasional snipers fired into the columns."[17]

Meanwhile, the XIX Corps of Hodges's First Army ran out of gas and was immobilized for several days. The U.S. 5th Armored Division continued to push forward, however, and on the evening of September 11, one of its patrols crossed the German frontier near Stalzenburg. The Americans probed deeper the next day, and discovered that the West Wall opposite the Ardennes was weakly manned and some of its fortifications were not occupied at all. Supply difficulties prevented an attack until September 14, and by that time, the situation had fundamentally changed. Model had been able to reinforce the threatened sector and stopped the U.S. attack, which penetrated the first line of defense on the outskirts of Pruem. The Americans were finally halted on the very fringes of the West Wall. (The map on the facing page shows the situation on the Western Front on September 16.)

Along the coast, the Canadian First Army, with six divisions, captured the city of Rouen near the mouth of the Seine on August 31, took the minor ports of Dieppe and Ostend a few days later, and prepared to attack the major Channel ports of Le Havre and Calais. In the zone of the British Second Army, the British VIII Corps—with two infantry divisions, two tank brigades, and most of the army's heavy and medium artillery—was still on the Seine, immobilized because of a lack of gasoline. The British XII Corps was still engaged in driving into the rear of Zangen's 15th Army but was meeting unexpectedly stiff resistance. This meant that out of the fourteen divisions and seven armored brigades in the 21st Army Group, Montgomery had only one corps left with which to continue the advance into Holland: Horrocks's XXX Corps, with the 11th and Guards Armoured Divisions. As good as it was, it was not strong enough to sustain the momentum of the drive.

WESTERN FRONT: September 15, 1944

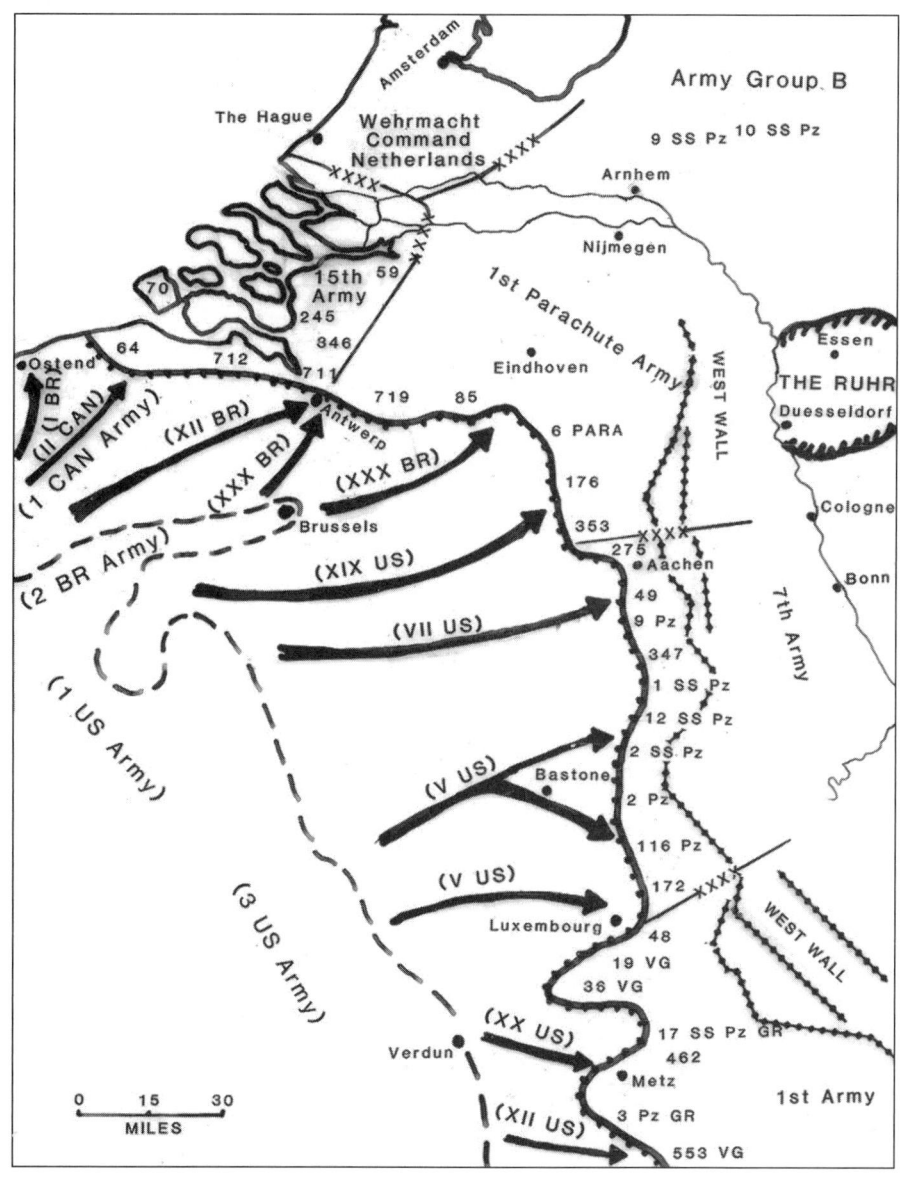

South of the Ardennes, Patton was also running into serious problems. His army had been largely paralyzed because of a lack of fuel for
several days. When he was at last able to resume his offensive on September 5, German resistance had stiffened. One American effort to
cross the Moselle at Pont-a-Mousson was beaten back with heavy losses.
Although one U.S. force was able to seize Toul in the Moselle bend,
the American Third Army in general was tied down in heavy fighting
between Metz and Nancy. Patton's great advance had come to an end.

It was the same story everywhere: just as suddenly as it had
started, it had stopped. The *Wehrmacht* was no longer on the run.
Despite the Mons pocket, Army Group B had managed to escape and
was now digging in behind the West Wall. Army Group G—consisting
of the 19th Army and LXIV Corps—had also escaped, bringing most
of its combat units out with it, more or less intact. The two army
groups linked up on September 10, establishing a continuous front
from the North Sea to the Swiss border. Most of it was behind the
West Wall, which extended from the Dutch border near Cleve to the
Swiss frontier just north of Basle. The Germans once again had a con-
tinous front, although it was not strongly held.

June, July, and August had been a disastrous period for the Third
Reich. It had lost 55,000 men killed and 340,000 missing in the west
and 215,000 killed and 627,000 missing on the Eastern Front. Count-
ing wounded—which generally amounted to three times the number
killed—the total casualties amounted to 2,047,000. OB West had also
lost the use of 200,000 more men who were cut off on the Channel
islands or in Hitler's so-called fortresses on the Atlantic coast. The
casualties suffered from June to September were roughly equal to the
losses the *Wehrmacht* suffered from the start of the war to February
1943, including Stalingrad. A quarter of a million horses had also
been lost. Twenty-nine divisions had been lost or rendered impotent
(including those trapped in the coastal fortresses), and three divisions had been disbanded in the Balkans, two in Italy, and ten in the
east—a total of forty-four divisions. In all, the Reich would lose 106
divisions in 1944, more than it possessed when the war began in
1939.[18]

Senior-officer losses on the Western Front had not been light. In addition to those already mentioned (which included two field marshals and two army commanders), they included

- Gen. of Artillery Theodor Geib, Army Rear Area commander, southern France; mortally wounded on July 30.
- Lt. Gen. Dietrich Kraiss, commander of the 352nd Infantry Division; mortally wounded near St. Lô on August 2 and died on August 6.
- Maj. Gen. Leo Mayr, leader of the 659th Field Administrative Headquarters; captured on August 20.
- Maj. Gen. Johannes Schraepler, commander of the 120th Artillery Command; captured by the Americans on August 21.
- Maj. Gen. Walter Gleininger, commander of the 586th Field Administrative Headquarters; committed suicide on August 21.
- Maj. Gen. Claus Boie, commander of the 497th Field Administrative HQ; captured by the British on August 24.
- Maj. Gen. Hans-Georg Schramm, director of the 533rd Field Administrative Headquarters; captured at Troyes on August 26.
- Maj. Gen. Edgar Arndt, commander of the 708th Infantry Division; killed in action in September.
- Maj. Gen. Detlef Bock von Wuelfingen, acting commander of the 681st Field Administrative Headquarters; captured near the West Wall in early September.
- Gen. of Infantry Erwin Vierow, former commander of Northwest France and chief of the ad hoc General Command Somme; captured on September 1.
- Maj. Gen. Fritz Reinhardt, commander of the 518th Field Administrative Headquarters; killed in action on September 1.
- Maj. Gen. of Reserves Hubertus von Aulock, *Kampfgruppe* commander in Paris and later northwestern France; captured on September 2.
- Maj. Gen. Paul von Felbert, commander of the 560th Field Administrative Headquarthers in southwestern France; captured on September 5.
- Maj. Gen. Axel Schmidt, commander of the 159th Reserve Division; killed near Belfort Gap on September 8.
- Lt. Gen. Conrad-Oskar Heinrichs, commander of the 89th Infantry Division; killed in action on September 8.

- Maj. Gen. Botho Elster, commander of the 541st Field Administrative Headquarters; captured on September 14.
- Maj. Gen. Erwin Jolasse, commander of the 9th Panzer Division; seriously wounded on September 16.
- Lt. Gen. Erwin Rauch, commander of the 343rd Infantry Division; captured in Brittany on September 18.
- Maj. Gen. Erich von Kirchbach, commander of the 622nd Field Administrative Headquarters; mortally wounded on September 24.

In addition, several commanders were sacked or forced into retirement. The best of these was Baron Hans von Funck, veteran commander of the 7th Panzer Division and XXXXVII Panzer Corps and one of Germany's best tank commanders. Others included Gen. of Infantry Walter Fischer von Weikersthal, commander of the LXVII Corps, relieved on July 24; Gen. of Infantry Erich Raschick, commander of *Wehrkreis X* (headquartered at Hamburg), retired on July 30; Gen. of Artillery Curt Gallenkamp, commander of the LXXX Corps, sacked on August 10; Maj. Gen. Ernst von Poten, commandant of Metz, sacked on September 8; and Wolfgang von Kluge, brother of the late field marshal, commander of the 226th Infantry Division, and commandant of Dunkirk, forced into retirement for political reasons on August 29. In addition, Hans von Kluge, the son of the field marshal, was demoted to the staff of a division and sent to the Eastern Front. He was later summarily relieved of duty and dismissed from the army.

In contrast to the *Wehrmacht,* Eisenhower landed more than 2,100,000 men and 460,000 vehicles on the European continent between June 6 and September 11. This amounted to forty-nine full-strength combat divisions, with more Anglo-Saxons joining the fight every week, and the French Army was reconstituting itself at a rapid pace for the Battle of Germany. Over the same period, Ike's forces had lost 40,000 killed, 164,000 wounded, and 20,000 missing—a total of 224,000 casualties, less than half what Hitler's legions had suffered. No wonder the morale of the Allies soldiers was very high in early September 1944, even though their fuel tanks were very low. Bradley and Montgomery were already planning the crossing of the Rhine, and even Eisenhower was wagering that the war would be over by Christmas. Not even the worst pessimist among them would have guessed that it would be five more months before they could even cross the Rhine.

HITLER'S NEW STRATEGIC PLAN

Even before the Falaise pocket was cleared, Adolf Hitler's mind was turning toward thoughts of resuming the offensive. On August 19, he met with Walter Buhle, chief of the army staff at OKW, and Albert Speer, the minister of armaments, and instructed them to begin preparing to send large allotments of men and equipment to the Western Front. At the same time, he told them that he intended to retake the initiative in the west in early November, when the Allies air forces would not be able to fly. He ordered General Jodl, the chief of operations of OKW to prepare a report on the conditions necessary for an all-out offensive in the west.

Jodl reported back on September 6 and concluded that a major offensive in the west would require an operational reserve of twenty-five divisions; would have to be launched during a period of bad weather, when Allied airplanes would be grounded; and would have to be focused in such a manner that it achieved overwhelming combat superiority in the sector chosen for the attack. Finally, Jodl stated that the offensive would not be possible before November 1.

Over the next two weeks, Hitler and Jodl took time each day to discuss the offensive and draft a very general plan. The first major step toward its execution was taken on September 14, when the Fuehrer ordered the organization of a new staff, to be designated Headquarters, 6th Panzer Army, which he placed under the command of his former bodyguard, SS Col. Gen. Joseph "Sepp" Dietrich. All of the SS panzer divisions in the west, the Führer instructed, were to be taken out of the line and rehabilitated under this headquarters. Meanwhile, Hitler and his staff calculated that the Allies had approximately sixty divisions on the continent, with another thirty-two in England and Scotland. An estimated thirty-nine divisions were still in the United States, although five were apparently on their way to Europe. Their disembarkment would take a considerable amount of time, he predicted, because of the Allies' lack of port facilities. The major Channel ports had not yet been cleared, and Antwerp would be useless until the Allies opened the Scheldt estuary. Hitler concluded that the Allies had no major strategic reserves on the European mainland. He was correct.

After his regular situation conference at the Wolf's Lair on September 16, Hitler invited his top advisers into the inner chamber for a second meeting. Present were Keitel, Jodl, Guderian, and Gen. of Fliers Werner Kreipe, the chief of the General Staff of the *Luftwaffe* and the successor to Gen. of Fliers Guenther Korten, who had died of the wounds he suffered on July 20. Jodl began the briefing by presenting the overall picture. Politically, the Reich was isolated. Italy had been eliminated as a military force; Romania and Bulgaria were gone; Japan was in retreat; and Finland had just broken off its alliance with Germany. He rehashed the casualty figures for the past three months and then turned to the positive side. The Soviet summer offensive seemed to be at an end, and on the Western Front, many of the troops were getting a much-needed rest as the Allied offensive stalled.

"Stop!" the Führer cried suddenly, raising his hand in a dramatic fashion. There was silence for two minutes. Then Hitler said, "I have made a momentous decision. I am taking the offensive. Here—out of the Ardennes!" Slamming his fist on the map in front of him, he added, "Across the Meuse and on to Antwerp!"[19] Suddenly, all of the care, worry, and illness seemed to leave him. Once again he seemed to be the dynamic, undefeated Führer, the genius of 1940. All that the *Wehrmacht* would have to do was hold the West Wall and contain the Soviets for several weeks while simultaneously taking many of its panzer divisions out of the line, rebuilding them, reequipping them, and forming enough new divisions to create a strategic reserve of twenty-five divisions. (The map on the next page shows the Siegfried Line and the location of the major battles fought in its defense.)

THE BATTLE OF THE SCHNEE EIFEL

On September 12, Col. Charles T. "Buck" Lanham's U.S. 22nd Infantry Regiment, the spearhead of the U.S. V Corps, pushed into the Ardennes, followed by the rest of the 4th Infantry Division, the 28th Infantry Division, and the 5th Armored Division.[20] They were pursuing the I SS Panzer Corps (1st and 2nd SS Panzer Divisions),

THE SIEGFRIED LINE CAMPAIGN: Sept. 11–Dec. 15, 1944

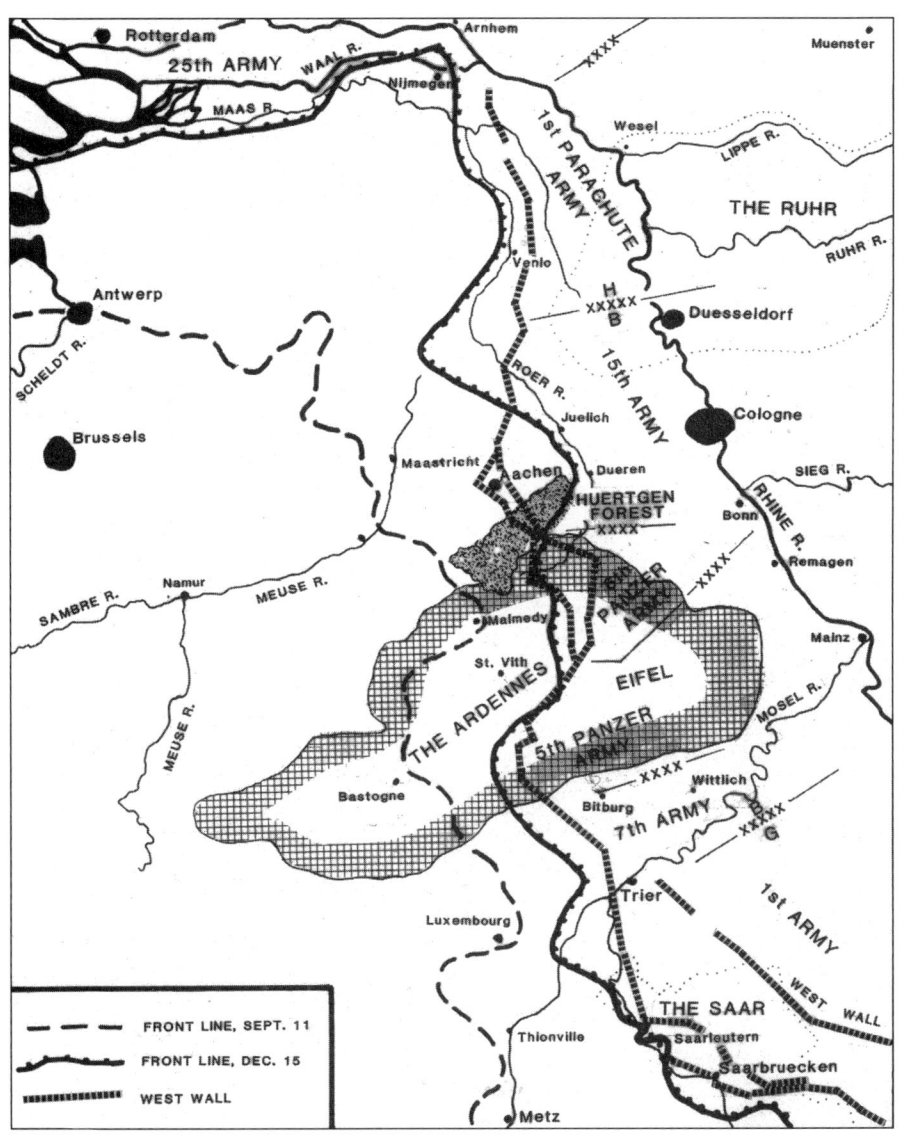

which blew up the Our and Sauer River bridges and fell back to the
West Wall, which disappointed the SS men when they first saw it.
"Damn it! Where are the bunkers?" SS Major Rink of the 1st SS
Panzer Division swore when he arrived. "Silence over the fields and
nothing else! We expected a lot more." Initially, he did not even
know where the minefields were; then he learned that there weren't
any. Local farmers had taken the barbed wire and were using some of
the bunkers as chicken coops.[21]

The I SS Panzer Corps was placed in charge of defending the
West Wall from Monschau to Dasburg, which included most of the
Eifel, as the German Ardennes is known. It was led by SS General
Keppler, who was described as "very energetic—and high handed."
Without enough men to man his positions, he set up roadblocks and
pressed army stragglers into the SS by offering them a choice: join
the SS or be shot. They all joined. He also had his men comb the rear
areas, including Wittlich, Bitburg, Trier, and other towns. They
drafted any soldiers they found.[22]

The Americans reached the edge of the West Wall on the evening
of September 13. They were led by General Gerow, who would later
become an American hero for his successful defense of Eisenborn
Ridge during the Battle of the Bulge. This corps commander knew
that the Germans were running and reasoned that they might keep
on running if pressed. If they did, he could break through the
Siegfried Line—as the Allies called the West Wall—within forty-eight
hours. He launched the first attack against it the following morning
when he sent the U.S. 22nd Infantry, supported by Shermans and
tank destroyers, up the western slopes of the Schnee Eifel (Snow
Mountains). Neither Gerow nor Maj. Gen. Raymond O. Barton, the
commander of the 4th Infantry Division, expected serious resistance.
These expectations seemed to be confirmed when the forward American patrols reported that they had captured the first bunkers on the
West Wall, which were undefended.

The first serious opposition came when the Americans ran up
against German positions just north of Brandscheid, a fortified hamlet northeast of the village of Buchet, on the southern flank of the
U.S. 4th Infantry. They were met by *Kampfgruppe* Kuehne, which was
led by SS Major Kuehne, who had 800 men, mostly from the army's

105th Training Battalion, and a battery of 88-millimeter antiaircraft guns—against Latham's 3,000 men. Brandscheid was surrounded by open fields, offering the Americans little cover. The SS quickly knocked out the first two Shermans, and the Americans, who would have been slaughtered had they continued forward, halted.

Unknown to them at the time, the Americans were facing the 2nd SS Panzer Division "Das Reich." Under SS Maj. Gen. Heinz Lammerding, who had now recovered from the wounds he suffered in Normandy, the division was a seriously depleted unit. Lammerding had about 750 men from his own division (grouped into four battalions) and 1,900 attached soldiers (in nine battalions), a total of 2,650 men. He also had fourteen 75-millimeter antitank guns, thirty-seven artillery pieces, one assault gun, one operational Panther tank, and two inoperative tanks in a nearby repair facility.[23]

The next morning, in a drizzling rain, the Americans renewed their attack, this time launching a frontal assault against Brandscheid itself. The hamlet, which lay on a small hill, would soon become known as "the Verdun of the Eifel," and it would change hands eight times over the next four months. The 2nd Battalion of the 22nd Infantry Regiment reached the hill but was repulsed when Kuehne launched a counterattack. The fighting was fierce. Lt. Col. John Dowdy, the 2nd Battalion's commander, was killed by an artillery shell burst.

As the Americans retreated through the forests of the Schnee Eifel, they came under well-directed German artillery fire. By the time they arrived back at the their jump-off point, one company had lost half of its men. The Americans had lost 800 men, the Germans about 680.

On the morning of September 16, the men of the U.S. 4th Infantry Division's 12th Infantry Regiment and the U.S. 28th Infantry Division also went over to the attack. They discovered that the 3rd SS Panzer Grenadier Regiment "Deutschland" of the 2nd SS Panzer Division "Das Reich" had taken positions north and south of Brandscheid. The Americans were again checked. The 28th Infantry, a division of Pennsylvania National Guardsmen, lost 1,500 men.

Meanwhile, Gerow reinforced Maj. Gen. Lunsford Oliver's 5th Armored Division with the 112th Infantry Regiment of the 28th Division and threw it into the attack. Oliver struck across the Sauer near the village of Wallendorf, which was defended by the hastily assembled Alarm Battalion Trier and Alarm Battery Trier. Subsequent investigations revealed that these units, which had been assembled from the thousands of stragglers who were making their way back to Germany and had been pressed into the I SS Corps, contained men from thirty different formations. They were certainly no match for a tough, experienced, full-strength and well-led U.S. armored division. Most of the Trier companies were soon in full retreat.

One company of Alarm Battalion Trier, however, launched a spirited counterattack. It was commanded by Capt. Karl Kornowski, a Catholic priest and a veteran of the Russian Front. He found the battalion commander, a major, huddled in a trench. The major ordered Kornowski to counterattack, but as the priest recalled, "He was too busy crapping his pants to show us [where]." Captain Kornowski personally led the counterattack and recaptured eight bunkers from the Americans. He then ran into an ambush and was captured. The Americans sent him to Wallendorf, where they took his few belongings, including a bottle of locally manufactured schnapps. Fearing that it might be poisoned, they made him drink some. They then took the bottle back but returned his tobacco pouch, rosary, and picture of the Virgin Mary.[24]

Alarm Battery Trier failed even more miserably than did its counterpart, leading to the court-martial of its commander. The proceedings revealed that he was a reserve *Luftwaffe* signals officer who knew nothing about artillery. His battery had little ammunition and almost no optical or observation equipment, and only three enlisted men in the unit had any artillery training at all.

General Oliver had been lucky enough to strike at three different boundary lines: between Army Groups B and G, between the 7th and 1st Armies, and between the I SS and LXXX Corps. He had also unwittingly struck through the Moselle Gate, one of thinnest and most vulnerable sections of the Siegfried Line. Here the German engineers of the late 1930s had depended on the mountainous and forested terrain and poor road network, rather than the strength of the West Wall, to halt an invader.

Elements of General Bayerlein's decimated Panzer Lehr Division lay behind Alarm Battalion Trier. He counterattacked with a company of PzKw IV tanks, but the Americans were waiting for him. The Shermans destroyed three panzers and six half-tracks and were soon pursuing the five surviving Mark IVs through the Siegfried Line and into Germany itself. At one point, Oliver's forward units pushed six miles into the Third Reich and were only three miles from Bitburg, a major road and railroad center.

By nightfall, the situation was so serious that Field Marshal Rundstedt took a personal interest in the battle. He telephoned General Knobelsdorff, whose 1st Army was responsible for this sector, and demanded, "How is it possible that the Americans could break through the West Wall like that?" Knobelsdorff tried to make excuses, but Rundstedt would have none of it. He took Gen. of Infantry Dr. Franz Beyer's LXXX Corps away from Knobelsdorff and gave it to 7th Army, making Beyer, Brandenberger, and Field Marshal Model responsible for the battle.[25] Rundstedt told his staff that it was time to "pull the club out of the sack." To hold the line until he could launch a counterattack, he reinforced Beyer with two grenadier battalions and a flak regiment of eleven batteries. He also dispatched the 19th Volksgrenadier Division from Knobelsdorff's army to the threatened sector. He reinforced the I SS Panzer Corps, which was responsible for the northern edge of the salient, with the 2nd Panzer Division, and ordered the 36th Volksgrenadier Division, the remnants of the 5th Parachute Division, and the 108th Panzer Brigade to the endangered sector, where they were to launch a counterattack.[26]

They need not have bothered. At 8:40 P.M., General Gerow ordered Oliver to call off the offensive. American logistics had failed. The U.S. First Army did not have the gasoline to continue the offensive long enough to achieve any decisive results. Hodges barely had enough fuel to extend his southern flank far enough to link up with Patton's Third Army.

Gen. Siegfried Westphal, the chief of staff of OB West, later recorded that the Allies had missed a golden opportunity to effect the immediate and total defeat of the Third Reich. "If the enemy had thrown in more forces," he wrote in 1951, "he would not only have broken through the German line of defenses which were in process of being built up in the Eifel, but in the absence of any considerable reserves on the German side he must have effected the collapse of the whole Western Front within a short time."[27]

From September 17 to October 4, the U.S. V Corps pulled back and abandoned the Wallendorf bridgehead and went over to the defensive throughout the Ardennes sector. General Beyer had no way of knowing what the American strategy was, so he and Keppler launched a series of attacks on the American salient. They were greatly hampered by the weather, which turned clear on the eighteenth and brought the return of the fighter-bombers. German forces were pounded in their assembly areas wherever they were identified. The 108th Panzer Brigade was hit especially hard, although exact casualty figures are not available. During the evening of September 23, Beyer launched an effective counterattack on Romersberg. The 19th Volksgrenadier Division advanced down the Sauer River, captured several American bunkers and moved behind the U.S. 5th Armored Division. They then knocked out fifteen Shermans with shots from behind. The LXXX Corps reported knocking out thirty-one of the sixty American tanks that had penetrated the West Wall. It also reported knocking out ten reconnaissance vehicles, shooting down nine airplanes, taking 52 prisoners, and finding 531 American dead.[28]

The German propaganda ministry reported dozens of horror stories about American behavior in the Wallendorf bridgehead. Goebbels reported that the Americans acted like the "barbarians of old." They were all ex-convicts, the scum of the American prison system. They mounted a "reign of terror" in the Wallendorf area, complete with rape, murder, pillaging, and arson. One story was entitled "The Raped Village," and another headline blared, "Women and Children Used as Human Shields." One story told how they beat a mother of four unconscious in the village of Kruchten. The villagers begged on their knees for the brutal Americans to stop. But they would not. After the mother lost consciousness, they burned every house in the village. "This is what we'll do with every German village we capture," one American reportedly declared. "Burn it to the ground!"[29]

The truth was quite different. A priest on the American side of the line later recalled that they lived as if on an island. They were not bothered by the American army nor by the Nazis, who had fled. There was no electricity, no government, no ration cards, and no money, but that didn't matter since no shops were open. They lived by bartering and eating local crops and animals. There was enough food, and it was good. The only thing they were short of, the priest recalled, was salt.

✠

Back in Germany, the Nazis belatedly tried to get every ounce of strength and production they could from the German people. On August 24, Hitler and Goebbels issued another wave of total war decrees. Effective September 1, all theaters, music halls, bars and cabarets were closed. All publishing houses were shut down except those publishing *Mein Kampf* or medical textbooks. All universities were closed except those training physicians for the military or SS. All boys and girls sixteen years of age or older were now eligible for active military duty or some other form of service in the case of girls. Most pilot training schools were closed because the imminent fall of Ploesti in Romania meant that there would not be enough fuel to train them. Excess air force and naval personnel, including U-boat men without submarines, were transferred to the infantry. This order may have affected up to 30 percent of all men in the German Navy. Several new penal battalions (*Strafbattalionen*) were created from men in military prisons.

Even before the August 24 decrees, many fourteen-year-old boys were already serving in flak batteries as auxiliaries or "flak helpers." Some of their former teachers tried to continue their education by riding out to the batteries on horseback to hold classes there. The auxiliaries, however, defeated these attempts by bribing the air force sergeants with cigarettes. Whenever a teacher appeared, an air raid alert was sounded. The auxiliaries went to the guns, and the teachers had to leave the area.

While the floodgates were creaking in the Ardennes, the Replacement Army in Berlin was working overtime to raise new combat formations for the Reich. The Replacement (or Home) Army and its subordinate *Wehrkreise* (military districts) have never been given the credit they deserve by historians for the way they performed during

World War II. This is partially because the Replacement Army was led by two very unsympathetic characters: Col. Gen. Fritz Fromm and Reichsführer-SS Heinrich Himmler. Himmler, of course, was a rabid Nazi who was largely responsible for the Holocaust, and Fromm was both pro-Nazi and anti-Nazi at the same time.[30] Despite their lack of character, however, both Fromm and Himmler were good organizers, and Himmler had inherited a very efficient organization when Fromm was arrested on July 21, 1944.

The Replacement Army and its *Wehrkreise* had tremendous responsibilities. They implemented the German draft; at least partially trained the new recruits; organized them into companies, battalions, regiments, and divisions; and provided replacements and new equipment for older divisions already in the field. Generally speaking, they did an excellent job, despite interference from Hitler.

The Home Army provided divisions for the field armies in bunches, which were called "waves." The Germans conquered Poland with Waves 1 through 4. By the summer of 1944, they had activated a total of twenty-nine waves. In the fall of 1944, they activated six Wave 30 divisions, of which the 12th, 16th and 36th were sent to the West. The five Wave 31 shadow divisions were quickly absorbed by the 25 Wave 32 divisions: grenadier divisions numbered 564 and 588. They, in turn, were absorbed by veteran infantry (now Volksgrenadier) divisions which had been depleted in combat.[31] Within four weeks, several of these would be on their way to the front.

These new divisions were smaller than the 1939-type divisions, to be sure, but they were equipped with a much higher proportion of automatic weapons and shoulder-fired disposable anti-tank weapons, which increased their fire power per man markedly.

AACHEN: THE FIRST ATTACKS

Aachen was the first German city to be seriously threatened by the Allied advance. One of the major seats of Catholicism in Germany and built by Charlemagne, Aachen was an old imperial city—thirty-two German emperors and kings had been crowned there—a symbol of German nationalism, and thus a significant part of Nazi mythology.

By the fall of 1944, there was little left to admire about the formerly beautiful old city. It had been struck by seventy-five large air raids, and the famous inner city was covered by 3,000,000 square meters of debris; 43 percent of its buildings had been destroyed, and another 40 percent had been badly damaged. Of the 162,000 people who lived there in 1939, only about 25,000 remained, most of them huddled in cellars.

On September 5, Eisenhower referred to it when he issued the following order:

> From the beginning of this campaign, I have always envisaged that as soon as substantial destruction of the enemy forces in France could be accomplished, we should advance rapidly on the Rhine by pushing through the Aachen Gap in the north and through the Metz Gap in the south. The virtue of this movement is that it takes advantage of all existing lines of communication in the advance towards Germany and brings the southern forces on the Rhine at Coblenz, practically on the flank of the forces that would advance straight through Aachen. I see no reason to change this conception.[32]

When J. Lawton Collins's VII Corps of 80,000 men approached the area on September 12, its objective was not the city itself, but rather the Stolberg Corridor, a few miles to the south. Collins planned for Maj. Gen. Clarence Huebner's U.S. 1st Infantry Division (the "Big Red One") to probe the defenses of Aachen on September 13, while Maj. Gen. Maurice Rose's 3rd Armored Division broke through the West Wall defenses in the corridor. Once the wall had been breached, the 1st Infantry would attack Aachen, while the tank division, supported by Maj. Gen. Louis Craig's 9th Infantry Division, outflanked the city to the east, taking Eschweiler and then the city of Dueren on the Roer River.

Lt. Gen. Friedrich-August Schack's LXXXI Corps, which controlled four divisions, defended the Aachen sector. Of the corps' divisions, the 49th Infantry Division was in remnants, and the 9th Panzer had been so reduced by casualties that it had the combat value of a regiment. The 275th Infantry and 116th Panzer, however, were in reasonably good condition. Schack was not a good choice to defend Aachen. Highly excitable, he had commanded the 272nd Infantry

Division in combat in Normandy, in the hell of Falaise, and in the retreat across the Seine, during which much of his division had been destroyed. He had been in command of the LXXXI only since September 4—the day Gen. of Panzer Troops Adolf Kuntzen had been relieved of his duties and sent into involuntary retirement. Understandably, Schack was suffering from stress and was, in fact, on the verge of a nervous breakdown as the Americans approached the West Wall.

On the specific orders of Field Marshal Rundstedt, Schack assigned the task of defending the city to what was considered his best division, Lt. Gen. Count Gerhard von Schwerin's 116th Panzer—the "Greyhound Division"—which he reinforced with the 105th Panzer Brigade and three fortress battalions.[33] Schwerin was one of the heroes of the Third Reich and only the third general in the German Army to be decorated with the Knight's Cross with Oak Leaves and Swords. He was also a fractious man, a disillusioned defeatist who had been privy to the conspiracy of July 20. (One of his relatives, Count von Schwerin und Schwanenfeld, had already been arrested and would soon be executed for his part in the plot. General Schwerin had been assigned to approach the Allies in the event the assassination attempt succeeded.)

Schwerin's defeatism had been noted weeks before. In Normandy, he had ignored an order to counterattack, and Baron von Funck, the commander of the XXXXVII Panzer Corps, had wanted to relieve him of his command as early as August 7. On August 23, Col. Gerhard Mueller, a veteran of the Afrika Korps who had lost an arm on the Eastern Front, replaced Schwerin as commander of the 116th Panzer. Mueller proved to be a better regimental commander than a division commander, however. The staff and senior officers of the division had revolted against Mueller and, in an event almost unprecedented in the history of the German Army, succeeded. Mueller was sent to the 9th Panzer Division, whose commander had been wounded, and Schwerin resumed command of the 116th on September 1, although Model and Brandenberger were now suspicious of him.

Upon assuming command of Aachen on September 12, Schwerin's first act was to reverse a Fuehrer Order. Acting on instructions from Hitler, *Kreisleiter* Rudolf Schmeer ordered the evacuation of the city; then, instead of supervising the evacuation, he fled Aachen with the National Socialist administrators and most of the police force.[34] Schwerin immediately halted the evacuation, which he considered senseless. Then, taking his life in his hands, Schwerin addressed a note to the American commander, unaware that the Americans' primary objective was the Stolberg corridor and not the city itself. Written in English, it called on Collins to treat the inhabitants in a humane way, implying that he had no intention of defending the place.

The German engineers who designed the West Wall recognized the importance of the Stolberg Corridor and the entire area around Aachen, which they referred to as the Aachen Gap. The fortifications around the city consisted of two deep and elaborate belts of pillboxes and bunkers, all with overlapping fields of fire. While the West Wall averaged only three miles in depth across most of the German frontier, it was up to ten miles thick in the Aachen Gap. The first belt of fortifications, the Scharnhorst Line, included a continuous band of pyramid-shaped concrete antitank obstacles known as "dragon's teeth."

The second belt, the Schill Line, lacked the dragon's teeth but was thicker than the Scharnhorst Line. Both belts had hundreds of pillboxes, which averaged about twenty-five feet in width, forty-five in depth, and twenty in height. Their walls and roofs were made of reinforced concrete, three to eight feet thick, and could withstand almost any artillery bombardment. They had a major weakness, however: they were built in the 1930s, when the 37-millimeter gun was the standard antitank weapon of the day. Although effective against the tanks of 1939, the 37-millimeter gun was practically useless against the Allied tanks of 1944. Moreover, West Wall pillboxes could not accommodate 75-millimeter and 88-millimeter weapons because their gun openings were too small. Some of the pillboxes could not even house heavy machine guns.

The U.S. 1st Infantry Division's probe on September 13 almost threw the nervous General Schack into a panic because it penetrated into Aachen's Staatsforst: one of the many woods surrounding the city. Schack promptly reinforced Schwerin with the 34th Assault Gun Brigade, which hurriedly unloaded at Aachen's main station, counterattacked (as Schack had ordered), and quickly threw the Americans out of the woods.

Schack had committed his reserves at the wrong point. The U.S. force that had reached the Staatsforst amounted to only a single infantry battalion while the main American attack was launched several miles south by the U.S. 3rd Armored Division, which was met by the vanguards of the 9th Panzer Division, most of which was still en route to the corridor. This veteran division was now under the command of Gerhard Mueller because General Jolasse had been wounded a few days before.[35] Although it was greatly reduced in numbers and consisted largely of young and inexperienced motorized infantry, the 9th Panzer retained its fighting spirit and would do so throughout the war. The division tied up the 3rd Armored in the dragon's teeth throughout the morning of September 13. Then, when the Americans at last penetrated the outer crust with a task force of twenty tanks, the panzer troops knocked out half of them near Mausbach with their self-propelled assault guns and *Panzerfausts* (shoulder-fired, single-shot, disposable antitank weapons). The Americans did not really begin to gain ground until nightfall restricted the visibility of the German crews in the pillboxes. Meanwhile, General Schack reinforced the Schill Line in the Stolberg Corridor with Lt. Gen. Paul Mahlmann's 353rd Infantry Division.[36] Until a few hours before, the 353rd had been a mere headquarters without any infantry battalions. Now it controlled a few local security units made up of older, inexperienced men whose morale was poor. Despite their low quality, Schack committed them to combat south of Stolberg.

That night, another Führer Order arrived in Aachen instructing Schwerin to resume the evacuation of the city. Almost simultaneously, the men of S.A. Major Zimmermann, a fanatical Nazi, began to arrive in Aachen with instructions to carry out Hitler's evacuation orders. Schwerin had no choice but to rescend his order of September 13 and allow the evacuation to start again. *Kreisleiter* Schmeer came back to Aachen to supervise the evacuation, but his return did not save him. Furious that he had fled, Hitler ordered Schmeer stripped of his party offices and sent to the front as a private in the infantry. He was not heard from again.

On September 14, the vanguard of the U.S. 9th Infantry Division joined the battle on the southern flank of the 3rd Armored, and the American troops began to make more rapid progress. They gained four and a half miles that day and by nightfall had captured a bridge across the Vicht River (south of Stolberg), which the 353rd Infantry Division had failed to blow up. Fighting was still heavy, especially against the 9th Panzer Division. The battalion spearheading the American advance was reduced to a strength of thirteen tanks—40 percent of its normal establishment. That night, however, most of the 353rd Infantry Division simply melted away into the darkness, leaving very little opposition to the American advance. By daybreak on September 15, General Schack was on the verge of a nervous breakdown. The Americans were across the Vicht and were within two miles of penetrating the West Wall, and most of his remaining pillboxes were empty. Frantically, he called his commander, General Brandenberger, for help.

Gen. of Panzer Troops Erich Brandenberger, the balding, bespectacled, full-jowled commander of the 7th Army, did not look the part, but he was just the type of leader for a crisis. He radiated calm but acted quickly, decisively, and almost always correctly. He had a superb record and had mastered many difficult situations on the Eastern Front. Fighting for the West Wall was not his idea; he favored an immediate retreat to the Rhine, mainly because he knew that the army he had inherited was too weak to hold the 100-mile-long front between Trier in the south and Aachen in the north. On his southern flank lay the I SS Panzer Corps, which included four *kampfgruppe*-size divisions: the 1st SS Panzer, 12th SS Panzer, 2nd SS Panzer, and 2nd Panzer Divisions—down to a total combat strength of 2,000 men and six tanks. The I SS Panzer also controlled the 172nd Replacement Division, a training unit of limited combat value. In Brandenberger's center, General Straube's LXXIV Corps had four "divisions": the remnants of the 347th Infantry and 3rd Parachute; the 89th Infantry, which was full of inexperienced replacements; and the 526th Replacement Division, a training unit just down from Aachen.[37] He had little with which to reinforce Schack on his northern flank except the 12th Volksgrenadier Division, a rebuilt unit which had just been assigned to the 7th Army and had not yet arrived from East Prussia. Unlike the other divisions in the 7th Army, this one was at full strength—almost 15,000 men—and had its full complement of artillery and seventeen assault guns. Brandenberger promptly diverted it to the threatened sector and ordered Schack to commit it to battle as a unit—i.e., not one battalion at a time as they arrived.

In the meantime, Schack frantically ordered General Mueller to close the gap with a counterattack. The inexperienced panzer grenadiers of the 9th Panzer promptly moved out, almost in parade-ground formation, and attacked the American flank at Zweifall three times. They were slaughtered by American artillery; by the end of the day, the fields around Zweifall were littered with German dead. The 9th Panzer had been severely damaged, and the Americans were almost through the West Wall. On the morning of September 16, standing between the U.S. 3rd Armored Division and open country-side were a handful of bunkers and a "stomach battalion." Despite their physical ailments, these middle-age men managed to impose a considerable delay on the 3rd Armored, as did the survivers of the 9th Panzer, who checked the Americans in street fighting inside Stol-berg. Meanwhile, the train carrying the men of the I Battalion of the 27th Fusilier Regiment of the 12th Volksgrenadier Division arrived at Juelich and found Schack's staff officers waiting for them. Within hours, they were thrown into battle at Verlautenheide, north of Eilen-dorf. The II Battalion, which arrived at Juelich an hour later, was immediately rushed to Stolberg, where it joined the battle there. Schack had ignored Brandenberger's order not to commit the 12th Volksgrenadier Division piecemeal.

Sunday, September 17, was another day of heavy fighting in the Stolberg Corridor, as General Schack committed the 27th Fusilier Regiment to counterattacks across the open fields between Verlaut-enheide and Stolberg, where the artillery of the 3rd Armored Division cut it to pieces. By noon, the 27th Fusilier was a broken force. The Americans had lost only two dead and twenty-seven wounded. Schack also committed the 48th Grenadier Regiment of the 12th Volksgrenadier to an attack at Weissenberg, but here the Germans achieved surprise and pushed the Americans back. General Rose managed to stop them only by committing his last reserves, but casualties in the 48th Grenadier were also high. One battalion lost 400 men killed or wounded in twelve hours.

Feeling that his corps commander was wasting his division in uncoordinated piecemeal attacks, the 12th's commander, thirty-eight-year-old Col. Gerhard Engel, telephoned Schack and, in an almost insubordinate tone, demanded that all further attacks be postponed until he could reorganize the division for a concentrated attack. A subdued Schack agreed. Colonel Engel, after all, had been one of the Führer's adjutants from 1937 to 1943, until he had become so inspired by one of Hitler's speeches that he volunteered for frontline duty. Hitler was known to have a soft spot for this idealistic young officer.[38]

By Sunday, September 17, Schwerin's note of September 13 had found its way into the hands of the Nazis. General Schack asked him to report to his headquarters. When Schwerin arrived, Schack relieved him of his command and, in the name of Field Marshal Model, arrested him. He told Schwerin that he had orders to deliver him to the nearest People's Court, which was attached to the 7th Army's headquarters at Munstereifel. The count played for time by asking Schack's permission to return to his division to say farewell. The corps commander agreed, but only on the condition that Schwerin return immediately to corps headquarters. Schwerin assented and left. He turned command of the division over to Col. Heinrich Voigtsberger, the commander of the 60th Panzer Grenadier and the division's senior regimental commander,[39] but he had no intention of returning. Schwerin believed that Aachen would fall in a matter of days, if not hours. The U.S. VII Corps was nearly through the West Wall, the 12th Volksgrenadier Division had been wasted, and LXXXI Corps had nothing left with which to oppose the Americans. Schwerin either did not know of, or did not appreciate the significance of, an event that took place earlier that day when three Allied parachute divisions were dropped behind German lines to the northwest, beginning the Battle of Arnhem. During this operation, code-named Operation Market Garden, the Allies would give Montgomery's assault forces supply priority, and the offensive in the Aachen sector promptly came to a halt. Brandenberger would have more than a week to sort out his units and prepare his defenses.

When Schwerin did not return, and with the front silent, a strong SS detachment, led by an SS lieutenant colonel, was ordered to the headquarters of the 116th Panzer Division to arrest the missing general. A group of PzKw IV tanks blocked its way. The SS leader furiously demanded to be allowed to pass, but the soldiers obeyed only their own officers. Through an intermediary, General Schack proposed to meet with Schwerin at his Schack's former headquarters, a farmhouse near Berensberg. Schwerin arrived late, after Schack had left, and was nearly captured by the hated German military police, who were known as "chained dogs" because of the silver crescent plate they wore around their necks. He escaped only by jumping out a back window, after which he hid out in Aachen, but only for a day or two. When the Americans still did not attack, Schwerin became convinced that he was risking the lives of his beloved Greyhounds by allowing them to hide him. At last, he agreed to surrender himself to General Brandenberger at the *Führerbunker*, a specially constructed complex in the woods east of Munstereifel from which Hitler had directed the campaign against France in 1940. Schwerin was then taken to Rundstedt's headquarters by a major who warned the count that he had orders to shoot him if he tried to escape. Remarkably enough, Schwerin got off with a warning and a severe reprimand, thanks to the intervention of Field Marshal Rundstedt. He was even given command of a new division, the 90th Panzer Grenadier, in Italy in December.

Lieutenant General Schwerin was not the only commander in the Aachen Gap to lose his job that week. The SS denounced Schwerin's replacement, Colonel Voigtsberger, as an accomplice to the "traitor" Schwerin, and he was also sacked.[40] He was succeeded by Maj. Gen. Siegfried von Waldenburg, the former commander of the 26th Panzer Grenadier Regiment, who had spent two and a half years as deputy military attaché to Rome and chief of staff to the German mission to *Commando Supremo* (1941 to early 1944).[41] This capable officer led the 116th Panzer Division for the rest of the war. Gerhard Mueller, who had received his promotion to major general only on September 1, was sacked as commander of the 9th Panzer Division by General Brandenberger on September 18, along with his operations officer, Lt. Col. Wilhelm Friedel. The 7th Army commander had been dissatisfied with Mueller's leadership in general and his conduct of the counterattacks of September 16 in particular. He was replaced by Maj. Gen. Baron Harald von Elverfeldt, an officer who had distinguished himself as chief of staff of the LVI Panzer Corps and 9th Army on the Eastern Front. Elverfeldt would lead the division until he was killed in action in March 1945.[42]

Finally, the highly excitable General Schack was relieved of the command of the LXXXI Corps on September 21 and replaced with Gen. of Infantry Friedrich Kochling, a more capable and less nervous officer.[43] Schack, who had been a corps commander for only seventeen days, was relieved without perjudice, and after a three-month medical leave to rest his strained nerves, he was given another corps command. Eventually, he would be promoted to general of infantry.

AN ARMY ESCAPES

And what was happening to the north, in the zones of the 1st Parachute and 15th Armies, while Brandenberger was trying to check the Americans around Aachen?

The British 11th Armoured Division captured Antwerp on September 4, taking the Germans by surprise. Hitler quickly gave the 1st Parachute Army under General Student the task of checking the British advance on the Albert Canal line. Meanwhile, panic broke out in Holland. It was triggered by the *Reichskommissar*, Dr. Arthur Seyss-Inquart, and Anton Mussert, the brutal leader of the Dutch Nazi Party.[44] As early as September 1, Seyss-Inquart ordered German civilians, including the Nazi administrators, to leave the western parts of the Netherlands. Mussert followed his lead, and both officials were among the first to flee. Seyss-Inquart established his new headquarters in a lavish bunker at Apeldoorn fifteen miles north of Arnhem. Mussert moved to Twente in Overijssel Province, even farther away from the Allied armies.

Although the initial evacuations caused a considerable amount of nervousness among the Nazis and their collaborators, the situation did not degenerate into an absolute shambles until Antwerp fell on September 4, when panic set in. There were more Nazis in Holland than any country outside Germany, and many of them were now fleeing for their lives, along with German civil administrators, labor battalions, *Luftwaffe* service personnel, *Osttruppen*, and even some German soldiers. Railroad stations were overwhelmed with people trying to escape to the Reich, many of them with their families. Some soldiers even threw away their weapons—or sold them to the Dutch. Some troops begged Dutch citizens for civilian clothing; others took it at gunpoint. Officers lost control of the situation, and discipline broke down completely. Gangs of German soldiers stole horses, wagons, automobiles, trucks, and bicycles—anything that would help them get to Germany more quickly—while Nazi officials and some officers and sergeants tried to make off with their loot. Most of the disorderly troops seemed to be drunk. One Dutch woman recalled seeing a German truck carrying off a large double bed–with a woman in it.[45]

"Scenes were witnessed which nobody would ever have deemed possible in the German army . . ." Walter Goerlitz wrote.

> Naval troops marched northward without weapons, selling their spare uniforms. . . . They told people that the war was over and they were going home. Lorries loaded with officers, their mistresses and large quantities of champagne and brandy contrived to get back as far as the Rhineland, and it was necessary to set up special courts-martial to deal with such cases.[46]

The Dutch civilians were also infected by the panic, but in another way. Liberation fever set in. Everywhere Dutch civilians were rejoicing, crowding the sidewalks, waving long hidden Dutch flags, yelling "Long Live the Queen!" and singing the Dutch national anthem. Rumors that the British were just down the road swept every Dutch city as crowds gathered, straining to catch their first glimpse of the liberating Allies.

But the Allies were not just down the road. They were back in Belgium.

Gradually, discipline reasserted itself. Although Germany's divisions had been scattered, its command system was still more or less intact, and highly trained and experienced divisional and regimental cadres were sent to the Netherlands, where they absorbed stragglers and restored order. New reinforcements—paratroopers, Hitler Youth, and two SS panzer divisions—appeared on the scene, obviously ready to kill for their Führer. On September 10, Heinrich Himmler promulgated an order which, in the opinion of Milton Shulman, did more than anything else to restore order: "Every deserter will be prosecuted and will find his just punishment. Furthermore his ignominious behavior will entail the most severe consequences for his family. Upon examination of the circumstances, they will be summarily shot."[47]

Lt. Gen. Kurt Chill, the commander of the 85th Infantry Division, which had practically been destroyed, was ordered to return to Germany to rebuild his scattered command. Instead, he stayed in Belgium and, on his own initiative, set up reception stations on the northern end of every bridge north of the Albert Canal, absorbed elements of two other divisions, and formed his units and stragglers into the ad hoc Battle Group Chill.[48] By September 4, Student's 1st Parachute Army could muster approximately 20,000 men, along with a few flak guns and twenty-five tanks—not enough to stop the British, but it was a beginning. It was joined later that day by Maj. Gen. Karl Sievers's 719th Infantry Division coming down from Dordrecht on the Dutch coast. Meanwhile, Trierenberg's 347th Infantry Division—or what was left of it after Normandy—rolled into Capellen seven miles north of Antwerp. Student was soon on the verge of mustering a real army. Col. Baron von der Heydte's rebuilt 6th Parachute Regiment arrived with about 3,000 men, followed by elements of the 2nd Parachute Regiment. They were soon joined by five more parachute regiments, a parachute antitank battalion, and about 5,000 service troops, transported from Bitsch in forty-three trains. These units became part of the ad hoc Parachute Training Division Erdmann, which was commanded by Student's own chief of staff, Lt. Gen. Wolfgang Erdmann.[49] Others were assigned to Battle Group Walther, led by Col. Erich Walther, a tough young paratrooper who had distinguished himself against the British Eighth Army in Sicily. By the middle of September, Student's center had been pushed back from the

Albert Canal to the Meuse-Escaut Canal, but he now had a real army. From west to east, he controlled the 719th Infantry Division, Battle Group Chill, and Battle Group Walther—all under the command of Gen. Hans Reinhardt's LXXXVIII Corps, which had been transferred from the 15th Army. To the east lay Division Erdmann and the 176th Replacement Division—7,000 men under the command of Lt. Gen. Berthold Stumm—both directly under the control of the 1st Parachute Army. Farther to the east were two new 15th Army divisions, the 59th and 245th Infantry, under Lt. Gen. Walter Poppe and Lt. Gen. Erwin Sander, which had just crossed the Scheldt and had been placed under Student's command. The 59th was actually in reasonably good condition. The crisis, it seemed, was over, at least in the zone of the 1st Parachute Army.

The situation was also much improved for Gustav von Zangen's 15th Army. Trapped west of the Schacht when Antwerp fell, it seemed that it had little chance of escaping. On September 4, the British 11th Armoured Division was only eighteen miles from the South Beveland peninsula, Zangen's last escape route. From there, it would have been a simple matter to bar the neck of the peninsula, which was only two miles across, and 15th Army would be "in the bag." The British did no such thing, however. "It was a multiple lapse—by four commanders from Montgomery downwards," B. H. Liddell Hart wrote later.[50] But the British generals were looking to the north and east, not to the west. Montgomery, Dempsey, Horrocks, and Roberts were all focusing on crossing the Rhine, capturing Berlin, and ending the war—not on clearing the Scheldt. Horrocks later frankly admitted as much:

> My excuse is that my eyes were fixed entirely on the Rhine and everything else seemed of subsidiary importance. It never entered my head that the Scheldt would be mined and that we would not be able to use Antwerp until the channel had been swept and the Germans cleared from the coastlines on either side. . . . Napoleon would no doubt have realized these things but Horrocks didn't.[51]

Unmolested, Zangen deployed the 245th and 711th Infantry Divisions, and later part of the 70th Infantry, in covering positions along the Bruges-Ghent Canal. He also posted the fresh 64th Infantry Division, just up from Germany, along the line of canals and waterways from the sea near Zeebrugge to the West Scheldt near Terneuzen. He placed the commander of the 344th Infantry Division, Lt. Gen. Felix Schwalbe, a deaf man, in charge of the actual evacuation.[52]

Schwalbe's evacuation fleet consisted of two obsolete Dutch freighters, sixteen Rhine River barges that could carry 250 men per trip, three large vehicle ferries, a few motorized rafts, and a handful of patrol boats. They were covered by the huge coastal guns on Walcheren Island and by antiaircraft gun concentrations at Breskens and Flushing. The Germans were surprised when the Allied navies made no attempt to disrupt the evacuation. Lt. Gen. Walter Poppe, the commander of the 59th Infantry Division, recalled that crossing the 3.5-mile-wide Scheldt in a completely blacked out convoy was "a most unpleasant experience."[53] He expected to be "blown out of the water" at any minute.

Proud, serious-minded, and capable, Schwalbe began his evacuation on September 6. To avoid heavy losses to the bombs of the Allied air forces, he operated only at night, unless the weather was poor enough to ground the fighter-bombers during the day. Had the Allies advanced another twenty miles and cut the South Beveland isthmus, Schwalbe had made contingency plans to evacuate the troops through the Dutch coastal islands to Dordrecht and Rotterdam—a dangerous journey of twelve hours, compared to the forty-five minute trip via Flushing. Had the isthmus been cut, the 15th Army would have had to abandon, at the very least, all of its vehicles, assault guns, and field artillery.

The 245th Infantry was the first division to cross. It joined the 1st Parachute Army on September 16 and was used to reinforce Battle Group Chill. The 59th Infantry crossed next and arrived just in time to counterattack the U.S. 101st Airborne Division on the Wilhelmina Canal bridge at Best on September 18. Zangen's headquarters units crossed on September 19, moving from Middelburg on Walheim Island to Dordrecht on the Dutch coast. The LXVI Corps crossed the Scheldt with the 346th and 711th Infantry Divisions on September 23, leaving the 719th Infantry as a rearguard along the Turnhout Canal line from near Antwerp to Turnhout. The next day, the 719th beat back an attempt by the Canadian First Army to force a crossing near Antwerp. By the time the ferry operation ended on September 26, Schwalbe had evacuated 82,000 men, 580 guns, 6,200 horses, and 6,200 vehicles.[54] And the guns of the 15th Army continued to bar the Scheldt to Allied supply ships, making Europe's second best port useless.

German field marshals Walter Model and Gerd von Rundstedt. U.S. ARMY

Dragon's teeth on
the Siegfried Line.

U.S. ARMY

Captured *panzerfaust*. U.S. ARMY

U.S. Gen.
Courtney Hodges.

U.S. ARMY

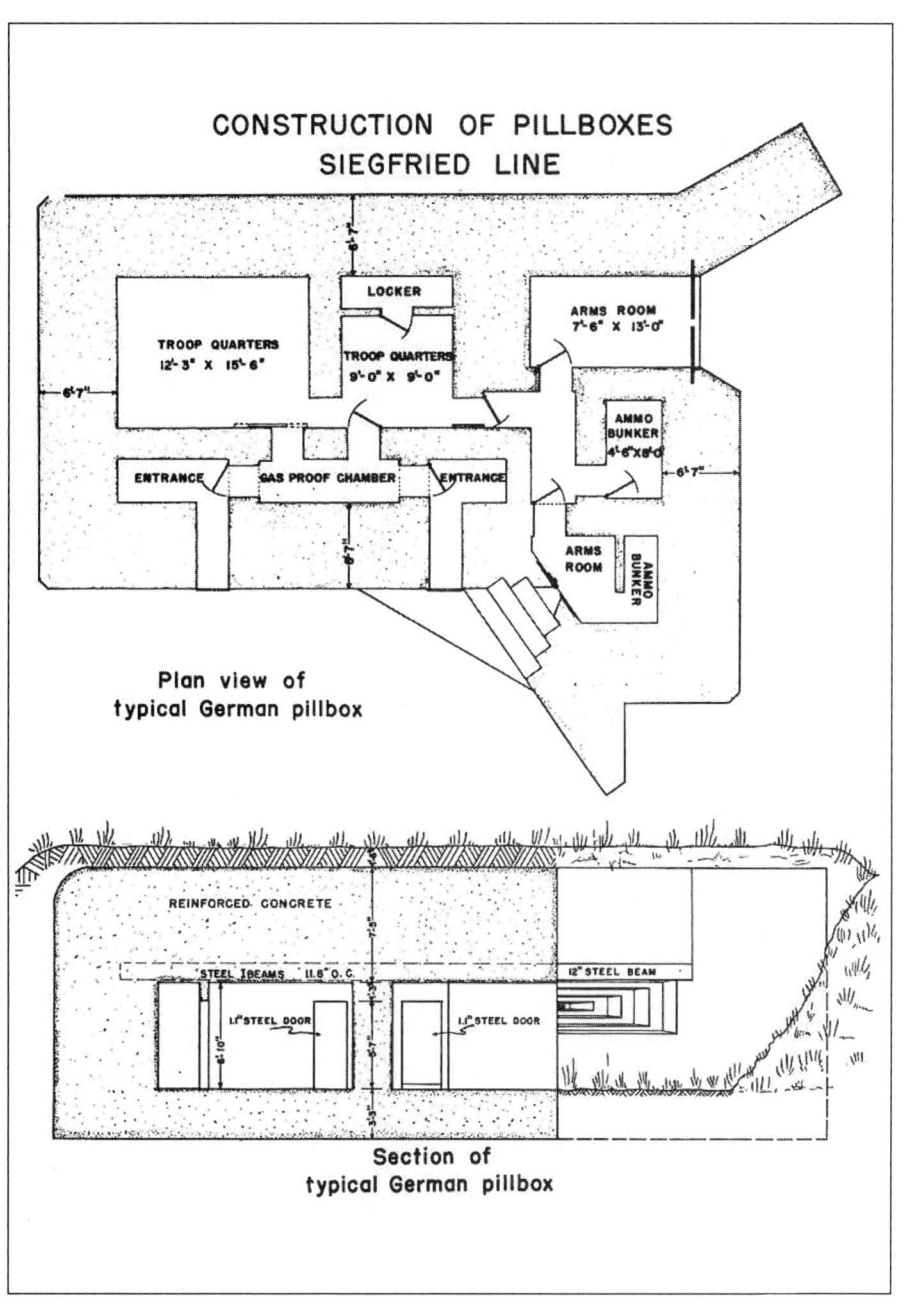

CONSTRUCTION OF PILLBOXES
SIEGFRIED LINE

LOCKER

ARMS ROOM
7'-6" X 13'-0"

TROOP QUARTERS
12'-3" X 15'-6"

TROOP QUARTERS
9'-0" X 9'-0"

AMMO BUNKER
4'-6"X8'-0"

ENTRANCE   **GAS PROOF CHAMBER**   **ENTRANCE**

ARMS ROOM

AMMO BUNKER

Plan view of typical German pillbox

REINFORCED CONCRETE

STEEL IBEAMS 11.8" O.C.

12" STEEL BEAM

1.1" STEEL DOOR

1.1" STEEL DOOR

Section of typical German pillbox

Plan of a typical German pillbox. U.S. ARMY

Dragon's teeth near Brandscheid. The Schnee Eifel is the wooded area at upper left.

U.S. Gen.
Leonard T. Gerow.

U.S. Gen. J. Lawton Collins.

U.S. Gen. Lewis Brereton.

U.S. Gen. Charles Corlett.

British Gen. Miles Dempsey (left) and U.S. Gen. James Gavin review plans for Market Garden. U.S. ARMY

U.S. Gen. Maxwell Taylor.

U.S. ARMY

German Gen. Kurt Student.

U.S. ARMY

The U.S. 82nd Airborne Division lands near Grave. U.S. ARMY

Aerial photo of
Aachen showing
key locations.

U.S. ARMY

The bridge at Nijmegen. U.S. ARMY

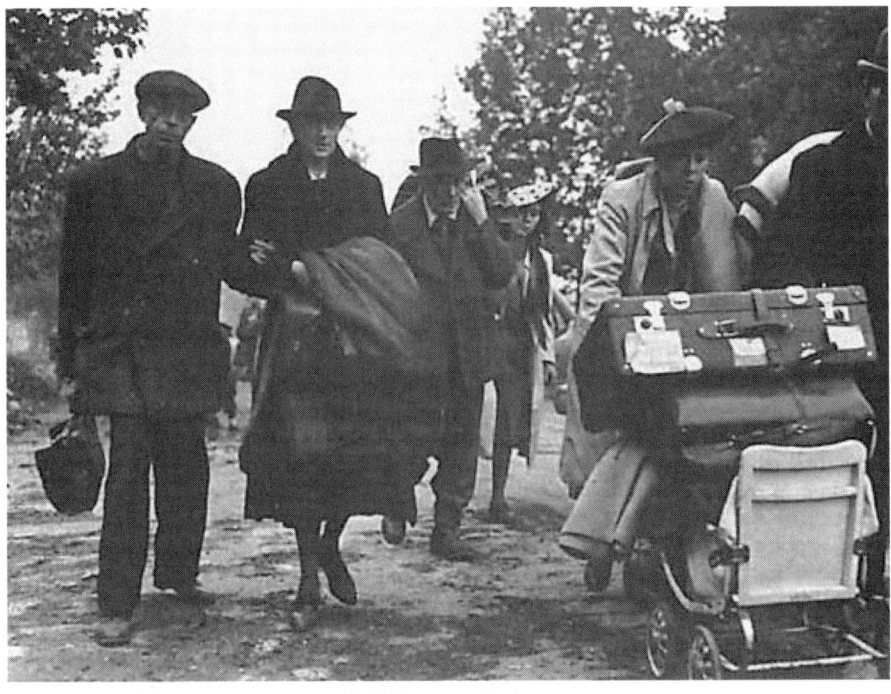

Civilians flee Aachen. U.S. ARMY

Col. Gerhard Wilck and his staff after surrendering Aachen.

German Gen. Gustav von Zangen.

Rimburg Castle.

Aerial photo of
Aachen showing
the extensive
damage it
suffered.

German Gen. Hasso von Manteuffel.

The Kall Trail.

American
troops struggle
up a hill.

U.S. ARMY

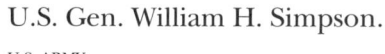

U.S. Gen. William H. Simpson.

U.S. ARMY

The Huertgen Forest.

U.S. ARMY

U.S. troops march through Siegfried Line fortifications. U.S. ARMY

U.S. Gen. Troy Middleton.
U.S. ARMY

An American vehicle
mired in the mud of the
Huertgen Forest. U.S. ARMY

CHAPTER 4

Arnhem

On September 4, SS Lt. Gen. Wilhelm "Willi" Bittrich,[1] the commander of the scattered II SS Panzer Corps, finally found the headquarters of Army Group B. Communications had failed, and he had been out of contact with army group for three days. Bittrich recalled later that he had not seen Model since they served together on the Eastern Front in 1941. "Monocle in his eye, wearing his usual short leather coat, Model was standing looking at a map and snapping out commands one after the other. There was little time for conversation."[2] His orders for Bittich would be of the greatest significance in the days ahead. He was to slowly withdraw his two divisions, the 9th and 10th SS Panzer, from the battle and move them north to a quiet sector where they could rest and refit. The location Model chose was quite arbitary: the Dutch city of Arnhem, located on the Rhine River seventy-five miles behind the front.

Field Marshal Bernard Law Montgomery was also making plans during the first week of the month. On September 10, he met with Eisenhower in Brussels, to discuss his latest and most controversial idea. The conference took place in Ike's airplane because the Supreme Commander had injured his good knee a few days before. Monty's plan was bold in the extreme: he wanted to use the First Allied Airborne Army, formed in August under the command of U.S. Lt. Gen. Lewis H. Brereton, to lay an airborne carpet as far north as Arnhem, where it would establish a bridgehead over the Rhine. The tanks of the British XXX Corps would break through the front of the German 1st Parachute Army and drive up this corridor, linking up with each airborne division in turn. When the operation was over, a powerful Allied armored force would be positioned on the edge of the North German Plain, thus outflanking the West Wall, which faded out northeast of Nijmegen. One more short thrust to the Zuider Zee would cut the Netherlands in half and isolate the German

OPERATION MARKET GARDEN: THE PLAN

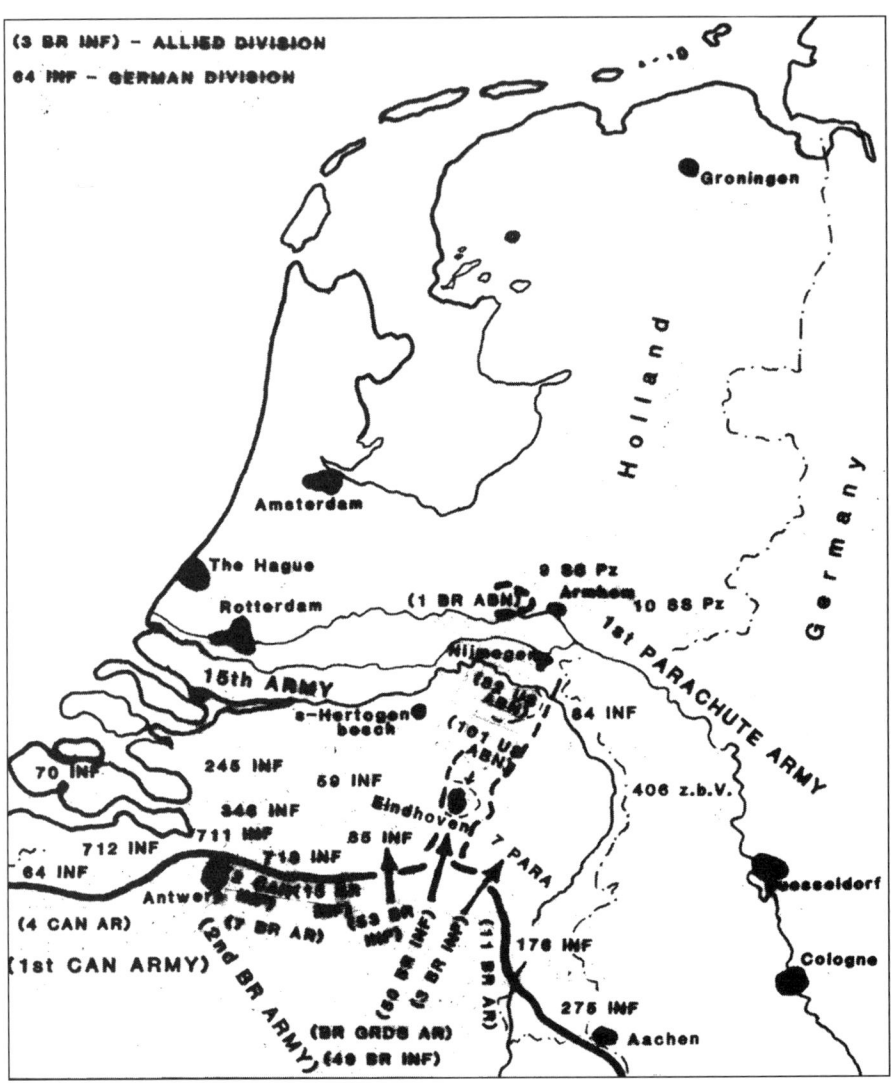

forces, including the 15th Army and half of the 1st Parachute Army, in western Holland. The British Second Army would then spearhead the single Allied thrust to the Ruhr and beyond.

The final Allied plan called for an attack almost due north through Eindhoven. It required the seizure of eleven bridges, including the Maas River bridge at Grave, the Waal bridge at Nijmegen, and the Lower Rhine bridge at Arnhem. Three Allied airborne divisions would be committed to the operation, the airborne part of which was called Market. The U.S. 101st Airborne, under Maj. Gen. Maxwell D. Taylor, would land north of Eindhoven between Veghel and Zon; the U.S. 82nd Airborne, under Brig. Gen. James M. Gavin, would land south of Nijmegen between the Maas and the Waal; and the 1st British Airborne, under Maj. Gen. Robert E. "Roy" Urquhart, would land west of Arnhem, just north of the Lower Rhine (Neder Rijn). A fourth division, the 52nd Lowland, would be brought into the battle zone by Dakota transport airplanes as soon as an airfield had been secured. The Polish 1st Parachute Brigade, under Maj. Gen. Stanislaw Sosabowski, was attached to the British 1st Airborne. Both the 1st and 82nd Airborne were under the command of the British I Airborne Corps. The operation would be supported by 4,700 airplanes, of which 2,023 were troop carriers. This figure excludes more than 2,500 gliders that were also assigned to the operation. In all, if everything went according to plan, 35,000 men would be deposited on the objectives in three days, one-third of them by glider. The operation—the largest airborne operation of all time—would be supported by almost 1,500 fighters and fighter-bombers.

The ground phase of the operation, dubbed Garden, would be the responsibility of Horrocks's XXX Corps, which included the Guards Armoured, 43rd Infantry, 50th Infantry, and U.S. 101st Airborne Divisions and the 8th Armoured Brigade. The Guards would spearhead the attack, followed by the 43rd (Wessex) and 50th (Northumberland) Divisions and the 8th Armoured Brigade. The Dutch Princess Irene Brigade would bring up the rear. The initial attack would be supported by 350 guns and waves of rocket-firing Typhoon airplanes. In all, Horrocks had some 20,000 vehicles—all on a single highway, heading north. Nine thousand engineers would also support the advance.

The unorthodox plan relied heavily on surprise and speed. It was also risky. The XXX Corps would have to push up a narrow sixty-four-mile-long corridor, and for a considerable distance, the entire ground force would be confined to one road. If the Germans were successful in delaying Horrocks or cutting the highway at any point, the paratroopers would be in very serious trouble. In addition, the plan called for the British 1st Airborne to land six to eight miles west of its principal objective, violating a cardinal principle of airborne warfare: "It is in general better to take landing losses and land on the objective than to have to fight after landing in order to reach the objective."[3]

The entire plan was colored by the euphoria of pursuit. No one seemed to realize that the pursuit was over; the *Wehrmacht* had already recovered its balance and was no longer running. Even the Allied military intelligence officers—normally a suspicious and pessimistic lot—were infected. Montgomery and Eisenhower continued to ignore the facts that the 15th Army was escaping, the Scheldt had not been cleared, and the port of Antwerp was not yet open. The intelligence officers also ignored some strong, albeit inconclusive, indications that there were powerful German tank units in the Arnhem area, and although they were aware that the II SS Panzer Corps had disappeared from the front, only one British officer seemed to connect the two events. His superiors promptly decided that he must be suffering from overwork and immediately sent him home on medical leave.

Perhaps the major flaw in Montgomery's plan was that it left little room for error. In his defense, it should be pointed out that he did achieve surprise and almost succeeded. One of the main reasons that it failed was that it was unlucky. In this battle, the intangible factor of luck was clearly on the German side. As of September 16, Army Group B had exactly three divisions in reserve behind a front of about 300 miles: one static infantry unit and the 9th and 10th SS Panzer Divisions. The odds against Model posting both of his mobile divisions in the very sector where the British paratroopers would drop are almost astronomical. Even more astronomical is the fact that during the second week in September, Field Marshal Model decided to relocate his headquarters. The site was selected by his General Headquarters administrative and transportation officer, a thirty-five-year-old lieutenant named Gustav Sedelhauser, who stumbled briefly across the stage of history. He located the new headquarters site in Oosterbeek, an upper-income residential village two and a half miles west of the center of Arnhem. Lieutenant General Krebs and the staff of Army Group B headquartered in the beautiful Hotel Hartenstein, while Model was billeted in the nearby but less ostentatious Tafelberg. The headquarters was operational by September 15, two days before the Allied paratroopers landed. It was located just two miles from one of the main British drop zone.[4]

✠

On September 14, Willi Bittrich, the commander of the II SS Panzer Corps, held a meeting with his two divisional commanders at his headquarters, a small castle on the fringe of Doetinchem, about twenty-two miles east of Arnhem. As was typical of SS officers, both of the commanders were young men. SS Maj. Gen. (*Brigadeführer*) Heinz Harmel,[5] the commander of the 10th SS Panzer Division "Frundsberg," was thirty-eight years old, and SS Lt. Col. Walter Harzer[6] was only thirty-one. Both were veterans, however. Bittrich informed Harzer that his division was being sent back to Germany to rebuild. It was to leave all of its operational panzers, assault guns, and armored personnel carriers behind to be absorbed by the 10th SS Panzer. The division was then to board trains and begin moving to Siegen, northeast of Koblenz, where its refitting would take place.

Neither division had come out of France in very good shape, but the 10th SS Panzer, which was the division nearest to the British drop zones, had been devastated. It was down to a strength of 3,500 men, about five tanks, and very few armored vehicles. (The map on the next page shows the dispositions of the Frundsberg Division on the eve of this, its most famous battle.) The 9th SS Panzer, on the other hand, had 6,000 men, twenty PzKw V tanks, forty armored personnel carriers, and a number of flak guns and artillery pieces, but Harzer had no intention of giving Harmel all of his operational tanks, assault guns, and APCs because he suspected that they would never be replaced. He decided to have his own men disable many of the vehicles so that they could be carried back to Germany for repair. He began his move on September 16.

Meanwhile, rumors abounded about the possibility of an Allied airborne or combined airborne-amphibious attack. Jodl was particularly concerned about a possible seaborne landing in Holland, but both Rundstedt and Model considered this extremely unlikely. On September 14, *Luftwaffe* Col. Gen. Otto Dessloch, the recently appointed commander of the 3rd Air Fleet, telephoned Model and warned him to leave the Arnhem area. The marshal responded by inviting him to dinner at the Tafelberg, but Dessloch declined, having no intention of being taken prisoner. "If I were you, I would get out of that area," he said. Model only laughed.[7]

DISPOSITIONS, 9TH SS PANZER DIVISION, September 17, 1944

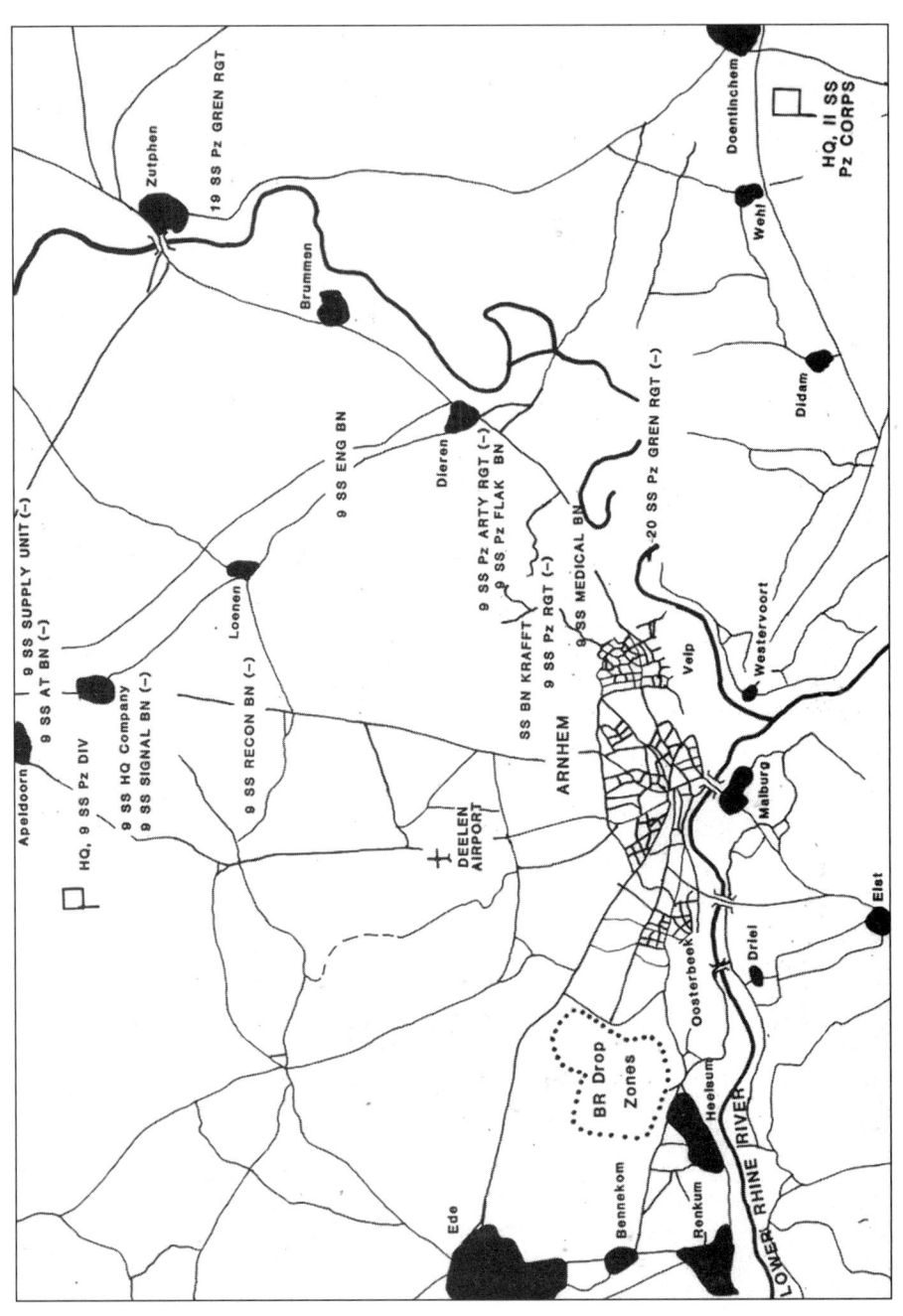

Maj. Gen. Walter Grabmann, the commander of the 3rd Fighter Division, visited Hans Krebs, Model's chief of staff, and expressed his concerns about the rumored airborne landings at Arnhem. Krebs told him that, if he continued talking nonsense, he was going to make himself look ridiculous. On the other hand, SS Lt. Gen. Hanns Rauter, the Higher SS and Police Leader (*Höhere SS- und Polizeiführer, or HSSPf*) of the Netherlands, took the rumors seriously.[8] Dozens of Dutch men and women were arrested, sent to concentration camps, or simply shot. All travel between provinces was prohibited, an earlier curfew was imposed, and Dutch citizens were summarily drafted into labor battalions to dig trenches for the *Wehrmacht*. Rauter warned that if more than five people were seen together, they would be fired on without warning. He also met with Model and Krebs and warned them to expect a major parachute landing in the Arnhem area. Model replied that he did expect a British ground attack but expressed the opinion that Montgomery was too cautious to use elite airborne troops "in a reckless adventure."[9]

The rumors, of course, were true. On the morning of September 17, almost 5,000 Allied airplanes took off from twenty-four airfields and headed for the drop zones. Hundreds of these were bombers and fighter-bombers, which blasted known German positions as well as Oosterbeek, Arnhem, Nijmegen, and Eindhoven. Entire blocks were reduced to rubble. Allied transports lifted off with more than 20,000 soldiers, 511 vehicles, 330 artillery pieces, and almost 600 tons of equipment in the initial wave.

Although the Allies took the Germans completely by surprise, the *Wehrmacht's* reaction was not slow. SS Maj. Sepp Krafft and his 16th SS Panzer Grenadier Training and Replacement Battalion had been displaced from the village of Oosterbeck when Model moved in with the headquarters of Army Group B. He moved his troops a few miles to the northwest to the woods and farms around the little village of Wolfheze. Unwittingly, he had placed his men on the very edge of the British drop zone, blocking the main road to Arnhem.

The British paratroopers began to bail out at precisely 1 P.M. As soon as Krafft them floating to earth by the hundreds, he immediately realized what was happening and knew that their objective had to be the bridges at Arnhem. Even though he was sick to his stomach with fright, he quickly deployed his understrength companies to

block the Ede-Arnhem and the Utrecht-Oosterbeek-Arnhem roads—
the two main highways into the city. To give the British the impression that he was stronger than he really was, Krafft at once began to
launch sharp hit-and-run platoon-size attacks on the fringes of the
drop zones and to shell them with four experimental, oversize, multi-
barrel mortars, which had a devastating effect on the British paratroopers. Although Krafft no doubt took the best possible action
under the circumstances, he did not have enough men to block the
southernmost secondary road leading from the drop zones to Arnhem along the northern bank of the Rhine.

As Krafft was issuing his orders, an alarmed Maj. Gen. Friedrich
Kussin, the commandant of Arnhem, rushed up to Krafft's headquarters in his staff car to determine what was happening. With a clear
view of the heath from Krafft's command post, the general was
shocked by the size of the British airborne operation. Desperately, he
promised to send reinforcements by 6 P.M. As the general started back
to the city, Krafft warned him not to take the Utrecht-Arnhem road,
because he already had reports of British soldiers in the area. Kussin
assured him that he would get through and sped off to the west at
high speed. Krafft was sure that Kussin's reinforcements would never
reach him, and he was right. The general was later found dead, his
body hanging out of his car, which was wrecked on the side of the
Utrecht-Arnhem road. He had been mowed down by British machine
guns.[10]

Field Marshal Model; his chief of staff, Lieutenant General Krebs;
and Col. Hans von Tempelhof, the chief of operations, were eating
lunch when a staff lieutenant colonel rushed in and announced that
gliders were landing at Wolfheze, only about two miles away. Model
instantly concluded that they were commandos out to kill or capture
him. He jumped to his feet and issued orders for the evacuation of
the headquarters. A few minutes later, he fled to the west, heading
for Bittrich's headquarters at Doetinchem and carrying only a small
suitcase containing his linen and toilet articles. General Krebs fled
with him—in such a hurry that he forgot his cap, belt, and pistol.
Colonel Tempelhof did not even remove or destroy the war maps in
the operations room.

At 1:30 P.M., while Model and his staff were making their getaway,
General Bittrich first learned of the landings and immediately put the

THE BATTLE OF ARNHEM, September 17, 1944

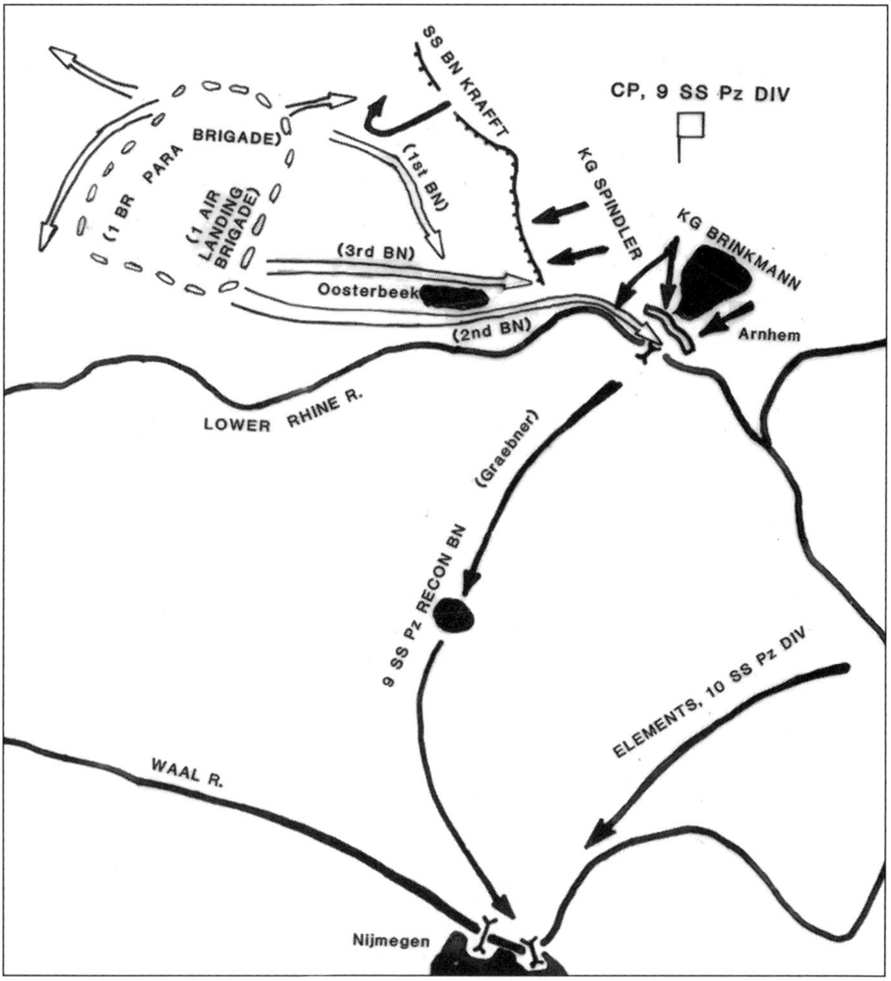

9th and 10th SS Panzer Divisions on full alert. He ordered the 9th SS to move out of its assembly areas to defend the Arnhem area and destroy the paratroopers west of the city in the Oosterbeek area. At the same time, he instructed the 10th SS to move to Nijmegen to defend the bridges there. Unfortunately, most of the 9th SS had already departed by train for Germany, and, the previous day, Bittrich had sent the 10th SS's commander, SS Major General Harmel, to Berlin, to try to persuade SS Gen. Hans Juettner, the chief of the Command Office of the Waffen-SS, to release more equipment for the II

SS Panzer Corps. The 10th SS did not really get moving until he returned, and Harzer's 9th SS still faced the problem of repairing the tanks and assault guns he had deliberately disabled, to avoid handing them over to the 10th SS Panzer. Five valuable hours would be wasted on this task.

On September 17, Harzer had only 2,500 men left in the immediate vicinity of Arnhem, as Table 4 indicates. While the 10th SS Panzer was paralyzed, he took immediate and aggressive action, throwing every available armored car, panzer, assault gun, and panzer grenadier platoon into blocking positions along the two major highways into Arnhem, the Ede-Arnhem road and the Utrecht-Arnhem road, in effect reinforcing Major Krafft. Like Krafft, however, he failed to cover the secondary road along the northern bank of the Rhine. It is unclear whether this was an oversight on his part or whether he did not know the road existed, but the failure of the 9th SS to block this road left the British with a single, uncontested route into Arnhem. (The map on the previous page shows the Battle of Arnhem on September 17.)

On the Allied side, General Urquhart, the commander of the British 1st Airborne Division, was generally pleased with the drop of his division. Only 36 of his 320 gliders had not arrived, although he had still lost a number of important, heavily armed jeeps. His total strength was about 5,200 men, meaning that he initially outnumbered the defenders two to one. His main problem was communications, which, because of number of foul-ups, soon broke down completely. Even so, Brigadier Lathbury's 1st Parachute Brigade moved out for Arnhem early that afternoon. The plan called for Brig. Philip "Pip" Hicks's 1st Airlanding Brigade to secure the landing zones while the three battalions of the 1st Parachute Brigade converged on Arnhem, each from a different route. Lt. Col. David Dobie's 1st Battalion would drive along the Ede-Arnhem road to seize the high ground north of the city. In the center, Lt. Col. J. A. C. Fitch's 3rd Battalion would head for the city from the north along the Utrecht-Arnhem road. Lt. Col. John Frost's 2nd Battalion would take the southernmost route, the secondary road along the Lower Rhine, to capture the main highway bridge and two secondary objectives—the railroad and pontoon bridges west of the main highway bridge.

TABLE 4: ORGANIZATION AND STRENGTH
OF THE 9TH SS PANZER DIVISION AT ARNHEM,
SEPTEMBER 17, 1944

Division Headquarters Company: 120 men

1 Platoon, 9th SS Field Police Company: 60 men

2 Alarm Companies, 9th SS Panzer Regiment
(one without tanks and fighting as infantry)

2 Alarm Companies, 19th SS Panzer Grenadier Regiment
(without heavy weapons)

2 Alarm Companies, 20th SS Panzer Grenadier Regiment
(without heavy weapons)

2 Alarm Companies, 9th SS Panzer Artillery Regiment
(without guns, fighting as infantry)

9th SS Panzer Reconnaissance Battalion: 400 men with armored
cars

1 Company of the 9th SS Anti-Tank Battalion
(without assault guns, fighting as infantry)

1 Company, 9th SS Flak Battalion with four 20-millimeter guns
and a few 88-millimter guns, the rest fighting as infantry

1 Company, 9th SS Panzer Engineer Battalion: 60 men

1 Company, 9th SS Panzer Signal Battalion: 80 men

1 Company, 9th SS Supply Battalion

1 Company, 9th SS Economic Battalion:
70 men, fighting as infantry

2 Companies, 9th SS Medical Battalion
(used as medical personnel)

SOURCE: Fuerbinger, *9.SS-Panzer-Division*, 418–19.

Fitch's 3rd Battalion and Dobie's 1st quickly ran into Krafft's men and the vanguards of the 9th SS Panzer, which immediately began to launch small, local counterattacks aimed more at pinning down the British paratroopers than destroying them. The German tactics worked: by nightfall, the northernmost British battalions had gained only two and a half miles and were still more than four miles from the vital bridge. To the south, however, Frost's battalion advanced without opposition. Shortly after 6 P.M., it reached its first objective, the railroad bridge southeast of Oosterbeek. It appeared to be undefended, but suddenly blew up in their faces. About a half an hour later, they reached the pontoon bridge, only to find that the center section had been removed, rendering it was useless. Then they pressed on toward the main highway bridge, which they expected to be demolished before they arrived. Earlier that afternoon, at II SS Panzer Corps Headquarters, SS General Bittrich had recommended to Field Marshal Model that the bridges at Arnhem and Nijmegen be destroyed at once, but Model refused even to consider it. The bridges might be needed for future counterattacks, he said. Bittrich argued, but the marshal was adamant.

Model quickly set up a temporary command post at Bittrich's headquarters at Doetinchem and immediately signaled Rundstedt for reinforcements. Although Rundstedt liked to comment privately that Model would make a good regimental sergeant major, he sent the live-wire field marshal everything he could. Model's rapid reaction to the British offensive would have a decisive effect on the campaign in the days ahead. His stubborn refusal to blow the bridges, however, almost led to disaster because it allowed the British paratroopers to capture part of the main highway bridge at Arnhem.

Shortly before 7 P.M., even as Frost's men approached the highway bridge, SS Capt. Viktor-Eberhard Graebner, who had been decorated with the Knight's Cross earlier that day, crossed the bridge at Arnhem with the approximately forty vehicles of his 9th SS Panzer Reconnaissance Battalion. Finding nothing out of the ordinary, he signaled divisional headquarters that there were no paratroopers in this sector and then proceeded to the south to sweep the road as far as Nijmegen. Less than an hour later, the surprised British paratroopers arrived, and found the bridge intact. They launched an immediate attack against the bridge, which was supposed to have been defended by twenty-five German security troops who had not seen action since World War I. These old men had deserted their posts, and the British were able to capture the northern end of the structure. They attempted to rush across and establish a bridgehead south of the Rhine but found this end defended by a small but heavily armed detachment of SS panzer grenadiers who had arrived only half an hour before. Both sides saw that it was suicide to try to cross the bridge, which became a no-man's-land. Content with half a bridge, Frost established a defensive perimeter encompassing eighteen buildings on the northern bank; here, with 600 to 700 men, he awaited relief from the British XXX Corps, which was scheduled to arrive in less than two days.

Unlike the security troops at the bridge, two female German telephone operators at the Arnhem Post Office did not run away; instead, they rang up the II SS Panzer Corps headquarters and informed General Bittrich that the Arnhem highway bridge was in British hands. The SS general was infuriated; he had specifically ordered Harzer's 9th SS Panzer to hold this bridge. Controlling himself, he quickly directed the 10th SS Panzer to cross the Rhine by ferry and proceed to Nijmegen. The bridge over the Waal had to be held, he said, before the British XXX Corps, advancing from the south, could seize it. He also ordered the 9th SS Panzer to recapture the Arnhem bridge and prevent the British paratroopers from reinforcing the men already in the city. (Later, he would remember the two operators and personally decorate them with the Iron Cross.)

North of Arnhem, the Germans reacted quickly. The Armed Forces Commander in the Netherlands, *Luftwaffe* Gen. Friedrich Christiansen, was a pioneer naval aviator in World War I, during which he had earned the *Pour le Merite*. Although it is generally conceeded that he was "over his head" in this corps-level appointment, which he owed solely to his friendship with Hermann Goering, he nevertheless performed well on September 17. As soon as he received the initial reports of the airborne landings, he organized his security and training battalions into an ad hoc division under the command of Lt. Gen. Hans von Tettau, the veteran paratrooper who had so distinguished himself as Student's operations officer in 1940 and 1941.

Tettau's mission was to come up on the right flank of the 9th SS Panzer Division and try to overrun the British drop zones. By nightfall on September 17, both the British landing zones and the battalion at Arnhem were under counterattack, as were the two battalions in between. Harzer, the 9th SS's commander, underestimated the strength of the defenders on the bridge, however, and concentrated his forces to prevent the British 1st and 3rd Battalions from reaching Arnhem, rather than against Frost's men in the city. During the night of September 17–18, not a single panzer or assault gun challenged the British hold on the vital Rhine River bridge. Frost held his perimeter fairly easily against the unsupported SS infantry, which suffered heavy casualties. The SS troops were impressed by the fierce resistance they met in Arnhem. "The only way to get the British out is to blast the buildings down, brick by brick," one of them reported. "Believe me, these are real men. They won't give up that bridge until we carry them out feet first."[11]

Meanwhile, more reinforcements headed for the Arnhem sector, including Knaust's 9th SS Panzer Grenadier Replacement Training Battalion, elements of the 102nd Heavy Rocket Launcher Battalion (from Bittrich's reserve), and—most importantly—Bruhns's 506th Heavy Panzer Battalion, dispatched by Field Marshal Model.

What was happening to the south, where the two American parachute divisions had dropped and the British XXX Corps was trying to drive up the airborne corridor to Arnhem?

Like the British 1st Airborne, the U.S. 101st Airborne Division made a highly satisfactory landing. Despite the loss of a few gliders to accidents and German flak, General Taylor had more than 6,600 men in his drop and landing zones. Unknown to him, his beautiful jump was watched with great envy by Col. Gen. Kurt Student and his chief of staff, Colonel Reinhard. Student, the "father" of the German parachute corps and one of the most prominent airborne pioneers in history, was headquartered in a cottage near Vught. Initially, Student and Reinhard were stunned by the scale of the Allies' drops. Then it became obvious to them that the objectives of the operation were to seize the bridges around Eindhoven, Grave, and Nijmegen and hold them until the long-awaited British ground attack could reach them. At the time, Student did not even think about the bridge at Arnhem.

He ordered Reinhard to contact Field Marshal Model, but it was too late: the lines were already cut. Within two hours, the American paratroopers had taken Veghel, their northernmost objective, and its four highway and railroad bridges across the Aa River and the Willems Canal. The bridge across the Dommel River at St. Oedenrode was also captured without much opposition, but the 101st Airborne's main objective—the bridge over the Wilhelmina Canal at Son, about five miles north of Eindhoven—was heavily damaged by German demolition squads. The American parachute engineers naturally lacked heavy bridging equipment and could construct only a wooden footbridge.

Heavy fighting broke out at Best, where elements of the U.S. 502nd Parachute Infantry Regiment had landed. The Wilhelmina Canal Bridge at Best was strictly a secondary objective, earmarked for capture just in case the main bridge at Son was blown. The Americans were unaware that they had landed only ten miles from Student's headquarters and that Lt. Gen. Walter Poppe's 59th Infantry Division (part of the 15th Army) was billeted in nearby Tilburg. The Americans pushed to within fifty yards of the canal before German engineers blew up the bridge and Poppe's vanguards counterattacked the Americans. It was the beginning of a bloody three-day battle that attracted both German and American units like a magnet.

The bad luck that plagued the Allies throughout the remainder of this operation began in the zone of the 101st Airborne Division when a small German patrol, investigating a downed American Waco glider, discovered a briefcase. Inside was the entire Allied plan of operations, including maps showing the drop zones, corridors, objectives, and even Montgomery's route of advance into the Ruhr. It was quickly forwarded to Student's headquarters, but because of broken German communications and the confusion caused by the Allied landings, Field Marshal Model would not learn of it for another ten hours.

In the center of the Allied airborne corridor, between the U.S. 101st and British 1st Airborne, the U.S. 82nd Airborne Division's landing was also almost a textbook operation. More than 4,500 men, several batteries of artillery, and tons of equipment from the 505th and 508th Parachute Infantry Regiments landed in less than twenty minutes, some of them within one and a half miles of the German border. They straddled the town of Groesbeek while, eight miles to the west, the 504th Parachute Infantry Regiment landed more than 2,000 men north of Overasselt. The division's main objective was the nine-span, 1,500-foot-long bridge over the Maas River near Grave, eight miles southwest of Nijmegen, which was captured almost immediately. A truckload of German soldiers was caught on the bridge and almost all of them were machine-gunned to death before they could get out of their vehicle. Then the demolition charges were ripped out, and the 82nd turned to its next objectives: three road bridges and one railroad bridge across the Maas-Waal Canal. These objectives were secondary, and three of them destroyed or severely damaged before the paratroopers could reach them, although the paratroopers were able to capture a crossing over the Maas-Waal Canal at Heumen, less than five miles due east of Grave.

The U.S. 505th and 508th Parachute Infantry Regiments secured the Groesbeek Heights area, just west of the Reichswald, and the 508th Parachute headed for Nijmegen, intent on securing another major objective, the 1,960-foot highway bridge across the Waal. Unfortunately, SS Captain Graebner's reconnaissance battalion arrived in the city well in advance of the Americans, reinforcing the ragtag army garrison at Nijmegen—750 older garrison troops, training staff personnel, and railroad construction troops, mostly sixteen and seventeen years old, all under the command of Colonel Henke—and checked the tough paratroopers in heavy streetfighting inside the city.

The huge Allied ground advance began along the Belgium-Holland border at 2:15 P.M. with a devastating bombardment from 350 guns. The artillery concentrated on only a single mile of frontage to a depth of five miles. The tanks of the British XXX Corps rolled forward at 2:35 P.M., closely supported by rocket-firing Typhoon airplanes. The forward German positions seemed to have been wiped out by the initial bombardment, and at first, all seemed to go well for the British. Then they were plastered from the rear by German gunners repeating one of their favorite tactics from Russia. The Germans let the initial wave of tanks bypass them without firing and then emerged from their hiding places and ambushed the succeeding waves of tanks and infantry. At least nine British tanks were knocked out in the first few minutes. To the complete surprise of British military intelligence, most of the prisoners were from the 15th Army, which they had written off. "Our intelligence spent the day in a state of indignant surprise," one colonel wrote. "One German regiment after another appeared which had no right to be there."[12]

After the initial surprise of the first glider-parachute drop wore off, the Arnhem campaign became nothing less than a race. Could the Allies reach the bridgehead before the Germans wiped it out? Could the Germans bring up enough forces to block the advance or at least slow it long enough to allow the 9th SS Panzer Division time to eliminate the bridgehead? And could the Allied tanks arrive in Arnhem before Frost's parachute battalion would completely wiped out?

During the night of September 17–18, SS General Harmel raced back to the Arnhem area and rejoined his 10th SS Panzer Division to find that Bittrich had ordered it to defend Nijmegen. Unfortunately, the 10th SS was on the wrong side of the Rhine, and there were no bridges east of Arnhem over which it could cross. Harmel therefore had no choice but to use the ferry at Pannerden, eight miles southeast of the bridge. Ferrying an SS panzer division over a river in this manner, Harmel knew, would be a tedious, time-consuming, frustrating, and dangerous operation, but he had no choice. He began immediately.

When dawn broke on September 18, the second day of Operation Market Garden, Brigadier Hicks's 1st Airlanding Brigade was under attack to the west by Division von Tettau and to the east by an SS *kampfgruppe* led by SS Maj. Ludwig Spindler of the 9th SS Panzer Division.[13] Meanwhile, the British 1st and 3rd Parachute Battalions continued to struggle to reach Frost, but were halted at the massive St. Elisabeth's Hospital, about two miles northwest of the bridge. Here the British were met by a *kampfgruppe* led by SS Capt. H. Moeller, the commander of the 9th SS Panzer Engineer Battalion, who had a handful of tanks and a few 88-millimter and 20-millimter guns from the 9th SS's flak battalion.[14] The British also had to deal with snipers on rooftops and murderous automatic-weapons fire. General Urquhart and Brigadier Lathbury went forward into this battle and were ambushed. Lathbury was seriously wounded and temporarily paralyzed by a German machine-gun bullet, and then he, Urquhart, and two other officers were surrounded in a house by the SS panzers. Fortunately for them, none of the Germans knew where they were-neither did the British. The 1st Airborne Division had temporarily lost its leadership.

Elsewhere, SS Captain Graebner completed his reconnaissance mission. Posting a few assault guns south of the Nijmegen bridge, he turned back to the north with the rest of his column. After leaving about half of his battalion at the town of Elst—roughly halfway between Nijmegen and Arnhem—he proceeded with the rest to the bridge at Arnhem. That morning, he attacked over the bridge with twenty-two vehicles, but the British paratroopers on the northern end were ready, armed with antitank guns. The first two half-tracks made it across the bridge, but the third was hit and its driver wounded; the man tried to reverse but succeeded only in ramming the vehicle behind him. British antitank shells soon destroyed both of them, and British mortar bombs caused others to burst into flames. Some of the half-tracks swerved to avoid others, and at least two jumped the protective rails and fell off the bridge onto the streets below, a fall which probably killed everyone on board. German infantry jumped out of disabled half-tracks, only to be cut down by British machine guns. It was a massacre. Only ten vehicles managed to escape back to the southern end of the bridge. Captain Graebner was not among them; he lay dead on the Arnhem bridge.

Fifty-seven miles to the south, the British XXX Corps resumed its advance at 6:30 A.M. It was already well behind schedule. The plan called for British armor to link up with the U.S. 101st Airborne three hours after the offensive began. The connection did not occur until September 18—eighteen hours late. The plan also called for the Americans to capture the Son bridge beyond Eindhoven intact, but the Germans blew it up. Now bridging equipment had to be brought forward, and this was not a quick or easy task, with an entire armored corps advancing down a single road. It was after 7 P.M. on September 18 before the British reached the Son, and the engineers came up and began constructing a temporary Bailey bridge. For the moment at least, the ground offensive was halted.

North of the 101st, the U.S. 82nd Airborne Division was having similar problems. The Americans repeatedly attacked the bridge at Nijmegen, but the SS troops were well dug in and repulsed every attack. The 82nd's problems multiplied as the day wore on. It occupied an area ten miles long (north to south) and twelve miles wide—too much for one division—even an elite one like the 82nd Airborne. Against it the Germans threw in several waves of low-quality infantry, including *Luftwaffe* troops, signals personnel, men on leave impressed into service for the emergency, and recently discharged convalescents. Sweeping out of the Reichswald, they broke through the 82nd's line on the east, overran supply and ammunition depots, and pushed Gavin's division slowly back to the west toward the vital Grave-Nijmegen Highway.

That afternoon, the second huge Allied airborne wave took off for Holland. It had been delayed several hours by fog in England, but it represented a straggering force—1,336 C-47 transports, 252 four-engine Liberator bombers and 340 British Stirling bombers—carrying cargo, paratroopers, or 1,205 Horsa, Waco, and Hamilcar gliders, all escorted by more than 800 fighters. They carried almost 6,700 airborne troops, 681 vehicles, 60 pieces of field artillery, and 600 tons of supplies.

Although the German antiaircraft gunners did little damage to the first (troop-carrying) wave, they scored heavily against the second lift by holding their fire until the fighter escorts had flown past; then they shot down at least 21 airplanes (most of them B-24s), damaged 130 others, and caused the cargo drop to be scattered over miles of territory. Fifty-four gliders were also lost. The bridgehead at Arnhem, however, had received significant reinforcements in the form of Brig. John W. "Shan" Hackett's 4th Parachute Brigade and managed to hold off Division von Tettau and the 9th SS Panzer for another day.[15]

During the night of September 18–19, the 9th SS Panzer Division continued to mount local attacks against the British airborne bridgehead, while the 10th SS continued its frustrating ferrying operations without a great deal of success. By the morning of the nineteenth, Harmel's engineers had managed to get only two panzer grenadier battalions across the river and on the Arnhem-Nijmegen road.

The SS men besieging Frost's 2nd Parachute Battalion—now reinforced with SS Captain Brinkmann's 10th SS Recon Battalion, a few tanks from the 10th SS Panzer Regiment, the 4th SS Panzer Grenadier Replacement and Training Battalion, and three *Luftwaffe* field companies, and some mortar and artillery units—changed their tactics on the afternoon of September 19 and began to systematically destroy every building in the British perimeter. They used phosphorous ammunition to set the buildings on fire and 150-millimeter guns to fire 100-pound shells into the Allied-held buildings.

Inside the perimeter, it was now clear to the defenders that something had gone terribly wrong. They had been told that they would have to hold out for only forty-eight hours, and so they had started the battle with rations for two days. Most of these had now been eaten, the Germans had cut off their water, and ammunition was beginning to run low. Many men were now on a steady diet of apples and pears taken from the Dutch cellars and storerooms.

The other two battalions of the 1st Parachute Brigade tried desperately to reach the bridge but could not overcome or bypass the defenders of St. Elisabeth's Hospital, and their only success was to reach the house where General Urquhart was trapped and free the divisional commander. Their losses were prohibitive. Back in the British drop zone, Brigadier Hicks, the commander of the 1st Airlanding Brigade and acting commander of the division, and Brigadier Hackett, the commander of the 4th Parachute Brigade, were also under heavy attack. From the north and northeast, Hicks was struck by Captain Bruhns's 506th Heavy Panzer Battalion; Krafft's battalion; Spindler's *kampfgruppe* (the alarm companies of the 19th and 20th SS Panzer Grenadier and 9th SS Panzer Artillery Regiments); SS Capt. Klaus von Allwoerden's 9th SS Anti-Tank Battalion (fighting as infantry); and the only available intact tank unit in the 9th SS Panzer Regiment, SS Lieutenant Harder's 7th Company. To the north and west, Hackett was attacked by General von Tettau's ad hoc division. Neither Hicks nor Hackett could hold their ground, and both were steadily pushed back toward the river, losing several drop zones in the process. Among the wounded were Lt. Col. Derek Heathcote-Armony, the General Headquarters liaison officer and future chancellor of the exchequer of the United Kingdom, who was shot in the leg.

Far to the south, Horrocks's tanks at last crossed the Wilhelmina Canal at Son, forty-six miles from Arnhem. They were now thirty-six hours behind schedule and had covered barely a third of the distance to the bridge.

✠

THE BATTLE OF ARNHEM, September 19, 1944

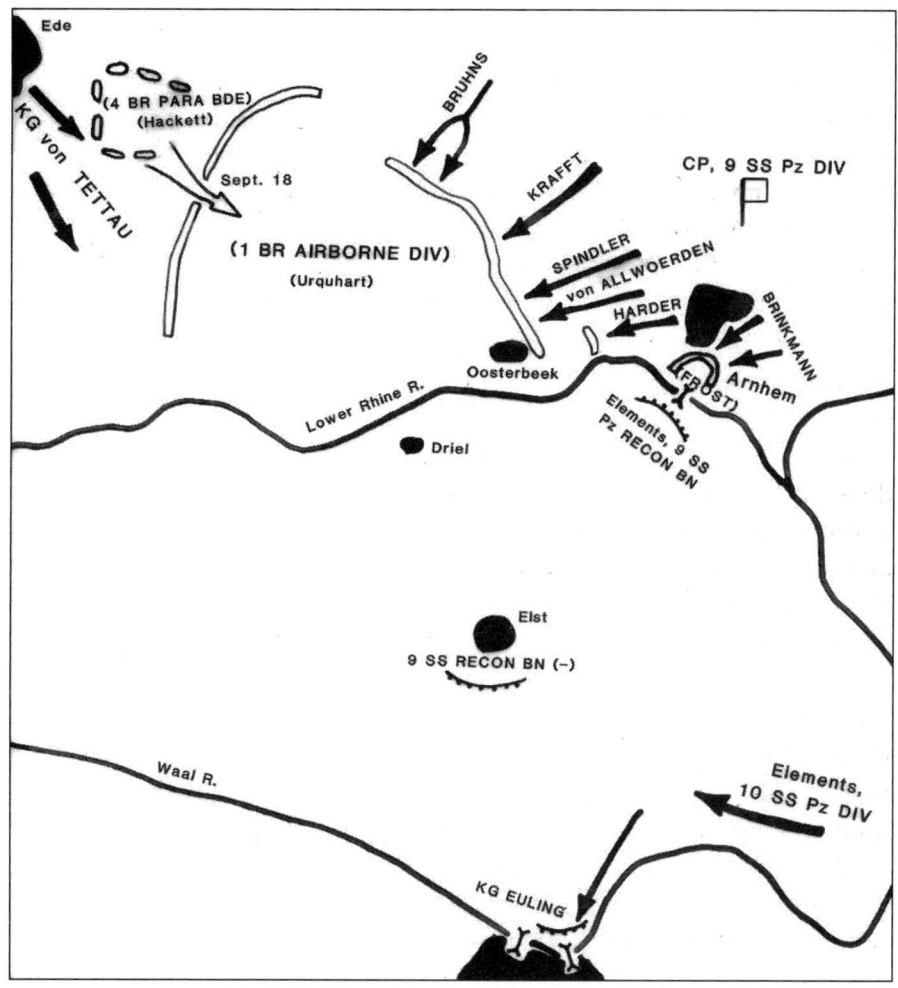

The third Allied airlift was carried out during the afternoon of September 19, and it was a disaster. Many of the planes and gliders were unable to take off because of bad weather. Of the 655 troop carriers and 431 gliders that got airborne, just over half got through. Flak, Messerschmitt fighters, and poor weather cost the Allies 112 gliders and 40 transports. Only 1,341 of the 2,310 troops bound for the 101st Airborne got through, and 28 of the 60 guns bound for the division were also lost. The 82nd Airborne lost 225 out of the 265 tons of supplies and ammunition dispatched to it. In the zone of the

British 1st Airborne, 163 cargo planes—British Dakotas and bombers used in a transport role—flew through a hail of antiaircraft fire and Messerschmitt attacks and dropped their loads on the assigned drop zones, which were now behind German lines. Because of their communication failures, the frantic British paratroopers were unable to advise the pilots of the true situation. Thirteen British bombers and Dakotas were shot down and 97 damaged, but only 21 tons of supplies and ammunition were recovered by the British. Part of the other 369 tons was destroyed, but most of it was collected by the Germans. One senior SS officer later commented that Arnhem was the cheapest battle they ever fought because they were supplied by the British.

Forty-six of the gliders carried elements of the Polish 1st Parachute Brigade. Only thirty-one of them reached the drop zone, and several of these were riddled by the machine guns of the German fighters. When they finally did land, the Poles found themselves under heavy fire because the Germans were on the very edge of the drop zone. The Poles lost most of their vehicles and supplies and eight of their eleven antitank guns almost immediately, but their troubles were just beginning.

At the same time, almost fifty miles to the south, General Taylor of the U.S. 101st Airborne Division threw the 502nd Parachute and 327th Glider Regiments, supported by British tanks from Horrocks's XXX Corps, against the 59th Infantry Division in the Battle of Best, finally settling the issue. General Poppe's division fell back rapidly, leaving behind more than 300 dead, more than 1,000 prisoners, and 15 artillery pieces. Horrocks's spearheads continued their road march to the north into the zone of the 82nd Airborne Division.

The Nijmegen Bridge was held by the I Battalion, 22nd SS Panzer Grenadier Regiment (10th SS Panzer Division), which was led by twenty-five-year-old SS Capt. Karl Heinz Euling.[16] Euling was the first to get his battalion across the Rhine at Pannerden, and General Harmel ordered him to hold the Waal River Bridge at Nijmegen at all costs. The captain ringed his perimeter and citadel with assault guns and turned back every attempt Gavin's paratroopers made to break his line. The British tanks had no better luck; Euling's guns were well sighted and beat back Horrocks's vanguard with losses.

Late that evening, General Gavin came up with a dangerous plan to capture the bridge. It must, he said, be attacked from both ends simultaneously. This meant that his paratroopers would have to make an assault crossing of the 400-yard-wide river against resistance that was almost certain to be stiff. Horrocks and Browning approved the plan, mainly because no one could come up with a better idea. Once it was approved, however, another long delay ensued because the assault boats were well back in the column. Since the XXX Corps was limited to a single road, it would take hours for the engineers to get them to Nijmegen. The attack was set for 1 P.M. on September 20.

To the north, the task of retaking the Arnhem bridge was assigned to *SS-Brigadeführer* Heinz Harmel, the commander of the 10th SS Panzer Division. Harmel rejected the haphazard approach Harzer had used; instead, he personally directed the tank and artillery commanders to systematically reduce every building in the British perimeter, one by one. "Aim right under the gables and shoot meter by meter, floor by floor, until each house collapses," he ordered.[17]

The forces Harmel deployed in Arnhem included Captain Brinkmann's elite 10th SS Panzer Reconnaissance Battalon and *Kampfgruppe Knaust,* which was not of the highest quality. It had been rushed from Holland to reinforce the 10th SS Panzer Division and was led by SS Maj. Hans Peter Knaust, a thirty-eight-year old officer who had lost a leg near Moscow in 1941. Like their commander, many of Knaust's men had been seriously wounded at one time or another, and many of them would not have been on active duty in 1940. The rest of the troops were seventeen- and eighteen-year-old volunteers who had just completed their eight weeks of basic training. They had thirty-five tanks, including several Tigers, which Knaust quickly committed against Frost.

By now, the British had lost eight of the original eighteen buildings inside their perimeter. Now a merciless bombardment began, with the panzers slamming shell after shell into the buildings on the east and west sides, while the SS artillery blasted those facing north. As Harmel predicted, the buildings collapsed from the rooftops downward. Even the SS men commented later that they felt sorry for the British. "Well, Padre," a wounded British sergeant said to his chaplain, "they're throwing everything at us but the kitchen stove." At that moment, the building shuttered under the impact of another heavy shell. The ceiling collapsed, and a kitchen stove fell into the cellar, landing right in front of the two men. "I knew the bastards were close, but I didn't believe they could hear us talking," the sergeant mused, shaking his head.[18]

The 9th SS Panzer Division—relieved of the task of taking the bridge and reinforced with the 191st Artillery Command (*Arko 191*, a reinforced regiment) and the bulk of the 102nd Mortar Battalion— now turned its full attention to destroying the rest of the British 1st Airborne Division in coordination with Division von Tettau. The 1st Parachute Brigade was indeed cut to pieces that day; it was reduced to a strength of 116 men, and Colonel Dobie was wounded and captured. All but about fifty of the 3rd Battalion's soldiers were casualties. Colonel Fitch was killed in action, and Brigadier Lathbury had already been captured. The 2nd Parachute Battalion was trapped and being crushed to death under the weight of German artillery. The battalions of the 4th Parachute Brigade and the 1st Airlanding Brigade were not much better off. The 2nd South Staffordshires were down to 100 men, the 11th Battalion had 150, and both battalion commanders were wounded. The other battalions were also severely punished. At the forefront of the battle, Lt. Col. Des Voeux, the commander of the 156th Parachute Battalion, was mortally wounded by a German mortar round and died shortly thereafter. That night, General Urquhart cancelled a planned attack to relieve the bridge and ordered the 4th Parachute Brigade to disengage—in effect abandoning Colonel Frost and the 2nd Battalion to their fate.

When darkness fell on September 20, the battered 4th Parachute Brigade pulled back into the Oosterbeek perimeter. All Urquhart could do now was try to hold a small bridgehead on the north bank of the Rhine and hope that the XXX Corps would arrive in time to save it. Back at the bridge, however, time was running out.

At dawn on September 20, Colonel Frost had, at best, 200 fighters left, and many of them were walking wounded. The cellars were full of wounded, and food, ammunition, and water were almost exhausted. Frost was wounded that morning when a mortar bomb exploded right in front of him and hurled him several yards through the air. He was struck in the left ankle and right shinbone and, barely conscious, was carried to a cellar; he was lucky to be alive.

By now, the 1st Airborne had partially solved its communications problems and had established contact with England. General Urquhart desperately needed reinforcements, and the 1,500 men of the Polish Parachute Brigade were scheduled to jump in the area between Heveadorp and Driel, near the southern bank of the Lower Rhine, because all of the drop zones on the northern side were either behind German lines or controlled by German fire. From there, the Poles would be ferried across the river into the bridgehead; however, the weather turned bad again, and the jump had to be cancelled. General Gavin also needed reinforcements, but the Glider Infantry Regiment—3,400 men—was also grounded in England.

In Horrocks's armored corridor, the situation also deteriorated badly on September 20. Having assembled every unit he could on both the eastern and western sides of the Allied salient, Model struck along the entire length of the corridor again and again, threatening the British lifeline with a series of ill-coordinated stabs.

The attacks from the west were directed by Gen. of Infantry Hans Wolfgang Reinhard's LXXXVIII Corps of Zangen's 15th Army, which now had 86,100 men and 616 guns across the Scheldt.[19] From the east, Kurt Student's 1st Parachute Army attacked with an assortment of units, including Lt. Gen. Gerd Scherbening's 406th Infantry Division, which contained four *Landesschützen* battalions, each with a combat strength of 500 over-age men; Meindl's II Parachute Corps, controlling six *Luftwaffe* battalions, two of which belonged to the 6th Parachute Division; a few low-quality battalions from Corps Feldt (Gen. of Cavalry Kurt Feldt); an ad hoc formation created by *Wehrkreis VI*; and the 107th Panzer Brigade. Neither Reinhard's nor Student's attacks amounted to much by 1940 standards, and the quality of the German troops involved was generally poor. Nevertheless, they represented a real threat to the British XXX Corps, which was overextended along the road to Nijmegen and was covered mainly by American airborne and glider regiments that lacked heavy weapons. The Germans also had surprise on their side: they could attack out of the heavily forested Reichswald and gain a local numerical superiority at any of a number of points. They used this advantage to infiltrate through the thin American lines and cut the road in several places. Maj. Gen. Gwilym I. Thomas, the commander of the British 43rd (Wessex) Infanty Division, had to turn his columns around, counterattack, and reopen Horrocks's only supply line. Maj. Baron von Maltzahn's 107th Panzer Brigade brought the critical Bailey bridge at Zon under fire and almost captured it before ten British tanks appeared, knocked out four panzers, and forced the Germans back. The Heumen bridge was also seriously threatened, and more British and American troops had to be diverted to counter the threat. The attack on the Nijmegen bridge was delayed even longer.

To the north, SS General Harmel set up his command post near the village of Doornenburg, two miles west of Pannerden and six miles northeast of Nijmegen, and conducted a reconnaissance to the south, finally getting a firm handle on the battle. One look convinced him that it would be impossible for either the Allied or German tanks to leave the Nijmegen-Arnhem Highway; it was therefore essential, he realized, for Knaust to destroy the British battalion in Arnhem and clear the bridge before the Allies took the bridges at Nijmegen. Realizing that it was only a matter of time before the Allied armor overran Euling's understrength battalion, Harmel decided to destroy the bridge. He hesitated, however, probably because of Model's orders not to blow it up. At 4 P.M., he received a report that a smoke screen had been laid across the Waal. That could only mean that the Allies were conducting a river crossing. He rushed back toward Nijmegen, intent on blowing the bridge before the Allies could cross it. He also intended for it to go down with as many British tanks on it as possible.

As Harmel realized, the American 504th Parachute Infantry Regiment was attempting to cross the river, supported by more than 100 guns and rocket-firing Typhoons and opposed only by Colonel Henke's emergency alarm battalion of boys as young as fifteen and men in their sixties. While they were in the water, however, the tough paratroopers were sitting ducks, and the defenders blasted them with machine-gun and mortar fire. Still the Americans kept coming. The slaughter was terrible. Half of the twenty-six boats were sunk, and many men drowned because the current was swift and they were heavily loaded with equipment. One they reached the other side, the paratroopers made short work of the defenders. Few prisoners were taken as Colonel Tucker's men stormed toward the northern end of the bridge. Simultaneously, other Allies attacked from the south. It seemed for a few minutes that even so, the Germans would hold. Then, the unit holding the railroad bridge suddenly broke and streamed across the bridge to the northern bank. The Americans on that side were now within range and met the Germans with a hail of bullets, killing them by the score. When the battle was over, more than 260 Germans lay dead, and dozens of others were prisoner.

On the highway bridge, meanwhile, Captain Euling and his SS men continued to fight against the Shermans and the British infantry. He signaled Harmel that he was surrounded and had only sixty men left. The SS general immediately realized that the highway bridge was as good as lost. Rushing to an engineer outpost on the north end, he waited until four tanks were on the structure heading for the north bank; then he gave the order. The engineer pushed the plunger down, but nothing happened. He tried again. And again. Still nothing happened. The British tanks were more than halfway across the bridge when Harmel and the engineers fled; as he retreated, the SS general was issuing orders in a rapid-fire manner. He wanted the roads between Elst and Lent blocked with every artillery piece and antitank gun they could lay their hands on.[20]

The road to Arnhem was not exactly open, but it was not heavily defended either. It was 7:15 P.M. on September 20, and Arnhem was only eleven miles away. Many of the American airborne officers wanted the British to continue their drive despite the terrain, but Maj. Gen. Allan H. S. Adair, the commander of the Guards Armoured Division, refused—for compelling reasons. The 43rd Infantry Division had been committed against Model's counterattacks to the south, and the British tanks had virtually no infantry support. Moreover, the terrain was terrible: "You can't imagine anything more unsuitable for tanks: steep banks with ditches on each side that could be easily covered by German guns." The fields on either side were covered with water, and the road, which occupied the higher ground, resembled an island.[21] Horrocks agreed with Adair: they would have to wait for the infantry, which would have to move through the columns of the Guards Armoured Division because the road was clogged with vehicles and at least some of the shoulders were mined. It would be eighteen hours before Horrocks could resume the attack. For the men of the British 2nd Parachute Battalion, time had already run out.

The British perimeter north of the Arnhem bridge was an inferno. About 4 P.M., three of SS Major Knaust's panzers broke through British lines and pushed their way to the bridge, which was at last back in German hands. The white flags did not appear until 7 P.M., and only then because a large group of wounded men were in danger of being roasted alive. The last pockets of resistance did not surrender until after dawn on the following day. The captured British paratroopers, most of whom were wounded, did not know what to expect from the SS men, and many feared the worst. They need not have worried. The Germans had been impressed by their heroic defense and heartily congratulated the British on their courage, passing out chocolates, cigarettes, and liquor to their wounded prisoners. This added to the bitterness of the captives because the cigarettes, candies, and liquor were British or American, having obviously come from the resupply drops that had fallen behind German lines.

Early on the morning of September 21, the SS engineers at last completed the task of removing the wreckage from the bridge, and *Kampfgruppe Brinkmann* and about twenty panzers headed south to block the Nijmegen-Arnhem road. They were followed by the 191st Artillery Regiment and a few companies of panzer grenadiers from the 9th SS Panzer Division. They were not a minute too soon. At 11 A.M., the British XXX Corps, spearheaded by the Irish Guards, resumed its advance, closely supported by Typhoons. The British pushed forward two or three miles without opposition until the four leading Shermans suddenly exploded, ambushed by assault guns in the woods to the left near Elst, where *Kampfgruppe Brinkmann* of the 10th SS Panzer Division had dug in during the night. Because of the muddy fields surrounding the highly elevated road, they were unable to advance farther.

The British tankers had to await the arrival of Thomas's 43rd (Wessex) Infantry Division, which was pinned down in the corridor by German attacks. Then they had to skirt the German positions to the west using secondary roads, before they would be in a position to relieve the paratroopers—or what was left of them. Because of traffic congestion on the main road, it took as long for the division to be transported by trucks as it would have if the infantry had simply marched.

The same day, the German attacks against the XXX Corps' corridor increased in intensity, with Reinhard's LXXXVIII Corps striking from the west and Obstfelder's LXXXVI Corps advancing from the east. Reinhard struck with *Kampfgruppe Huber*, a regiment-size battle group from the 59th Infantry Division, led by Major Huber. Obstfelder struck with *Kampfgruppe Walther*, which controlled the 1st Para-

THE BATTLE OF ARNHEM, September 21, 1944

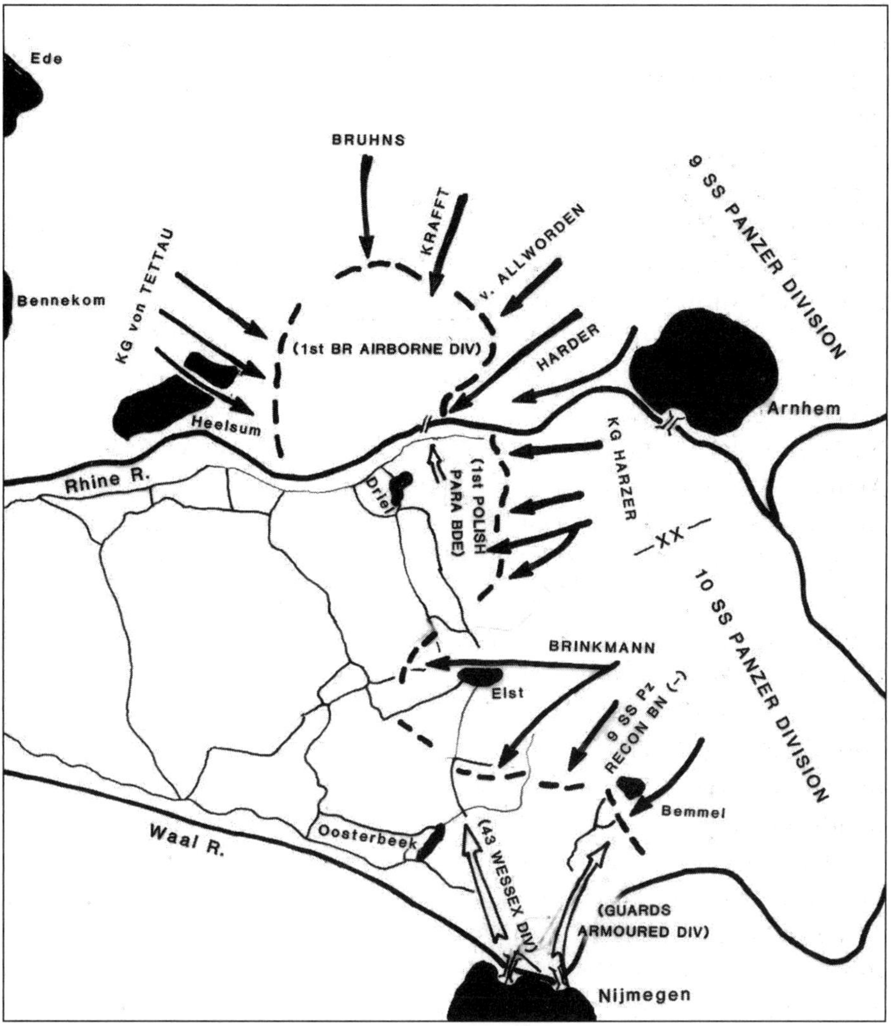

chute Regiment; the 107th Panzer Brigade; *Kampfgruppe Heinke,* a small battle group from the 10th SS Panzer Division; an artillery battalion; and the advanced infantry battalion of the 180th Reserve Division, which had hurriedly been sent to the battlefield by *Wehrkreis X.* Over the next two days, Obstfelder was joined by the 105th Panzer Brigade, von der Heydte's 6th Parachute Regiment, elements of the 2nd Parachute Regiment, the 245th and 59th Infantry Divisions (both at *kampfgruppe* strength), and the 180th and 190th Reserve

Divisions. More British troops had to be poured into the corridor and, like all of the others, had to be resupplied over only one major road. The traffic congestion was terrible and further delayed the last push to Arnhem.

In a desperate effort to keep the 1st British Airborne Division from being destroyed, the Allies decided to drop the Polish 1st Parachute Brigade south of the pocket near the southern bank of the Lower Rhine in hopes that they could reinforce the British paratroopers via ferry. As the Polish commander, Brig. Gen. Stanislaw Sosabowski, feared, the Poles flew into a maelstrom of flak, tracer bullets, and Messerschmitts. "It was as if all the enemy guns lifted together and let fly simultaneously," one observer reported. The slaughter was terrible.

The Poles landed two and a half miles south of the Oosterbeek perimeter shortly after 5 P.M. and were instantly caught in a German crossfire. Somehow they managed to survive until nightfall, when Sosabowski and his men tried to set up a ferry across the Rhine but were frustrated by German fire and a lack of equipment. Sosabowski determined to try again the following night.

September 22 was another tough day for the Allies in the Arnhem sector. General Obstfelder's relentless attacks against the corridor continued to increase in intensity, while Bittrich reinforced Brinkmann with *Kampfgruppe Knaust*, which included twenty-five Tiger tanks. Meanwhile, the 10th SS Panzer Division launched counterattacks against the Allied bridgehead at Nijmegen, and the 9th SS Panzer—now reinforced with the ten self-propelled guns of the 280th Assault Gun Brigade; the SS Landstorm Nederland Brigade; and the 642nd Marine Battalion, a naval unit—continued to slowly compress the 1st British Airborne. Of the 10,000 airborne and gliderborne troops dropped at Arnhem, Urquhart now estimated that he had fewer than 3,000 men left, excluding wounded.

The 43rd (Wessex) Division finally crossed the bridge at Nijmegen on the twenty-second and joined the Guards Armoured Division, which was stalled south of Elst. The infantry, supported by Shermans, attacked on a two-brigade front at about 9:30 A.M., but were checked by Brinkmann and Knaust. It was late afternoon before they could capture the village of Oosterhout. They would not be in a position to rescue the 1st Airborne the following day.

On the twenty-third, Obstfelder launched another major attack and cut the Arnhem road—now called "Hell's Highway" by the Allied soldiers—north of Veghel, in the zone of the U.S. 101st Airborne. Taylor's division, lightly equipped and depleted by five days of fighting, was now having a difficult time holding its positions. To the south, two more British corps continued their attacks in an effort to expand the corridor: the British VIII Corps (11th Armoured and 3rd Infantry Divisions) struck west of the road while the British XII Corps (7th Armoured, 15th Infantry, and 53rd Infantry Divisions, plus the 4th Armoured Brigade) attacked east of the highway. They were met by elements of the 15th and 1st Parachute Armies, respectively, and neither scored appreciable gains.

With the corridor cut, Horrocks was effectively surrounded and without means of resupplying his men and tanks by ground. He had little choice but to turn around the tanks of his 32nd Guards Brigade and send them south to reestablish contact with Taylor and the 101st. This caused further delays in reaching the Rhine. Urquhart signaled that he might not be able to hold out another twenty-four hours.

Saturday, September 23 was the seventh day of the battle. The weather finally cleared, and the Allies were finally able to reinforce Gavin with the 325th Glider Infantry Regiment, which had 3,385 men. Taylor's hard-pressed 101st Airborne was also reinforced with about 3,000 men, but the Polish brigade at Driel could not be reinforced. The Germans were too close to their drop zones and had already overrun some of them. An effort to resupply the British 1st Airborne Division was a disaster: of the 123 cargo planes involved, 6 were shot down and 63 damaged by German flak and machine-gun bullets. When they dropped their supplies, about 90 percent landed behind German lines.

SS Colonel Harzer and SS General Bittrich were also having their problems. They had Oosterbeek surrounded, but the suburb's narrow streets provided no maneuver room for the Tigers, and the 9th SS had been low in infantry strength when the battle began. In addition, Field Marshal Model was breathing down their necks, demanding that the British bridgehead be eliminated within twenty-four hours.

At last supported by fighter-bombers and rocket-firing Typhoons, the British managed to work their way around *Kampfgruppe Brinkmann,* and the 130th Infantry Brigade of the 43rd (Wessex) Division finally reached the Polish Brigade by nightfall. Using rubber boats, they managed to establish a ferry to the 1st Airborne and reinforced Urquhart during the night. It was clear, however, that the shallow bridgehead was in danger and, even if reinforced, was not going to be a vehicle Monty could use to launch a drive on the Ruhr. On the afternoon of Sunday, September 24, General Dempsey met with Horrocks and Browning at St. Oedenrode, where they made the difficult decision to admit defeat and withdraw the paratroopers from the bridgehead. Even as they were meeting, Model's troops cut the corridor again. Horrocks had to fight his way through German lines just to get back to his headquarters, which was now located at Nijmegen.

Things were, of course, worse within the airborne pocket, which was now small enough that every German shell or mortar round had a reasonably good chance of finding a target. Among those who fell that day was Brig. John Hackett, commander of the 4th Parachute Brigade. He was critically wounded when shrapnel from a mortar round hit him in the thigh and a piece about two inches square lodged in his lower intestines. He would have to be abandoned to the mercy of the enemy when the British retreated.

On the morning of September 25, General Urquhart received the order to evacuate the bridgehead. Although this order brought with it the bitter knowledge of defeat, Urquhart knew retreat was the only realistic course—he had only 2,500 men left. He managed to hold his lines during the day, and the evacuation began that night. By now, Horrocks had brought much of the XXX Corps' artillery within range of the bridgehead to pound German positions and give the SS the impression that Horrocks intended to launch another crossing the following morning. This made the retreat across the Rhine much easier.

Nature finally intervened on the Allied side for a change. The night of September 25–26 was dark, cold, and wet, and the retreating

THE BATTLE OF ARNHEM, September 24, 1944

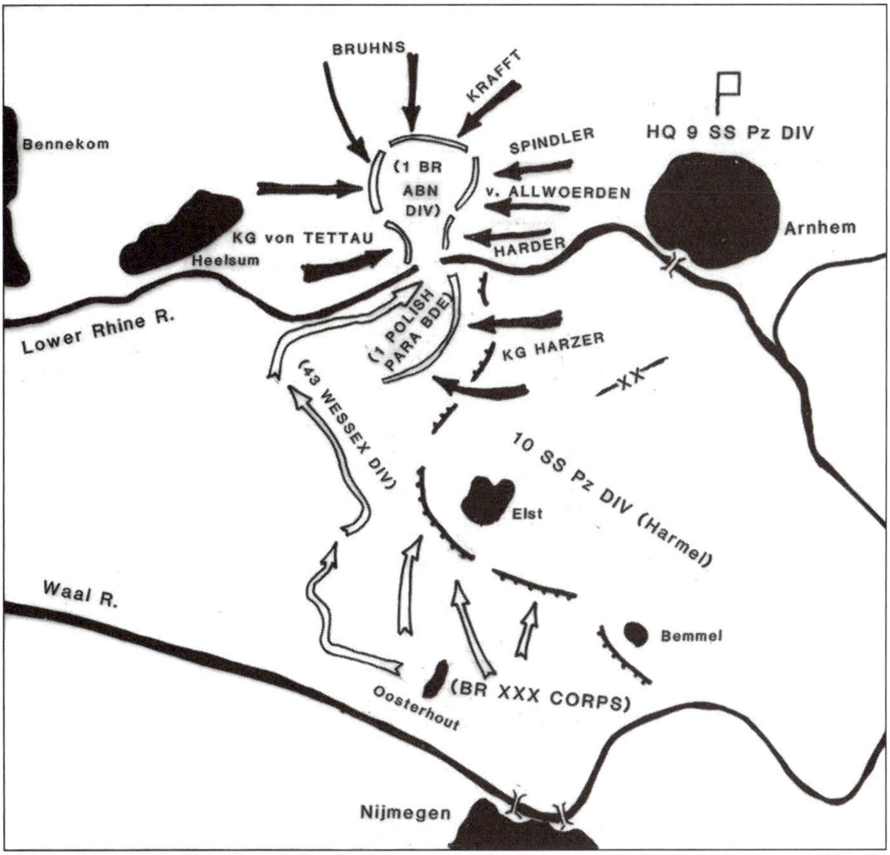

paratroopers were covered by a driving rainstorm. The evacuation was completed before dawn, and the next morning, the 9th SS Panzer and Division von Tettau found the British foxholes abandoned. The Battle of Arnhem was over.

Despite Montgomery's efforts to put a positive spin on the battle—he called it "90 percent successful"—Operation Market Garden had failed. All the British had gained was a fifty-five-mile corridor leading nowhere—a strategic dead end. Urquhart's 1st British Airborne Division lost 7,842 of the 10,005 men involved in the operation, including 1,200 dead. Some of the missing paratroopers, however, hid out with

Dutch families and eventually made their way back to British lines or, like Brigadiers Lathbury and Hackett, escaped later. Before he was captured, Hackett disguised himself as a corporal because he correctly believed that this would make it easier for him to escape. In the hospital, a German doctor declared that operating on him would be a waste of time and suggested that he be given a lethal injection. He was operated on by another prisoner, Capt. Dr. Alexander Lipmann-Kessel, a brilliant South African surgeon, who saved his life. Hackett escaped, hid out with the Dutch Resistance, and eventually reached British lines in February 1945.

Total Allied ground and airborne losses are estimated at more than 17,000 killed, wounded, captured, or missing, including air forces losses. According to Goebbels's propaganda ministry, German losses totaled 3,300, of which 1,300 were killed. A more realistic estimate would be at least 7,000 total casualties—probably more. By any measure, however, the operation was an Allied disaster, in more ways than one. The Germans defending Aachen and Metz had had time to recover, the bulk of the 15th Army had escaped; the Scheldt, which could easily have been opened in early September, was now barred by strong, well-rested troops; Antwerp was still useless; and the Germans defending Aachen and Metz were given time to recover. The Allied supply problem had become acute, and Eisenhower was now going to have to deal with it before he had any hope of conquering the Third Reich. The net effect was that Adolf Hitler would now have time to launch his long-planned counteroffensive in the Ardennes.

In addition, the West Wall had not been outflanked as Montgomery had envisioned—and now could not be because of the strong forces Model, Student, and others had positioned in and around Arnhem. It was now obvious that to defeat Germany, the Anglo-Americans were going to have to launch larger-scale attacks on the Siegfried Line. Germany, many German soldiers believed, still had an outside change of winning the war. But to do so, they would have to hold the Siegfried Line as long as they could.

CHAPTER 5

Aachen

SUPPLY PROBLEMS AND CHANNEL PORTS

All along, Eisenhower believed that the opening of the ports of Marseilles and Antwerp were absolutely necessary before his divisions could drive into Germany, although he allowed Montgomery to persuade him to launch the Arnhem operation before clearing the Scheldt. Even before Operation Market Garden, Montgomery's own chief of staff, Maj. Gen. Francis de Guingand, felt that the advance could not be sustained without opening the port of Antwerp.[1] The defeat at Arnhem made the opening of the port vital to the Allied cause.

An Allied divisional slice—i.e., the division plus the corps and higher-level units attached to support it—normally required approximately 600 tons of supplies per day, as opposed to 200 tons per day for the typical German division, which was both smaller and nonmotorized; in addition, the average German soldier was not as lavishly supplied as his Western counterpart. With thirty-eight divisions on the European mainland, the Allied ground forces alone required 22,800 tons of supplies per day, and the U.S. Ninth Air Force alone required another 13,000 tons per day. In addition, the Allies had to feed the civilian population, with Paris alone needing 2,400 tons a day. The heaviest requirement was in gasoline. The average Allied field army needed 1,000,000 tons of fuel per day in the pursuit. Eisenhower's logistical staffs could not furnish anything like these figures. On the last day of August, for example, Patton's Third Army—which was only thirty-five miles west of Metz and seventy miles from the Saar, the Third Reich's second leading industrial district—requested 400,000 tons of fuel of which it received only 31,000 tons.

As of the end of August 1944, 95 percent of all Allied supplies available on the mainland were in or near Cherbourg, on the beaches at Arromanches (the artifical port in the British sector), at Bayeux, and at Omaha Beach. There were virtually no supply depots between those locations and the army dumps, which were now 300 miles away. Turnaround time for trucks was now five days.[2] To complicate matters, Cherbourg was in ruins and could not even be opened until September 29; its capacity did not reach 15,000 tons per day until November. Also, the French railway system had been demolished (mainly by Allied bombers), and they had to rely exclusively on trucks.

In short, with the Allied spearheads 300 miles from the beaches, Cherbourg could support only about thirteen divisions. Antwerp, one of the best ports in the world and very close to the German frontier, could support fifty.[3]

The supply situation was only slightly mitigated by the capture of some of the smaller Channel ports. Rouen was captured on August 31, followed by Dieppe on September 1 and Ostend on September 9. The port of Le Havre was attacked by the British 49th Infantry and 51st Highland Divisions on September 10 after an aerial bombardment of 5,000 tons; it fell two days later. Boulogne, another minor port, was assaulted by the Canadian 3rd Infantry Division on September 17. Hitler had definitely picked the wrong man to command this "fortress." Ferdinand Heim, blamed for the Stalingrad encirclement and discharged from the army in 1943, was reactivated on August 1, 1944, as commandant of Boulogne.[4]

He defended the city to the utmost of his ability and inflicted moderately heavy casualties on the attackers, but he was hardly willing to "fight to the last man" as the Führer had commanded. Heim capitulated on September 23.[5]

The Canadians had neither the men nor supplies to attack all of the Channel ports simultaneously. Their next attack was against Calais, which fell on October 1 after a week-long battle. Five thousand Germans surrendered.[6] The strong garrison of Dunkirk was attacked by the Canadian 2nd Infantry Division on September 8, but the Germans repulsed the assault. It was not attacked again because it was not considered worth the casualties it would cost. The Dunkirk garrison did not surrender until the end of the war.

Capturing the Channel ports was by no means synonymous with opening them, and even when they were opened, their capacity was inadequate to sustain the Allied advance. Dieppe, which had a capacity of 6,700 tons per day, was opened on September 7; Le Havre, opened on October 9, could not unload 5,000 tons a day until November; Boulogne, 11,000 tons, was opened on October 12. Ostend, opened on September 28, was able to accommodate only 5,000 tons. Calais was not able to open until November, and then only to LSTs and smaller landing craft. On the other hand, Antwerp alone had a capacity of 100,000 tons a day. Clearly, it would have to be opened before Eisenhower's supply problems could be solved. Because of Market Garden, this operation could not even begin until October 2, and no one knew how long it might take to complete it. Naturally, Bradley, Hodges, Collins, Patton, and other American commanders could not wait until Antwerp was opened to resume their own offensives, especially in the Aachen Gap and Metz Gap sectors.

THE SECOND BATTLE OF AACHEN

It will be recalled that the American VII Corps was on the verge of breaking through the West Wall when absolute supply priority was shifted to Montgomery in order to support his Arnhem offensive. Collins was forced to suspend his attacks for a week, during which the Germans recovered. As a result, the first American effort in the Aachen sector was a failure, gaining only twelve miles at a cost of 20,000 casualties.

After a lull of a week, Hodges's First Army finally began to receive supplies again during the third week of September. He assigned his XIX Corps the task of capturing the sector from Cologne to Duesseldorf while the VII Corps was to secure Bonn to Remagen and the V Corps would capture the Koblenz to Bonn-Remagen zone. First, however, Hodges had to take care of a few items of unfinished business. To secure his right wing, he wanted to capture high ground in the vicinity of the Monschau corridor north of the Huertgen Forest, which meant that the Huertgen must be cleared of Germans. Also, Aachen would have to be taken, and the Peel Marshes northwest of Aachen would have to be cleared.

Hodges planned to seal off Aachen from the east. North of the city, Maj. Gen. Charles H. Corlett's XIX Corps—spearheaded by the U.S. 30th Infantry Division and supported by the 29th Infantry and 2nd Armored Divisions—would penetrate the West Wall northeast of Aachen and then push almost due south. Simultaneously, Collins' VII

Corps would attack with the U.S. 1st Infantry Division, supported by the 3rd Armored Division.[7] They would break through the West Wall south and east of the city in the vicinity of Eilendorf. The 1st Infantry would then push on through Verlautenheide to Wurselen, where it would link up with the 30th Infantry Division coming down from the north. While all of this was going on, the U.S. 9th Infantry Division would clear the Huertgen Forest, and the U.S. VIII and British XII Corps—including the British 51st Highland, 4th Armoured, 53rd Infantry, 15th Infantry, and 11th Armoured and U.S. 7th Armored and Belgian 1st Divisions—cleared the Peel Marshes.

On the other side of the line, General Koechling, who had recently replaced Schack as commander of the LXXXI Corps, defended Aachen with 20,000 men and 239 guns.[8] Under his command were, from south to north, Lt. Gen. Hans Schmidt's 275th Infantry Division; Colonel Engel's 12th Volksgrenadier Division; Col. Gerhard Wilck's 246th Volksgrenadier Division, which had just arrived in Aachen to replace the 116th Panzer Division, which had been sent to the rear to rebuild; Lt. Gen. Wolfgang Lange's newly arrived 183rd Volksgrenadier Division; and the remnants of Lt. Gen. Siegfried Macholz's 49th Infantry Division, which had just been reinforced with more than 4,300 replacements, including two *Landesschützen* battalions made up mostly of men forty-five years of age or older, two ad hoc battalions of stragglers, two infantry replacement battalions, and four security battalions. In reserve, Koechling had the 341st and 217th Assault Gun Brigades (both at battalion strength), the 506th Heavy Panzer Battalion, and the 108th Panzer Brigade. The last two units, however, had been heavily engaged in the Arnhem fighting and could muster only eleven tanks between them. Despite odds of more than four to one against him, Koechling was confident that he could hold the ancient imperial city, for Rundstedt had promised him that he would receive the 3rd Panzer Grenadier Division and the rebuilt 116th Panzer Division during the first week of October. These divisions would add 24,000 men to the defense.[9]

Koechling assumed that the Americans would attack on a broad front southeast of Aachen, driving northeast from the Stolberg corridor in an effort to capture the Roer River towns of Dueren, Juelich, and Linnich. He therefore concentrated his efforts on reinforcing the 246th and 12th Infanty Divisions in and south of Aachen. The main American attack, however, came nine miles northeast of the city and three miles southwest of Geilenkirchen, near the villages of Rimburg and Marienberg, taking General Koechling and the defenders by surprise.

The American offensive began at 9 A.M. on October 2 when 360 medium bombers (A-20 Havocs and B-26 Marauders) and 72 fighter-bombers (P-38 Lightnings and P-47 Thunderbolts) attacked German positions—or at least they thought they did. Actually, the airmen miscalculated, and more than half the bombs fell well behind German lines and did no damage whatsoever. So inaccurate was the attack that later, under interrogation, when one German prisoner of war was questioned about the effect of the bombing, he responded in amazement, "What bombing?" One group of medium bombers missed their targets by twenty-eight miles and blew away a Belgian village behind Allied lines, killing thirty-four civilians in the process. Even the napalm bombs, America's newest secret weapon, which were dropped accurately did little damage because the woods were too wet for the oil to burn properly.

Following the abortive aerial bombardment, twenty-six American artillery battalions plastered the forward German positions with much greater accuracy but without much greater effect. All but the heaviest shells simply bounced off German pillboxes. Then General Hobbs's U.S. 30th Infantry Division attacked along a one-mile front between Rimburg and Marienberg. Its first obstacle was the Wurm River, which was only two to four feet deep and fifteen to eighteen feet wide. It had little effect on the American infantry, which quickly forded it; however, their supporting tanks quickly bogged down in the thick, black mud. The Americans pushed forward without tank support.

The German 49th Infantry Division did not make a good fight of it at first. The first line of pillboxes was captured with a loss of only two American dead, and hundreds of Germans were taken prisoner. Only the German artillery seemed to be effective; it caught a U.S. infantry company advancing over the flat terrain, taking out 93 of the company's 120 men in a matter of minutes.

Slowed mainly by shell-cratered open ground and muddy beet fields and turnip patches, the Americans captured pillbox after pillbox and slowly pushed the defenders back to Palenburg. Here

Macholz's men made a stand and were still holding the southern half of the village when night fell. The U.S. advance was also checked in front of Rimburg Castle, a thick-walled baroque structure, complete with moat. (Its owner was a cousin of Field Marshal Brauchitsch, the commander in chief of the German Army until Hitler sacked him in 1941.) Without armored support, the American infantry stopped here for the night.

Deceived by the U.S. 29th Infantry Division's feint northwest of Geilenkirchen, the U.S. 30th Infantry Division's offensive had been in progress for several hours before the German generals became aware that it was, in fact, the main thrust. When they finally realized this was the long-awaited main attack, the 49th Infantry Division was on the verge of collapse, so General Koechling ordered the 183rd Volksgrenadier Division to counterattack as soon as night fell to keep it from being smashed by fighter-bombers. Unfortunately, General Lange, the commander of the 183rd, had only one battalion in reserve, and it was not ready to advance until midnight—when it was promptly disorganized by an American artillery bombardment. Reluctantly concluding that neither the 49th Infantry nor 183rd Volksgrenadier Divisions were suitable for anything but defensive missions, Koechling ordered Lange and Macholz to seal off the bridgehead until he could assemble more effective forces for the counterattack.

The next day, October 3, the Americans captured Rimburg Castle and cleared a dozen pillboxes, fully breaching the first band of West Wall fortifications. Their 119th Infantry Regiment, however, was checked in the nearby Rimburg Woods, while the 117th Regiment was stopped in house-to-house fighting at Uebach, a village about a mile east of the Wurm, where they were plastered by German mortar and artillery fire. The weather was so poor that the fighter-bombers were grounded, and the German gunners could operate freely. Meanwhile, the 2nd Armored Division managed to get its Combat Command B across the Wurm, but it also failed to take Uebach. General Koechling planned to counterattack that night and ordered several fresh units to the threatened sector, including both of his reserve assault gun brigades, two infantry battalions from the 49th Infantry Division, and an infantry battalion from the 246th Volksgrenadier Division. The German units of 1944 were not of the same high quality as those of 1941, and it was daylight on October 4 before they were ready to attack. At first, they pushed back the American center but became disorganized by their own artillery, which accidently dropped several shells into their ranks. By the time they hit the U.S. 119th Infantry Regiment the second time, the Americans were ready, and the attack was repulsed.

Fierce fighting continued in Uebach all day, with little quarter being given or asked for by either side. CCB finally took the ruined town at 4 P.M., and the American advance began to pick up speed. Field Marshals Rundstedt and Model and General Brandenberger visited Koechling at his command post and concluded that the forces in this sector were insufficient to check the Americans. They promised to send him reinforcements as quickly as possible. In the meantime, they ordered him to throw every unit into the battle that he could possibly spare. Before nightfall, Koechling sent a *Landesschützen* battalion, his last assault gun battalion, an artillery battalion from the 12th Volksgrenadier Division's sector southeast of Aachen, the entire 404th Grenadier Regiment, and an antitank company from the 246th Volksgrenadier Division to Aachen. Meanwhile, Brandenberger scraped the bottom of the barrel to reinforce the Uebach sector. He took an infantry battalion from the 275th Infantry Division (now part of the LXXIV Corps and heavily engaged in the Huertgen Forest); a static machine gun battalion; and an artillery brigade, which consisted of one battalion of very heavy howitzers and two batteries of 150-millimeter howitzers. He also sent Koechling the cadets of the army NCO training schools at Dueren and Juelich as ad hoc infantry battle groups. Koechling used them to relieve the 343rd Grenadier Regiment of the 183rd Division, which had been fighting the U.S. 29th Infantry Division northwest of Geilenkirchen. He planned to use it to counterattack.[10]

As was typical for the German Army at this stage of the war, these reinforcements looked more impressive on paper than in reality. Many of them were of mediocre quality, and almost every unit was very much understrength. In addition, assembling them for a coordinated counterattack took significantly more time than Koechling anticipated. The 404th Grenadier Regiment, for example, did not arrive until noon on October 5. By then, the Americans had cut the Geilenkirchen-Aachen highway, and the LXXXI Corps had lost its best chance to defeat the offensive. Koechling had to commit his reinforcements piecemeal as they arrived, just to try to check the U.S. advance. A local counterattack by the 148th Grenadier Regiment of the 49th Division on the morning of October 6 did regain four pill-boxes and net more than 100 prisoners, but that was all. Before the end of the day, all of the pillboxes were back in American hands.

Angry at the lack of success, Koechling instructed his corps artillery, the 117th Artillery Command, to ignore its steadily dimin-ishing stockpile of ammunition and blast the American bridgehead with everything it had. This desperate measure increased the Ameri-cans' casualties but did not halt them. That afternoon, General Cor-lett committed the entire U.S. 2nd Armored Division to the battle and gained ground rapidly.[11] By nightfall on October 7, the Ameri-can tankers had cut another major road, the Aachen-Linnich high-way, and were pursuing a beaten 49th Infantry while the U.S. 30th Infantry Division drove into the rear of the 246th Volksgrenadier Division. Koechling tried to block the 2nd Armored's advance on Als-dorf by throwing in a battalion from the 12th Volksgrenadier Divi-sion, but it was overrun by Sherman tanks. By nightfall, the U.S. bridgehead was six miles long and almost five miles deep, and Amer-ican spearheads were within three miles of Wuerselen, where they were scheduled to link up with Collins's VII Corps—a development that would result in the encirclement of Aachen. American casualties had been high: more than 1,800 killed, wounded, and captured in the U.S. 30th Infantry Division alone; CCB of the 2nd Armored Divi-sion had lost fifty-two tanks. But all of the roads to Aachen had been severed, save one: the Aachen-Juelich-Düsseldorf highway. The Amer-icans seemed to have won the battle.

Spearheaded by the U.S. 1st Infantry Division, Gen. "Lightning Joe" Collins's VII Corps began its offensive on October 8. Its objective was to link up with the XIX Corps and complete the encirclement of Aachen. It appeared to the Americans that the operation would be an easy one. The four divisions of the German LXXXI Corps were down to an infantry strength of fewer than 18,000 men, about 240 guns, and a handful of tanks, and the tips of the American pincers were only two and a half miles apart when the attack began. Only three major obstacles stood between the 1st Infantry and Wuerselen: the village of Verlautenheide in the Schill Line; Crucifix Hill (Hill 239), 1,000 yards north of Verlautenheide; and the Ravelsberg (Hill 231).

At dawn on October 8, eleven American artillery battalions blasted Verlautenheide. The veteran U.S. infantry followed close behind the bombardment and took the village before most of the defenders could emerge from their foxholes. By the morning of the tenth, the 1st Infantry had captured all three of its intermediate objectives and was a little more than a mile from Wuerselen.

Inside the rapidly closing pocket lay Colonel Wilck's 246th Volksgrenadier Division—or at least what was left of it. In a vain attempt to halt the XIX Corps, Koechling had taken away the entire 404th Grenadier Regiment and a battalion from each of the 352nd and 689th Grenadier Regiments, leaving Wilck with only three of his original seven infantry battalions. The reinforcements promised by Rundstedt and others had been seriously delayed by Allied air attacks on the railroads, and it seemed unlikely that they would arrive in time to save Aachen. General Huebner, the commander of the U.S. 1st Infantry Division, thought that the city was doomed and sent the commandant, Lt. Col. Maximilian Leyherr, a surrender ultimatum— in addition to showers of surrender leaflets—threatening a massive aerial and artillery bombardment if he did not capitulate within twenty-four hours. Leyherr knew what would happen to his family if he accepted, so he flatly turned it down. He also refused to receive a delegation of local citizens which also wanted him to surrender. Meanwhile, the Americans took Haaren, Aachen's northeastern suburb.[12]

The next day, October 11, the Americans made good on their threats: dozens of Lightnings and Mustangs, each carrying 500 pound bombs, attacked the city, which had only a handful of antiaircraft guns left. Within an hour, sixty-two tons of bombs fell on the city. Then twelve artillery battalions poured 5,000 shells—169 tons of high explosives—on Aachen. But still the city would not surrender.

The Americans were not as close to winning the second battle for Aachen as appearances indicated. Their assault battalions were nearly exhausted, and neither Huebner nor Hobbs had any reserves to speak of.[13] The 117th Artillery Command (*Arko 117*, the artillery command of the LXXXI Corps, which included the 460th Heavy Artillery Battalion, 1301st Army Fortress Artillery Battalion, 63rd Forward Observation Battalion, and 246th Artillery Regiment) continued to pound the American spearheads, which were less than five miles apart, so locating targets was easy, and the German artillery in this sector was extremely effective. Most of the U.S. infantrymen were now living in cellars or captured pillboxes, coming out to man foxholes only when a German attack appeared imminent. Meanwhile, during the night of October 10–11, the first elements of the 3rd Panzer Grenadier and 116th Panzer Divisions arrived northeast of Aachen in the form of the 60th Panzer Grenadier Regiment. The 3rd Panzer Grenadier had 12,000 men, thirty-one assault guns, and thirty-eight artillery pieces. The 116th Panzer had been hastily rebuilt to a strength of 11,500 men, but its panzer regiment had only 41 of its authorized 151 PzKw IV and Panther tanks. Both divisions were under the control of Gen. of Waffen-SS Georg Keppler's I SS Panzer Corps.[14] Field Marshal Rundstedt insisted that these divisions be committed as closed units (i.e., not piecemeal), so it was obvious that they could not join the battle until October 12 at the earliest.

On October 11, the 108th Panzer Brigade launched a counterattack against Bardenberg with the intention of cutting the supply route to the American spearhead, which was now driving on Wuerselen. Although the 108th pushed into the town and scared the American command, the brigade was slaughtered by fighter-bombers and elements of the U.S. 30th Infantry Division. Meanwhile, General Hobbs's forward regiment advanced more than a mile and entered the northern suburbs of Wuerselen—within half a mile of the last vital road to Aachen. This was enough for Model, who persuaded Rundstedt to lift his restrictions on the use of the 3rd Panzer Grenadier and 116th Panzer Divisions. Brandenberger, the commander of the 7th Army, immediately organized a series of counterattacks designed to blunt the American drives. He reinforced the 60th Panzer Grenadier with *SS Kampfgruppe Diefenthal*, a miscellaneous collection of troops from the 1st SS and 12th SS Panzer Divisions under the command of SS Capt. Josef Diefenthal; the remnants of the 108th Panzer Brigade; and two assault gun battalions totaling thirty guns. Their task was to widen and then defend the corridor to Aachen—a major compromise for Rundstedt, who had originally intended for the I SS Panzer Corps to wipe out the American bridgehead and restore the West Wall north of Aachen.

A series of piecemeal German attacks began late on October 11 when a battalion-size battle group from the 1st SS Panzer Division under SS Maj. Herbert Rink struck the American spearhead in northern Wuerselen. The SS men were in an ugly and violent mood because they had passed through Dueren just after an American air raid. Here they saw German women "literally smeared against the walls of houses by the bombs." They swore to exact revenge on the Americans at Wuerselen. After a fierce battle, they threw them out of the town. German losses had been very high: out of 306 enlisted men engaged, 139 were killed or seriously wounded—almost half of the battalion.[15] After eliminating the immediate threat to Aachen, *Kampfgruppe Rink* continued into the city, where, on the personal orders of the Fuehrer, it reinforced the 246th Volksgrenadier Division.

German counterattacks continued the next day, when the reinforced 60th Panzer Grenadier Regiment dissipated its strength in a series of worrisome but uncoordinated attacks against the flanks of the 30th Infantry Division. The Americans turned back each one but gained no further ground that day—or the following two days. Showing a complete lack of appreciation for the true situation at the front, General Hodges, the U.S. First Army commander, suggested to General Corlett that he relieve General Hobbs. Corlett did not do this, but he did put considerable pressure on the hard-pressed general, whose exhausted division had already lost more than 3,000 men.

On the German side of the lines, Field Marshal Model, who was afraid that Aachen might be sealed off before reinforcements arrived, authorized the piecemeal employment of both the 116th Panzer and 3rd Panzer Grenadier Divisions. Faced with the possibility that the gap might be closed at any time, General Brandenberger threw each unit into the battle almost as quickly as it arrived—a major mistake by a man who was normally one of the most competent commanders in the German Army. "A comprehensive plan for a coordinated counterattack thus became infected with the fungus of counterattack by installments that quickly ate away what could have been an effective reserve force," the U.S. official history recorded. "German counterattacks now had no genuine relationship other than a common goal of widening the corridor into Aachen."[16]

On October 15, Maj. Gen. Walter Denkert, the commander of the 3rd Panzer Grenadier Division, committed his 29th Panzer Grenadier Regiment, along with ten to fifteen Tiger tanks from the 506th Heavy Panzer Battalion, east of Verlautenheide, with the objective of recapturing Crucifix Hill.[17] Within six minutes of the start of the attack, the U.S. VII Corps concentrated the fire of six artillery battalions on the advance, forcing the German infantry to take cover. The Tigers pressed forward, however, and overran two infantry companies before they were driven off by the American reserves. To the south, the 8th Panzer Grenadier Regiment launched a similar attack, which was smashed by seven artillery battalions from the 1st Infantry Division and VII Corps, as well as several batteries from the U.S. 3rd Armored Division. The fragmented attacks continued on the sixteenth, but never posed a serious threat to the invaders. Late that evening, the 3rd Panzer Grenadier Division withdrew to regroup, having lost a third of its combat strength—compared to fewer than 400 casualties for the U.S. 1st Infantry Division. The Germans had wasted their reserves.

Meanwhile, the U.S. 30th Infantry Division had gained only a thousand yards in three days of fighting. On October 15, General Hobbs ordered Colonel Sutherland of the 119th Infantry Regiment to sidestep Wuerselen to the west. That night, Sutherland recrossed the Wurm with two of his battalions and proceeded south along the west bank until he reached the village of Kohlscheid, which he attacked at dawn. The village was captured by noon. Sutherland then drove onward to a point more than a mile south of Wuerselen. He attacked across the river early that afternoon.

Simultaneous with Sutherland's attack on Kohlscheid, his third battalion launched an attack along the east bank toward Hill 194, just across the Aachen-Wuerselen-Linnich highway from the Ravelsberg (Hill 231). Here resistance was much heavier because the hill was defended by an understrength SS battalion—part of *Kampfgruppe Diefenthal*—and the 2nd *Landesschützen* Battalion, a relative fresh local defense unit made up of men forty-five years of age and older. Covered by a smoke screen laid by chemical mortar units, the Americans took the vital Hill 194 shortly after 3:30 P.M. Forty-five minutes later, they linked up with the forward elements of the U.S. 1st Infantry Division. Aachen was surrounded at last.

✠

On October 12, on the orders of Adolf Hitler, Col. Gerhard Wilck,[18] the commander of the 246th Volksgrenadier Division, arrived in Aachen to take personal command of the city, and Colonel Leyherr returned to his regiment.[19] Wilck arrived in Aachen with the 246th on September 25 and immediately earned a dressing down from Field Marshal Model because Wilck pointed out that the city could not be defended and should be abandoned. "The Führer has commanded that we will not give up one inch of ground," the red-faced marshal bellowed. "His command is holy for us!"[20] Upon taking command, Wilck was summoned to the 7th Army headquarters at Munstereifel, where his old friend, General Brandenberger, handed him a document to sign. It was a formal declaration that he would not surrender Aachen; if he violated this oath, the Fuehrer was empowered to execute his family. Wilck signed. Both officers knew that Wilck dearly loved his wife and children; both knew that Aachen would be defended to the utmost. After he affixed his signature, Wilck noticed that Brandenberger had tears in his eyes.

Wilck made the dangerous trip back into Aachen during the night of October 12–13 and set up his headquarters in Quellenhof, a luxurious hotel. At the time, only one road, Highway 57, connected Aachen with the rest of Germany. Inside the city, Wilck found that he had 2,000 men from nine different units, varying in quality from Rink's SS battalion to untrained elderly policemen, hastily incorporated into the *Wehrmacht* a few days before. He also had about 3,000 *Volkssturm* (home guards) and several batteries of flak artillery, a few panzers, and the remnants of the 341st and 217th Assault Gun Brigades, which had several operational tank destroyers. He immediately posted a more or less reliable rifle battalion along Highway 57 and a battle group from his own 246th Volksgrenadier Division to guard the high ground to the northwest. The rest of the perimeter was held by ad hoc *kampfgruppen*. Wilck kept the assault gun brigades and the Rink's SS battalion in reserve.

Wilck was delighted that the Americans continued with their efforts to encircle the city rather than launch an immediate frontal assault. During this seventy-two-hour respite, Brandenberger sent several truck convoys into Aachen to resupply Wilck with desperately needed ammunition. The encirclement was completed during the afternoon of October 16, and preceded by a massive artillery bombardment, the final offensive on Aachen began the next morning. Three U.S. infantry divisions would be engaged in the final assault.

At the Quellenhof, Colonel Wilck and SS Major Rink met for the first time, and it was acrimonious. "I take my orders directly from the *Reichsführer SS*, Heinrich Himmler, colonel," the stiff and arrogant Rink declared. "For that reason, I can only place myself conditionally under your command."

Wilck immediately grasped the implications of this remark: Rink had been ordered to spy on him and intercede if Wilck tried to surrender the city. His face turned red; Gerhard Wilck was not the type to avoid confrontations. "You are directly under my command, major!" he barked. "I am battle commandant here, and you are serving in this section of the front. How you combine that with any special orders you may have received from the *Reichsführer-SS* is your problem!

Rink immediately began to protest, but at that moment, an American infantry detachment, which had broken through unnoticed, attacked the Quellenhof, and both Rink and Wilck were soon fighting just like infantry privates, throwing "potato masher" grenades and firing machine pistols. The Americans were turned back.[21]

The battle for Aachen continued to rage without respite on October 18. Field Marshal Rundstedt telephoned General Koechling and told him to remind Colonel Wilck "with the utmost emphasis that he will hold this venerable German city to the last man. If necessary, he will allow himself to be buried in its ruins." The old Prussian marshal also implied to Koechling that his own career might depend on whether he successfully relieved the garrison or not.[22] Later that day, Koechling launched a hasty attack against the encircling American ring with the 3rd Panzer Grenadier and 116th Panzer Divisions. It failed, and Koechling did not have enough strength to try another. With that, OB West wrote off Aachen as doomed.

Most of the *Volkssturm* deserted as soon as they could safely do so. By the night of October 18–19, Colonel Wilck had only 1,200 men and one self-propelled gun left, and he was running out of medical supplies and shells for the artillery. He had already been forced to abandon his headquarters, the cellar of which was filled with dead and wounded. He ordered his men to blow up the main railroad bridges in the city and issued the last of his ammunition.

In the predawn darkness of October 19, German field kitchens issued their last hot rations: a little sausage; hunks of hard, straw-filled bread; and bitter, black ersatz coffee, called "nigger sweat" by the troops. The relentless Americans attacked again at dawn. By now, the German pocket in Aachen was only about one square mile, and it compressed even further that day, as the Americans finally took the Quellenhof, which was defended to the end by a detachment of German paratroopers, who threw champagne bottles at the Americans when they ran out of ammunition. They were finally forced into a cellar by a 155-millimeter gun, and those who did not surrender were killed.

Also encircled was SS Major Rink and his battalion, which was down to a strength of fifty unwounded men. It had suffered 90 percent casualties in two weeks. Even so, the young SS men were full of fight. They broke out of the smaller American trap and took up new positions on the Weyherstrasse on the steep southwestern slope of the Lousberg. There the survivors of Rink's SS battalion were attacked by the Shermans of the U.S. 3rd Armored Division. Separated from Wilck and seeing no need to sacrifice his own battalion, Rink decided to try to break out during the night. He sent a patrol to find a gap in American lines, but it never returned. He also sent out a column of wounded in half-tracks, which tried to escape via side streets but were captured by the Americans. There was no way out of the dying city.

By now, 80 percent of the houses of Aachen had been destroyed or damaged beyond repair. The city was now without electricity and had been without water for three days, and soldiers and residents alike were reduced to drinking from ponds or puddles, or from the ubiquitous shell and bomb craters. Fortunately for them, most of the battle was fought in a driving rain, supplying the Germans with water and robbing the Americans of their invaluable fighter-bombers.

Colonel Wilck, his staff, and his exhausted, dirty garrison continued to resist, fighting on with nothing to sustain them but adrenaline tablets. To boost morale, Wilck recommended 162 men for the Iron Cross. He had only 800 men left, and the Americans were within 600 yards of his command post.

The American advance was slow. Rather than sacrifice the lives of their infantry, they let the artillery do the work whenever possible. By the end of the day, they were within 200 yards of Wilck's bunker, which they shelled with 155-millimeter guns. The next morning, Saturday, October 21, Colonel Wilck sent his last messages: "All ammo gone after severe house-to-house fighting. No water and no food. Enemy close to command post of the last defenders of the Imperial City. Radio prepared for destruction." A few minutes later, he signaled: "We are reporting out. Best wishes to our comrades and loved ones." Then the radio went dead.[23]

From his thirty or so remaining American prisoners, Wilck selected two volunteers to approach the U.S. lines with a message: the commandant of Aachen was prepared to capitulate. They came out of the bunker under a white flag but were promptly fired on by nervous Americans who mistook them for Germans. Fortunately, these shots missed, and after a few exclamations, they were transported to the rear. The details of the surrender were quickly worked out, and Aachen capitulated at 12:05 P.M. on October 21. The first major German city had fallen to the Allies. Each side had suffered about 5,000 killed, wounded, or missing, about 5,000 Germans were captured.

Aachen had imposed a significant delay on the U.S. First Army and a considerable drain on Allied supplies. In addition, it was by no means a decisive victory, for General Brandenberger's 7th Army was now in better shape to meet another Allied offensive than it had been seven weeks before.

To the west, south, and north, several panzer and SS panzer divisions had been withdrawn to the east into the interior of the Reich. Here they were being hastily rebuilt and equipped with the best material Germany had to offer in this, the fifth year of the war. Preparations for Hitler's top-secret Ardennes offensive had already reached an advanced stage, and the Battle of Aachen, coupled with the German victory at Arnhem, Monty's failure to clear the Scheldt, and Hodges's obsession with the Huertgen Forest, played almost exactly into the Führer's hands.

CHAPTER 6

The Battle of the Huertgen Forest (Part 1)

Just south of the Aachen Gap lay the Huertgen Forest, part of the Ardennes-Eifel region, which is characterized by deep valleys, steep hills, treacherous gullies, and dense forests. The Huertgen Forest is the worst part of the Eifel region, which is called the Ardennes in Belgium. Due east the terrain levels off and becomes a gently undulating plain extending to the Rhine River. The Roer River, which rises near the picturesque town of Monschau, sixteen miles south of Aachen, forms the southern and eastern boundary of the forest, and its western end begins roughly along the German-Belgian border. (Monschau was a favorite place for German honeymooners and Adolf Hitler.) The northern edge of the forest is ill-defined and begins where the Stolberg corridor ends. Just north of Monschau lies the Monschau Corridor—seven miles long and four miles wide—which extends northeast toward Dueren and the Roer.

In the Huertgen, all of the advantages of terrain and nature accrued to the defense, and two of the Allies' most effective weapons—the fighter-bomber and the tank—were virtually neutralized. Because of the pilots' inability to see through the 100-foot-tall trees, the Americans could not use close support aircraft; mines, primitive roads, deep gullies, and thick woods rendered the Shermans useless most of the time. Moreover, the forest multiplied the effectiveness of German shelling because tree bursts scattered lethal fragments everywhere, making artillery and mortars much more deadly. American artillery, on the other hand, was usually ineffective because the Germans were defending pillboxes and bunkers that offered overhead protection—something the advancing American infantry naturally did not have. The deep, dark forest also had a negative effect on American morale, which was further undercut by the more or less constant rain and the ability of the Germans to infiltrate their lines at night to set up ambushes in their rear. After they sprung their ambushes, they melted away again into the dark and forbiding forest. Sometimes they left mines behind. Today, most American military historians agree that the Battle of the Huertgen Forest should never have been fought.

On September 11, during the first battle for Aachen, General Collins gave the U.S. 9th Infantry Division the task of sweeping the Huertgen Forest and pushing on to the Monschau corridor. No one expected serious resistance.[1] The task of defending the Huertgen fell to Col. Karl Roesler's burned out 89th Infantry Division. After the retreat from France, one of its grenadier regiments had only 350 men,[2] and Roesler's artillerymen, engineers, and other troops had long since been incorporated into the infantry. When he arrived on the West Wall in September, Roesler was given another infantry regiment made up of 1,300 low-quality security and local defense troops and men from replacement-training units, as well as seventy-five anti-tank guns. His total artillery strength stood at six guns: four 122-millimeter Russian howitzers, one German howitzer, and one medium Italian howitzer for which there was no ammunition.

Unfortunately for the Americans, both their commanders and Colonel Roesler picked the same terrain feature as the key to the battle: the Hoefen-Alzen Ridge. Here Roesler posted his veterans, the 1056th Grenadier Regiment, which held up the U.S. 60th Infantry Regiment, the forward unit of the 9th Division, for five days. The ridge was not captured until September 18. Then the Americans pushed on toward Hill 554 and the villages of Lammersdorf and Huertgen but had not reached these objectives on September 22 when they were hurriedly sent north to deal with an attack that Engel's 12th Volksgrenadier Division had launched against Schevenhuette. This turned out to be a serious mistake. By the time the 60th Infantry and other elements of the 9th Infantry Division arrived at Schevenhuette, the German attack had been repulsed, and they were not needed. Meanwhile, Gen. of Infantry Erich Straube, the LXXIV Corps' commander, sent Lt. Gen. Paul Mahlmann's 353rd Infantry Division into "the Green Hell."[3] By the time the American attack resumed on September 25, the Germans were ready for them. By September 26, the U.S. 9th Infantry Division had lost 1,000 men but had gained only a few hundred yards in heavy fighting. Hill 554 finally fell on September 29 to a combined infantry-tank attack, but it was clear that German resistance in the forest was by no means broken.

On September 29, General Hodges nevertheless ordered Maj. Gen. Louis A. Craig, the commander of the 9th Infantry, to get on with the job of clearing the Huertgen. None of the German commanders understood the apparent American obsession with clearing the Huertgen Forest. All the Allies had to do, Brandenberger observed, was to block the roads on the western fringe of the woods and bypass the forest itself. Secretly concentrating armor in the forest for a counterattack against the American flank never entered his mind because he had no armor, the forest had too few roads for the employment of armor in the counterattack, and the roads that he did have could easily be blocked by felled trees and mines, pinching off any possible counterattack. Even though he saw no reason for the American attacks, General Brandenberger was quick to reinforce his forest defenses; if the Americans wanted to fight in ideal defensive terrain, he was more than willing to accommodate them. The longer the Battle of the Huertgen Forest lasted, the better for the 7th Army.

To command the German forces in the Huertgen Forest, Brandenberger and Straube selected Lt. Gen. Hans Schmidt, the commander of the 275th Infantry Division, whom historian Charles MacDonald described as "a physically robust officer [who] was level-headed and never rattled under fire."[4] Schmidt's division absorbed the combat troops of the 353rd Infantry Division while Mahlmann and his staff were sent to the rear with their support units to organize a new 353rd Infantry. With the absorption of the 353rd, Schmidt's total strength was only 6,500 men, 5,000 of which were in combat units. He also had twelve howitzers and six assault guns.

The U.S. 9th Infantry Division began its advance October 6. General Craig's specific objective was the village of Schmidt, located three and a half miles southeast of Huertgen on one of the highest ridges west of the Roer and within three miles of the western edge of the forest. His men still had a great deal to learn about forest fighting. When German shelling began, they instinctively threw themselves to the ground as they had been trained to do. This is a perfect correct action under normal circumstances but not in forest. German shells, set for instantaneous detonation, exploded 75 to 100 feet above them, and a man lying on the ground thus exposed a far greater percentage of his body to shell fragments that one standing upright. The Germans, operating out of bunkers, pillboxes, and foxholes covered with logs, had no such problems. One U.S. battalion, advancing just behind the spearhead, suffered 100 casualties on the first day of the attack and did not engage a single German with small-arms fire.

On October 7, the second day of the advance, two American infantry battalions threatened the lateral highway running through Germeter and Richelskaul. Schmidt responded with a counterattack the following morning but without success. Finally, on the ninth, American engineers succeeded in clearing a tank tail to Richelskaul, which their infantry took earlier that day. The next day, the U.S. 39th Infantry Regiment captured the village of Wittscheidt, cutting the Lammersdorf-Huertgen highway. The 39th Infantry lost more than 500 men in five days of heavy fighting, and the town of Schmidt was still more than three miles away. This did not seem far to those still engaged in "pursuit thinking," but it seemed like light years to the men in the Huertgen Forest.

During the night of October 11–12, Hans Schmidt was reinforced with an ad hoc 1,200-man force called Regiment Wegelein. Commanded by Col. Wolfgang Wegelein, a veteran of the Eastern Front, it consisted of young men, half of whom were tabbed for officers' training school. It also had an unusually high number of mortars and heavy machine guns. General Brandenberger ordered it to assemble in the woods west of Wittscheidt and attack to the south. Simultaneously, Schmidt's own division, temporarily under the command of Col. Helmut Bechler,[5] was to attack to the north, up the Weisser Weh Valley, while General Schmidt directed the entire operation. Wegelein and Bechler were to join hands in the American rear, cutting off most of the U.S. 9th Infantry Division. Unfortunately for the Germans, Wegelein's regiment could not assemble until well after midnight. Wegelein wanted to delay the attack, but Schmidt refused; if they did not strike immediately, he declared, the opportunity would be lost.

The attack began at 7 A.M. on October 12, and initially, everything when well. Wegelein's men took the Americans by surprise and broke through their lines, cutting off the 39th Infantry Regiment in the process. Wegelein's communications soon failed completely, and he was not even able to control his own artillery fire. In addition, Bechler's attack was late and was rather easily contained by the U.S. 60th

Infantry Regiment. By nightfall, confusion reigned on both sides. Schmidt wanted to continue the attacks the next day until he received an order instructing Wegelein to return all of his officer cadets—about half his troops—to the rear. To make matters worse, Wegelein apparently got lost in the darkness and was killed by an enemy infantryman. General Schmidt now had no choice but to go over to the defensive the next day, when he was able to prevent the Americans from gaining any more ground.

By October 16, a lull descended on the battlefield. The U.S. 9th Infantry Division had gained 3,000 yards in eleven days of heavy fighting but had lost 4,500 men in the process. The Germans had lost about 3,000 men, most of them poor quality draftees, some of whom surrendered at the first opportunity.

On October 18, General Eisenhower met with Bradley and Montgomery and outlined his plan for the next phase of the campaign. Basically, it was a continuation of his broad-front strategy. Montgomery's 21st Army Group was to clear the Scheldt and open the port of Antwerp. Bradley's 12th Army Group, spearheaded by Hodges's First Army, was to make the main effort and force a crossing of the Rhine south of Cologne. In the meantime, a new U.S. army, the Ninth, under the command of Lt. Gen. William H. Simpson, was given a zone of operations north of the U.S. First Army to protect Hodges's northern flank, while, south of the First Army, Patton's Third Army launched a secondary attack in Lorraine.[6] For this offensive, Hodges had to give up the XIX Corps, but he was reinforced with Middleton's VIII Corps and another division. The offensive was to begin on November 5. Before that date, General Hodges decided, the Huertgen Forest had to be cleared.

Hodges could easily have outflanked the Huertgen Forest by sending the V Corps south of the Roer River dams, but he apparently never even considered doing so. He assigned the task of clearing the forest to Gerow's V Corps; ordered the 9th Division relieved by the 28th Infantry Division, a veteran Pennsylvania National Guard unit; and set the attack date for November 2. Again the village of Schmidt was the main objective. The principal supply route of the German 89th Infantry Division, now under Maj. Gen. Walter Bruns, passed through the village while another highway led downhill to the Schwammenauel Dam.

The German High Command realized that Schmidt had to be held because it was only a few miles north of the zone earmarked for Hitler's surprise offensive. The loss of Schmidt and the high ground around it would seriously jeopardize the northern flank of the great counterattack and threaten the offensive altogether. Even if this had not been the case, Hodges's plan was badly flawed because the 28th Infantry Division was the only Allied unit attacking along a 170-mile stretch of front. The plan practically invited the Germans to commit reserve forces.

Bradley's offensive to force a Rhine crossing ran into trouble before it began. He was supposed to have received new divisions, but they were slow in arriving, so he postponed the jump-off date until November 10—or the first day of clear weather thereafter. Nevertheless, the 28th Infantry jumped off on schedule at 9 A.M. on November 2, following a 12,000-round artillery bombardment. It was spearheaded by the U.S. 109th Infantry Regiment, which attacked along a narrow frontage of only one mile. Attacking along either side of the Germeter-Huertgen highway, one battalion made surprisingly rapid headway initially and captured the ridge overlooking the village of Huertgen early that afternoon. The rest of the regiment, however, ran into a thick minefield near Wittscheidt; the American engineers could not clear it because it was extremely well protected by German mortars and heavy machine guns, firing from bunkers and pillboxes. The 28th Division's other infantry regiments, the 112th and 110th, were committed to the battle by the end of the day but were unable to break the stalemate. Charles MacDonald later wrote:

> The forest . . . had begun to look like a battlefield designed by the Archfiend himself. Shelling had made a debris-littered jungle of the forest floor and cut naked yellow gashes on the trunks of trees. Here opposing lines were within hand-grenade range, the Germans waiting behind thick entanglements of concertina barbed wire, alive with trip wires, mines, and booby traps. Log-covered bunkers and foxholes almost flush with the ground augmented the pillboxes. Over it all hung a dim, macabre light filtered by dripping branches of dark green firs.[7]

On November 2 and 3, the Americans tried to breach the mine-field and cut tank trails to follow the main advance but failed on both flanks. In the center, two battalions of the 112th Infantry advanced through a gap in the German lines, took Kommerscheidt, crossed the small but swift and cold Kall River, and were on the outskirts of Schmidt before they met serious opposition. The town was defended by an understrength German infantry battalion, which was quickly defeated. The former Pennsylvania Guardsmen now controlled one of the vital villages in Europe, but they were cold, wet, and tired after two days fighting in the dark forest. They made themselves at home in the warm houses and did not take elementary precautions against a possible German counterattack. A few mines were laid, but the men were neither dug in nor camouflaged. They dug a few foxholes but did not construct a systematic defensive perimeter with strongpoints and overlapping fields of fire, nor did they send out any patrols to ascertain what the Germans were preparing to do next.

They were preparing to counterattack.

The key to holding Schmidt was the cart trail across the Kall gorge, which was now defended by one of the two battalions which had broken through. Unfortunately, the U.S. engineers were unable to make it suitable for use by tanks, so the defenders of Schmidt were without armored support. The Americans were also unaware that Field Marshal Model had expected them to try to capture the village; for that reason, he had Maj. Gen. Walter Bruns's 89th Infantry Division in the Monschau sector replaced by a *Volksgrenadier* division and sent to the Schmidt sector. Two of the 89th's Infantry battalions had passed through Schmidt only a few minutes before the American battalion arrived. The two German battalions spent the night within a mile of the village, and a third battalion, which approached Schmidt after midnight, found its way blocked, so it dug in on the highway west of the village.

Characteristically, General Brandenberger reacted energetically. He had just been given Maj. Gen. Siegfried von Waldenburg's 116th Panzer Division, which had recently been rebuilt,[8] so he ordered Waldenburg to send his panzer regiment—about thirty tanks—to Schmidt to reinforce the 89th Division, while two panzer grenadier regiments assembled in the Huertgen sector. Both forces were ordered to counterattack at dawn on November 4.

Just as day broke, a German artillery barrage woke up the American defenders at Schmidt; then the attack came in, supported by thirty PzKw IVs and Panthers. Within three hours, it was all over; the American battalion had been routed, and the survivors were racing toward Kommerscheidt or into the woods, pursued by the Germans. The U.S. 112th Infantry Regiment rallied at Kommerscheidt, where it was reinforced by nine tank destroyers and half a dozen Shermans that had at last managed to negotiate the Kall trail. They and the fighter-bombers enabled the Americans to hold their positions on November 5, which was the first clear day in more than a week. Every time a German tank emerged from the forest to attack Kommerscheidt, it was pounded by fighter-bombers. In the meantime, the 116th Panzer Reconnaissance Battalion cut behind the defenders and severed the Kall trail, forcing the U.S. 28th Division's reserves to fight in order to restore contact with Kommerscheidt.

The battle reached its climax on November 7. General Gerow had already dispatched the U.S. 4th Infantry Division to the endangered sector, but Bruns and Schmidt attacked before it could arrive. In the morning, fifteen panzers attacked but were beaten off by the Americans, who destroyed five of them; however, two Shermans and three tank destroyers were also knocked out. By noon the American position began to crumble, and when a German tank blew apart the house that served as the command post for both U.S. battalions defending Kommerscheidt, the defense collapsed. By nightfall, the American penetration beyond the Kall had been wiped out.

The second battle for Schmidt had been one of the most costly actions fought by an American division in World War II. The 28th Infantry Division lost 6,184 men. General Schmidt lost about half that number.

CHAPTER 7

Operation Queen: The Allied November Offensive

In November 1944, German war production neared its peak. Satisfied with the speed of his Ardennes buildup, Hitler decided to make sure his offensive was not threatened by an American capture of Schmidt. He therefore reinforced Brandenberger and Schmidt with several new *Volks* artillery corps (equivalent to about a regiment of artillery) and *Nebelwerfer* (rocket launcher) brigades. He also temporarily assigned the 5th Panzer Army, under Gen. of Panzer Troops Hasso von Manteuffel, the task of defending the Stolberg Corridor and the sector east of Aachen to deceive the Allies into believing that it was already committed.[1] Then the 5th Panzer was secretly withdrawn and sent south to assume its real mission: directing one of the two major drives into the Ardennes. Meanwhile, Gen. of Infantry Gustav-Adolf von Zangen's 15th Army, temporarily dubbed Gruppe von Manteuffel, in accordance with the German deception plan, took charge of the northern wing of Brandenberger's sector, including the LXXXI Corps in the Stolberg corridor and the northern tip of the Huertgen Forest.[2] At the same time, Army Group B was reinforced with a new reserve: the XXXXVII Panzer Corps, with a tank and a panzer grenadier division. Model, who could not believe that the Americans intended to launch their main offensive in the Stolberg Corridor–Huertgen Forest sector, posted these divisions farther to the north on the Roer River plain.

The Allies' November offensive against the Siegfried Line, dubbed Operation Queen, was a huge affair involving both the U.S. Ninth and First Armies, as well as the British XXX Corps on the northern flank—seventeen divisions in all. General Bradley said that it might be "the last offensive necessary to bring Germany to her knees,"[3] and General Hodges expressed the same opinion in almost the same words. The main attack, which was launched by Collins's VII Corps, began on November 16—the last possible date, according to Bradley's timetable. It was preceeded by a carpet-bombing attack by more than 1,200 heavy bombers from the U.S. Eighth Air Force, which blasted the German assembly areas, field installations, and communications and supply lines, as well as the city of Eschweiler in the Stolberg Corridor and the town of Langerwehe in the northern tip of the Huertgen Forest. At the same time, more than 1,000 British bombers destroyed Dueren and other targets on or near the Roer River, while 600 medium bombers from the U.S. Ninth Air Force attacked smaller towns in the Stolberg Corridor. The ubiquitous fighter-bombers blasted the German front lines. In all, more than 4,500 airplanes took part in the attack, about half of them heavy bombers, and more than 10,000 tons of bombs fell on German positiosn and installations. It was the largest air attack in direct support of ground forces during the war.

The air attack was followed by an artillery bombardment by 1,246 guns, and then the main attack, which was supported by more than 300 tanks and tank destroyers. For his attack, Collins controlled the U.S. 1st, 9th, and 4th Infantry Divisions, as well as the 3rd and 5th Armored Divisions. The 4th Infantry, reinforced by Combat Command Reserve of the 3rd Armored Divison, was committed to the Huertgen Forest with the objective of clearing it and capturing Dueren. The other divisions were to push through the Stolberg corridor to the Roer.

To defend against this massive offensive, General Koechling's LXXXI Corps had, from north to south, the 246th Volksgrenadier Division; the 3rd Panzer Grenadier Division; and the 12th Volksgrenadier Division. General Schmidt's 275th Infantry Division, still part of the 7th Army, was also subjected to massive attacks in the Huertgen Forest.

The 246th Volksgrenadier, which was to face the attack of the U.S. Ninth Army, was the worst of the lot, although it had been partially rebuilt after Aachen, absorbing the survivors of the now-defunct 49th Division. Under the command of Col. Peter Koerte, it was organized like most *Volksgrenadier* divisions and consisted of three infantry regiments of two battalions each, an artillery regiment, an engineer battalion, and an assault gun (antitank) battalion.[4] Because many of its troops were seventeen-year-olds with only six weeks of training, it was rated fourth class—suitable for limited defensive missions only—in spite of the fact that it now mustered 11,141 men.

The 3rd Panzer Grenadier Division, under the command of Maj. Gen. Walter Denkert, had about 11,000 men, many of them *Volksdeutsche*, and was a third-class unit—suitable for unlimited defensive missions. It consisted of two panzer grenadier regiments, the 8th and 29th; a motorized artillery regiment, the 3rd; and a tank battalion, the 103rd, equipped mainly with assault guns. It also controlled the 103rd Panzer Reconnaissance, 3rd Tank Destroyer, 3rd Motorized Engineer, and 3rd Motorized Signal Battalions.

In the Stolberg Corridor, opposite the main U.S. attack, was the 12th Volksgrenadier Division, which had a strength of 6,381 men.[5] Even though it had lost more than half of its men since September, the 12th was still rated as second class—capable of limited offensive action—because of its high state of morale and training. It was well led by Gerhard Engel, Hitler's former army adjutant, who had been promoted to major general on November 1. The units of the LXXXI Corps were supported by sixty-six 105-millimter and thirty-one 150-millimter howitzers, plus an assortment of thirty-one other guns, including 122-millimter Russian howitzers. They also had fifty-four assault guns, eleven 88-millimeter antitank guns, and forty-five antitank guns of small caliber.

In addition to these forces, Lt. Gen. Max Bork's 47th Volksgrenadier Division was just arriving in the corps sector by train and beginning the process of relieving the 12th Volksgrenadier at the front. About half of its men were former *Luftwaffe* and naval personnel recently transferred to the infantry; most of the rest were seventeen- and eighteen-year-old boys who had been rushed to the front with only six weeks' training. Although its equipment and weapons were good, most of the troops were unfamiliar with them; the artillerymen, for example, had only one week of training with their guns before they were sent to the front. The antitank weapons would not arrive until long after the 47th was sent into battle.[6]

The unlucky 47th, much of which was just getting off the trains when the American offensive struck, took the worst of the bombardment. One artillery battalion at Juelich was almost completely wiped out along with the city. The signal battalion and General Headquarters units were devastated in Dueren, which was so badly damaged that it was said to resemble a Roman ruin.[7] Some infantry units were also marching to the front when the Americans air attack began and were pulverized by medium bombers and fighter-bombers. "I never saw anything like it," one German sergeant later told his American interrogator. "These kids . . . were still numb forty-five minutes after the bombardment. It was our luck that your ground troops did not attack us until the next day. I could not have done anything with those boys of mine that day."[8]

The 12th Volksgrenadier, however, was in much better shape. Contrary to Allied expectations, it was relatively unhurt by the bombardment. Engel's frontline troops had been in their positions for some time, had burrowed deep into the German earth, and were protected by bunkers and pillboxes. Prisoners later estimated that the forward regiments suffered casualty rates of 1 to 3 percent. Their communications were completely disrupted, however, and they would be without hot food for days, because the bombardment had destroyed most of their field kitchens, supply vehicles, and horses. Despite being outnumbered five to one in infantry, Engel's troops managed to hold Hamich on November 16 and 17 against repeated American attacks. One U.S. infantry battalion suffered 70 percent casualties before it withdrew. The town finally fell on November 18, but the U.S. 1st Infantry and 3rd Armored Divisions still had to face persistent counterattacks from the 48th Infantry and 12th Fusilier Regiments.

German reactions to the offensive were both slow and incorrect. Zangen's 15th Army had taken over this sector only on November 15, but Manteuffel's 5th Panzer Army Headquarters had not yet departed. These two capable generals set up an informal combined headquarters and directed the battle as a team until November 20, when Manteuffel left for the Ardennes. Zangen and Manteuffel tried to create an army reserve by combining what was left of the 47th Volksgrenadier Division with a small *kampfgruppe* from the 116th Panzer Division, but Field Marshal Model ordered this force to counterattack and retake Hamich, despite the objections of Zangen and Manteuffel. Model still believed that the main Allied offensive would come farther north, near the boundary of the XII SS Corps and LXXXI Corps—not in the southern sector of the LXXXI Corps and on the northern boundary of the 7th Army. Model therefore committed the local reserves too soon and did not reinforce the threatened sector with his main reserve force, Gen. of Panzer Troops Baron Heinrich von Luettwitz's XXXXVII Panzer Corps.[9]

Shortly after nightfall on November 18, the remnants of the green 47th Volksgrenadier Division formed up into two battle groups. At 5:30 A.M. the next morning, they attacked the U.S. 1st Infantry Division and pushed it back to the outskirts of Hamich but could not eject it from the village. By now, it was obvious that the great breakthrough was not going to occur and that Operation Queen was not going to bring Nazi Germany to its knees, as Omar Bradley and Courtney Hodges had hoped.

To the north, the British XXX Corps was also in trouble. Its objective was to pinch off the Geilenkirchen salient and then push on to the small Wurm River, capturing the fortified villages of Hoven, Wurm, Mullendorf, and Beek in the process. At first everything went well. The green U.S. 84th Infantry Division advanced one and a half miles and took the village of Prummen while the veteran British 43rd Infantry Division on the left flank advanced two and a half miles, completely encircling Geilenkirchen and elements of the 183rd Volksgrenadier Division. The XXX Corps resumed its drive in the predawn darkness of November 18, attacking the thick minefields in front of the West Wall. This attack was spearheaded by elements of the British 79th Armoured Division and illuminated by "Monty's Moonlight"—powerful searchlights shining on the clouds, which reflected the light downward onto the battlefield. The 79th Armoured's specially designed tanks cleared the mines by using chain flails, which extended two yards in front of the tanks, causing the mines to explode harmlessly. Using this ingenious method of attack, the British breached the minefields within two hours, and by noon, the 43rd Wessex Division had been committed to the battle, attacking the forward line of pillboxes in the Siegfried Line. Then the trouble began. The American-made Sherman tanks with their narrow tracks bogged down in the mud, but the Germans, profiting from their lessons in Russia, had no such problem. Both the British 43rd and U.S. 84th Divisions were soon counterattacked by Lt. Gen. Eberhard Rodt's veteran 15th Panzer Grenadier Division.[10] "It was galling to see their tanks with their broad tracks maneuvering over muddy fields impassable to our own," Brig. Hubert Essame, the commander of the 43rd, recalled.[11] The American attack bogged down in the Siegfried Line, but the 43rd Infantry pushed on as far as the Wurm in four days of heavy fighting. "Years after the event," the historian of the Duke of Cornwall's Light Infantry wrote,

> those who survived could recall the intensity of the enemy fire and the sloppy ground over which they had to move to reach their objective. What is difficult to describe is the physical agony of the infantryman. . . . The November rain seemed piercingly cold. After exertion when the body warmed, the cold air and the wet seemed to penetrate the very marrow of the body so that the whole shook as with ague, and then after shaking would come a numbness of hand and leg and mind and a feeling of surrender to forces of nature far greater in strength than any enemy might impose.[12]

On November 22, Horrocks, the commander of the XXX Corps, ordered one final effort, and the British spearhead, the Duke of Cornwall's Light Infantry (DCLI), attacked the village of Hoven. But they were met by a hail of fire from Harmel's 10th SS Panzer Division, which Rundstedt had hurriedly brought down from Holland on November 16. "They went down everywhere, the muddy fields littered with crumpled dead," historian Charles Whiting wrote later.[13] Despite its heavy casualties, the men of DCLI pushed into Hoven but were soon virtually surrounded by the SS, who broke through into their rear. The U.S. 84th Infantry Division on the right flank tried to help but could not break through a German bunker line on the heights around the village of Suggerath, which the men of the tough 15th Panzer Grenadier Division had been ordered to hold at all costs.

Inside Hoven, the DCLI was smashed by the 10th SS Panzer. The town was leveled by the panzers, and two British companies were overrun. The entire battalion would probably have been destroyed had it not been for their PIATs, a spring-loaded form of the bazooka. The battle was so intense that the DCLI ran out of ammunition but fought on with weapons taken from dead Germans. The battalion commander was killed and both remaining majors were wounded, but still the light infantry struggled for survival. By now, the cellars were full of British and German wounded.

The battle continued until the next day, when the survivors of the DCLI broke out of the encirclement, led by their two wounded majors. One company had lost 105 of its 120 men. The northernmost thrust had been blunted. "The steam was going out of the whole huge . . . action," a British historian wrote later.[14]

Between the British XXX Corps and the U.S. First Army, the U.S. Ninth Army advanced across a relatively open plain dotted with villages and strongpoints. Although the terrain in this sector was much less formidable than that over which the First Army advanced, resistance was also stiffer because Model expected the main Allied offensive to come in this zone and had stationed some of his best units here. The defenders were all under the command of Zangen's 15th Army and included Gen. of Infantry Guenther Blumentritt's XII SS Corps,[15] with Colonel Landau's 176th Infantry Division, General Lange's 183rd Volksgrenadier Division, the 388th Volks Artillery Corps, the 301st Panzer Battalion (thirty-one Tigers), and the 559th Assault Gun Battalion (twenty-one guns). Immediately behind the XII SS Corps lay Luettwitz's XXXXVII Panzer Corps—Army Group B's main reserve—with the 9th Panzer Division, elements of the 15th Panzer Grenadier Division, and the 506th Heavy Panzer Battalion (thirty-six Tigers).

On November 16, the first day of the offensive, the 2nd Armored Division of the U.S. XIX Corps practically annihilated the 330th Grenadier Regiment of the 183rd Volksgrenadier Division and pushed to the edge of Juelich but lost thirty-five tanks in the process—fourteen to mines, ten to assault guns, six to artillery fire, and one each to mortar fire, mud, *panzerfausts*, and mechanical failure. Another was lost to a combination of mines and antitank gunfire. Elsewhere, the XIX Corps gains were limited to about a mile. The next day, the 2nd Armored Division was counterattacked by Maj. Gen. Baron Harald von Elverfeldt's 9th Panzer Division, and a real tank battle ensued. By the end of the day, at least eleven Panzers and Tigers had been knocked out, but the Americans had lost eighteen Shermans destroyed, sixteen damaged and out of action, and nineteen Stuart light tanks knocked out or destroyed. In the end, the 2nd Armored retreated and was relieved that the 9th Panzer did not follow.

On November 18, the U.S. 29th Infantry Division joined the fighting around Juelich, and the tide of battle began to turn in favor of the Americans. The 2nd Armored continued to fight indecisively with the 9th Panzer, but the 29th Infantry Division managed to push forward and, by the end of the day, had taken the villages of Siersdorf and Bettendorf from the 246th Volksgrenadier Division and had broken the first defensive ring around Juelich. By nightfall on November 21, it had cracked the second ring and was within a mile and a half of the Roer, where it was checked. On Novemher 22, Zangen committed two regiments of Col. Theodor Tolsdorff's fresh 340th Volksgrenadier Division—one at Linnich and the other at Juelich.[16] The third regiment of the division was committed at Juelich the next day, and the American advance was halted, despite the arrival of the U.S. 30th Infantry Division. On November 23, the 9th Panzer Division was withdrawn from the battle and sent to the rear to rehabilitate for the Ardennes attack.

On November 26, General Koechling's LXXXI Corps launched a major counterattack in the Juerlich sector, using two grenadier regiments of the 340th Volksgrenadier, the 301st Heavy Panzer Battalion, and the 341st Assault Gun Brigade, all supported by fourteen artillery battalions. Fortunately for the Americans, the German artillery was hamstrung by a shortage of ammunition, which was being horded for the Ardennes offensive. The Americans fired an estimated 27,500 rounds against the Germans and broke the back of the counterattack. They were still bogged down west of the river, however.

Everywhere the story was the same: unexpectedly stiff German resistance, unexpectedly high casualties, and no major breakthroughs anywhere. The story of Combat Command B of the U.S. 3rd Armored Division was fairly typical. Led by Brig. Gen. Truman E. Boudinot, it jumped off at H-Hour, 12:45 P.M., on November 16 between the U.S. 1st and 104th Infantry Divisions.[17] It attacked in the Stolberg Corridor—excellent terrain for armor—with the objective of capturing four villages on the western edge of the Hamich Ridge. None of the four were more than two miles from the combat command's front line when the offensive began. The 89th Grenadier Regiment of the 12th

Volksgrenadier Division defended the villages. Once it had captured the four villages, CCB was to be relieved by infantry and was to return to its parent unit in reserve in order to prepare for the next phase of the operation, the pursuit.

Struggling through the mud, CCB took all four objectives in three days of heavy fighting, but its losses were prohibitive. The armored infantry suffered 50 percent casualties, and tank losses were worse. Of the sixty-four medium tanks available at the start of the operation, only twenty-two were still operational when it concluded. Seven light tanks had also been knocked out, for a total loss of forty-nine tanks. Of these, German antitank fire had claimed twenty-four, *panzerfausts* had knocked out six, artillery fire had destroyed six, mines accounted for twelve, and an American airplane mistakenly attacked one. "These did not look much like statistics of a breakthrough operation," the U.S. official history noted later.[18] Certainly, CCB was no longer in any shape to undertake its next mission, but then it was no longer necessary. It was clear by now that there would be no pursuit. On November 19, the units of the U.S. First and Ninth Armies were, on average, no more than two miles from their jump-off points, and no unit had gained more than ten miles. The Ninth Army did not reach the Roer until November 28 and did not finish clearing the west bank until December 9, after a twenty-three-day battle in which it pushed forward twelve miles at its maximum point. Before the Siegfried Line, the west bank of the Roer, and the Huertgen Forest were cleared, the Allies would suffer more than than 80,000 casualties.[19]

CHAPTER 8

The Battle of the Huertgen Forest (Part 2)

And what was happening in the Huertgen Forest during this time? Simply put, another American division was being chewed to pieces. This time it was Maj. Gen. Raymond O. Barton's 4th Infantry Division, one of the best units in the U.S. Army.[1]

It had been committed piecemeal. The division's 12th Infantry Regiment had been hurriedly thrust into the battle during the night of November 6–7, when it seemed that the 28th Infantry Division was about to collapse. By November 15, it had only gained a few hundred yards but had suffered more than 1,600 casualties, including dozens of cases of combat fatigue or trench foot, a disease with symptoms similar to frostbite. When men live days on end in cold and wet conditions and are unable to clean or dry their feet, the flesh often peels away and the toes turn purple. Sometimes amputation is necessary. Trench foot reached epidemic levels in the Huertgen Forest.

On November 16, the remaining regiments of the 4th Division and CCR of the U.S. 5th Armored Division were committed to the attack in the Huertgen. They were ordered to push three and a half miles through the rest of the forest and then continue another three and a half miles to the Roer River. General Barton, an excellent battlefield commander, was appalled by this idea and begged for reinforcements. General Hodges rejected his appeal.

The 4th Infantry Division jumped off as ordered at 12:45 P.M. on November 16, and ran into a meat grinder. The defenders were Hans Schmidt's 275th Infantry Division, the same unit that had defended the Huertgen since early October. It was well accustomed to forest fighting. German guns pelted the Americans of the "Ivy Division" with a fire that Charles MacDonald described as "incrediby accurate."

In three days, the 22nd Infantry Regiment lost all of its battalion commanders (killed or wounded), most of its battalion staff officers, almost half of its company commanders, and many other important officers and NCOs. Then, suddenly, on November 18, they gained a mile and took the Weisser Weh.

After two months of almost constant combat, General Schmidt finally ran out of men. He had been wounded earlier in the day but, in view of the critical situation, had remained in command of his division. On the night of November 18–19, he desperately appealed to General Straube, the commander of the LXXIV Corps, and General Brandenberger for help. Straube had no reserves, and Brandenberger stretched his lines almost to the breaking point in order to send Schmidt one division, Col. Georg Kossmala's weak 344th Infantry (the rebuilt 91st Air Landing Division),[2] which could not arrive until the night of November 19–20. He also promised to send him the 353rd, once an expected *Volksgrenadier* division arrived. Had the Americans continued their attack on November 19, they would have finished off the 275th Division and won the battle. General Barton did not know this, and in any event, his own troops were exhausted. He waited until his engineers had constructed a bridge over the Weisser Weh and did not resume his attacks until November 20. By that time, Colonel Kossmala had come up with his relatively fresh troops, and the 4th Division was again checked in heavy fighting.

By nightfall on November 20, several American rifle companies were down to 30 percent of their normal strength, and it was obvious that the 4th Infantry could not clear the forest alone. General Hodges responded in what was now typical fashion: he threw another division into the battle. This time it was the turn of Maj. Gen. Donald Stroh's 8th Infantry Division. By November 22, it was attacking toward the village of Huertgen through rain mixed with snow, slowly pushing back the 344th Infantry Division. Again, however, the Americans could score no major breakthroughs in three days of heavy fighting.

By November 25, the Americans had pushed to within a mile of the edge of Huertgen village, and Hans Schmidt's 275th Division had lost most of its combat value because its infantry regiments had been virtually annihilated. That night, General Schmidt at last pulled the remnants of his division out of the battle, but the 344th Infantry continued to resist.[3] The 121st Infantry Regiment of the U.S. 8th Infantry Division finally took the ruined village at nightfall on November 28, along with 200 German prisoners.

✠

On November 20, the remnants of the 47th Volksgrenadier Division had slowly retreated into the northern reaches of the Huertgen Forest, pursued by the U.S. 1st Infantry Division. An American historian would later call the 47th Volksgrenadier a "suicidally stubborn unit."[4] Since it had been smashed by the aerial bombardment of November 16, it had fought with surprising determination and still blocked the road leading to Dueren. It checked the 1st in and around the village of Heistern for two days and held the woods to the east for two days after that. By the night of November 24–25, however, almost all of its men were either killed or wounded. The adjacent 12th Volksgrenadier Division on its northern flank was in similar condition, so Zangen combined them into *Kampfgruppe Engel*. He also begged Model and Rundstedt for reinforcements, declaring that *Kampfgruppe Engel* would soon collapse and the road to Dueren would be open. Zangen wanted to use at least one division from Hitler's reserve, which was now getting ready for the Ardennes offensive.

Zangen's request was relayed to OKW, which promptly turned it down, but OKW did agree to let Zangen have Lt. Gen. Richard Schimpf's 3rd Parachute Division, which was now on its way from Holland. It arrived on November 26 and 27, just in time to prevent the Americans from breaking through the Huertgen.

Like all of the German airborne units in late 1944, the 3rd was a parachute division in name only. Most of its men were between the ages of sixteen and nineteen and had little or no combat experience. Over the next three days, they attacked with little tactical skill and suffered hundreds of unnecessary casualties, but they also inflicted losses on the Big Red One—losses the 1st Infantry Division could not afford. The 1st and its attached units had been in constant combat for two weeks and had gained not quite four miles from Schevenhuette to Langerwehe at a cost of 4,000 battle casualties, excluding more than 1,000 cases of trench foot and battle fatique.

On November 29, Lt. Col. Derrell M. Daniel, commanding the American spearhead, made one final effort and pushed into Merode, a village located on the edge of the forest on the slope where the Huertgen gives way to the Roer River plain. Daniel, supported by five tanks, led his two forward companies downhill into the village, which was defended by a battalion of paratroopers. They were met by a firestorm of artillery and antitank fire. Not one of the American tanks survived. Daniel was soon cut off in the village, but no one seemed to realize how serious his position was because the batteries in his radios, weakened by continuous use, failed. At long last, a weak message came through: "There's a Tiger tank coming down the street now, firing his gun into every house. He's three houses away now . . . still firing into every house. . . . Here he comes."[5] Then the radio fell silent. Three hours later, a sergeant and twelve men reached American lines. They were all that was left of the two companies cut off in the village.

Following the decable at Merode, General Collins ordered the 1st Infantry Division to go over to the defensive. The Roer River was still more than three miles away.

Meanwhile, General Brandenberger at last secured the relief of the 353rd Infantry Division, brought it from the southern wing of his 7th Army, and committed it to the Huertgen Forest. Here it faced the U.S. 4th and 8th Infantry Divisions, as well as the newly committed Combat Command A of the 5th Armored Division. Like most of the German frontline divisions that had not been rebuilt for the Ardennes offensive, General Mahlmann's 353rd Infantry was seriously understrength, but it met the continuing American attacks with considerable courage. On November 29, the U.S. 22nd Infantry Regiment of the 4th Division, reinforced with CCA of the 5th Armored, launched a series of attacks on the village of Grosshau. One German medical corpsman recalled the battle:

> The earth trembles; the concussion takes our breath. Two wounded are brought to my hole, one with a torn-up arm, the other with both hands shot off. I am considering whether to cut off the rest of the arm. I'll leave it on. How brave these two are. I hope to God all this is not in vain.

To our left, machine guns begin to chatter, and here comes the Ami. In broad waves you can see him come across the field. Tanks all around him are firing wildly. . . . Can't stick my head out of the hole.

Finally here are three German assault guns. With a few shots we can see several tanks burning. Long smoke columns are rising. The attack slows. It's stopped.[6]

As nightfall approached, the Americans attacked again. The German medical corpsman recorded:

Unbelievable with this handful of men we can hold out against such attacks! . . . Our people are dropping like tired flies. . . .

Suddenly, hordes of Amis are breaking out of the forest. Murderous fire meets them, but he [*sic*] does not even take cover any more. We shoot until the barrels sizzle . . . but we cannot hold them any longer.[7]

The U.S. 22nd Infantry Regiment outflanked Grosshau to the north and, at dusk, attacked it from the north and west simultaneously. It overwhelmed the defenders and cleared the village that night, capturing the medical corpsman in the process. The next day, the 22nd Infantry tried to break out of the forest but was too weak to do so. Its condition was similar to the other regiments in General Barton's division. Since November 16, the 4th Infantry had gained just over three miles at its point of maximum advance. In the process, it had lost 4,053 men killed, wounded, or missing, plus another 2,000 non-battle casualties—a cost of 2,000 men per mile. Two days later, it was taken out of the battle and replaced with the fresh 83rd Infantry Division.

The battle was also taking a tremendous toll on the Germans. In early December, one commander noted that some soldiers were found stiff in their foxholes, dead from sheer exhaustion. Nevertheless, they continued to cling to the forest. On December 3, after losing the village of Brandenberg, General Brandenberger at last got permission from Berlin to use the fresh 272nd Volksgrenadier Division (minus one grenadier regiment), provided it was returned in time to absorb replacements and participate in the Ardennes offensive, which was now set to begin on December 16. CCR of the 5th Armored Division captured the important village of Bergstein on December 5 but was down to a strength of 400 men, sixteen tanks, and six tank destroyers, and was unable to push on to Castle Hill, which dominated the village to the east. After nightfall on the sixth, the 272nd Volksgrenadier Division, temporarily commanded by Colonel Kossmala and supported by five tanks, counterattacked and pushed into Bergstein. The battle lasted until dawn, when the Germans were at last forced to retreat. On December 7, the 272nd Volksgrenadier attacked twice more and was beaten back both times. By the end of the day, CCR had only seven operational tanks left.

During the night, special American reinforcements arrived in the form of the famous 2nd Ranger Battalion. Early on the morning of December 8, it stormed Castle Hill, which it held for two days, despite fierce shelling from the 272nd Artillery Regiment. Tree bursts took an especially heavy toll on the elite battalion. By the time it was relieved by a regular infantry battalion on December 10, it was down to 25 percent of its original strength.

By December 10, the Americans had conquered all but the last fringes of the Huertgen Forest. They began their last offensive that day, spearheaded by the fresh 83rd Infantry Division, which was supported by the 5th Armored. Fighting was heavy, as usual, but on December 13, the U.S. 329th Infantry Regiment broke out of the forest and pushed into the western suburbs of Dueren.

Although about one-eighth of the forest remained in German hands, the Battle of the Huertgen Forest was over. Three days later, the Battle of the Bulge would begin.

Since September 14, a succession of American units had been locked in a fierce battle for the control of this dense European jungle, including the 1st, 4th, 8th, 9th, 28th and 83rd Infantry Divisions and the 5th Armored Division, as well as numerous smaller units, including the 2nd Ranger Battalion, the 4th Cavalry Group, and the 1171st Engineer Group. More than 140,000 Americans fought in the battle, 24,000 of whom were battle casualties; another 9,000 were felled by trench foot, battle fatigue, or illness.

The Germans committed six divisions to the battle: the 47th, 89th, 275th, 344th and 353rd Infantry, as well as the 116th Panzer, plus most of the 272nd Volksgrenadier and elements of the 12th Volksgrenadier. An estimated 80,000 German soldiers fought in the Huertgen, but because many of their records were destroyed at the end of the war, their losses are not known, although they were significantly less than American losses. What is known is that they accomplished their objective: they held up the American advance in the Eifel-Ardennes region until Hitler was ready to launch his massive offensive. They also continued to hold the Roer River dams and thus presented the Fuehrer with a secure northern flank, for no Allied drive north and east of the Roer was possible until the dams had been either captured or destroyed. If the Allies crossed the Roer north of the dams and the Germans blew them up, the ensuing floodwaters would cut off any Allied forces on the wrong side of the river for at least two weeks—during which they would undoubtedly be destroyed. Because they were obsessed with clearing the Huertgen Forest, the American generals, especially Courtney Hodges, overlooked the importance of these dams. Now it was too late. No attack to the north could possibly disrupt Hitler's offensive. Even though he had lost the battle, General Brandenberger had won a major victory for the Third Reich.

CHAPTER 9

Metz and Alsace-Lorraine

While Montgomery's attempt to outflank the Siegfried Line was failing at Arnhem and Hodges was trying to batter his way through it at Aachen and in the Huertgen Forest, three other major Allied forces were also trying to continue the advance in accordance with Eisenhower's broad front policy. These were the Canadian First Army, which was trying to clear the Scheldt; Patton's Third Army, which was trying to push into Germany via the Metz Gap; and Devers's 6th Army Group, consisting of the U.S. Seventh and French First Armies, which was trying to push through the Vosges Mountains in eastern France to the Rhine.

THE BATTLE OF METZ

In August 1944, following the breakout from Normandy, the bulk of Gen. Patton's U.S. Third Army pushed rapidly to the east, bypassing or overrunning static German units as it went. At the end of the month, the Third Army consisted of the XX, XII, and VIII Corps, although the last unit remained in Brittany besieging the German garrisons at Brest and St. Nazaire. In all, Patton had a strength of almost 315,000 men, divided into seven motorized infantry and two armored divisions and supported by the 600 fighter-bombers of Brig. Gen. Otto Weyland's XIX Tactical Air Command (TAC).

By the end of the month, however, Patton had virtually run out of gas. There was enough fuel in Normandy, but not enough trucks to carry it to frontline units. The suddenness of the German collapse had taken the Allies by surprise, and they simply did not have enough transportation units on the mainland to maintain the momentum of their advance. In addition, the French railroad network had been thoroughly smashed by the Allied air forces prior to and during the Normandy campaign—a major Allied victory, to be sure, but a double-edged one, because now that the Allies had the railroads in their hands and needed them to continue the advance, they were practically useless. This problem was compounded by a lack of locomotives, most of which had been destroyed by the fighter-bombers or the Germans. The army pipelines were not yet complete and could carry only a fraction of the fuel their armies required. The fact that Patton and Lt. Gen. John C. H. Lee, the commander of the Service of Supply, despised each other did not help the Third Army.[1]

To maintain its advance, the Third Army needed 400,000 gallons of fuel per day. On August 28, it received only 300,000 gallons, which fell to 32,000 gallons two days later. Indeed, without captured German supplies, Patton would not have reached the Meuse. He was already using food and medical supplies from captured German warehouses, which allowed him to commit more of his vital trucking to the task of transporting petroleum, oil, and lubricants. But it still was not enough. The shortage was so bad that it was affecting tactical operations. On the last day of August, a detachment of seventeen tanks from the U.S. 7th Armored Division set out to seize the critical Meuse River bridge at Verdun. Fourteen of the tanks ran out of gasoline before they reached the town.

On September 2, Maj. Gen. Walton H. Walker, the commander of the XX Corps, sent two task forces from the 7th Armored Division toward Sedan, advancing on either side of the Meuse. Both of them ran out of gas before they could reach the city and had to wait two days until they could be refueled. "My men can eat their belts, but my tanks have gotta have gas!" Patton cried.[2] If properly supplied, he declared, he could break through to Rhine. His protests were backed up by General Bradley, who did not like the idea of giving Montgomery supply priority, and together, he and Patton pressured Eisenhower into giving him permission to push on to the Moselle as soon as he received enough fuel to make the move. Patton was delighted. He "forgot" to tell the Supreme Commander that he had just captured another 110,000 gallons—enough to get the XII Corps as far as the river.

"Any army wishing to move toward the Rhine south of the Ardennes had to pass through the Metz gap between the Ardennes hills and the Vosges, a basic fact of military geography," Anthony Kemp wrote.[3] The natural route of Patton's advance would carry him east across the Moselle, through Metz, to Saarbruecken, and on to the Rhine River at Mannheim. The city of Metz was constructed on islands in the Moselle River and is surrounded by hills, and both the French and Germans built extensive fortifications over the years. It had never been taken by direct assault, and as late as 1870, Field Marshal Count Helmuth von Moltke, the chief of the Prussian General Staff for thirty years and the man who captured Paris in 1871, said that Metz was worth 120,000 men.

Naturally, Gen. of Panzer Troops Otto von Knobelsdorf, the commander of the 1st Army, knew all about the value and importance of Metz, but he very much doubted that he could hold it. When he inherited the 1st from General von der Chevallerie, it was, like most of the rest of OB West, a beaten force, on the run, just trying to get out of France.

At the end of August, the entire 1st Army could muster only nine infantry battalions, two batteries of artillery, ten tanks, and a few assault and flak guns.[4] He was soon reinforced with the 3rd and 15th Panzer Grenadier Divisions from Italy, with several battalions of police and two new *Volksgrenadier* divisions. When he fell back beyond the Meuse, Knobelsdorf was also given control of the remnants of the exhausted and depleted 17th SS Panzer Grenadier Division "Goetz von Berlichingen," now under SS Col. Otto Binge, which was in the process of rebuilding in his area. Knobelsdorf immediately posted it west of the city on the Verdun-Metz road to block Patton's approach to the Moselle. On September 2, when much of the U.S. Third Army was immobilized because of a lack of fuel, patrols from Patton's cavalry reconnaissance squadrons pushed to the Moselle and reported that the bridges were undefended. One detachment from the 3rd Cavalry Group actually entered Thoinville and cut the demolition wires to the vital bridge there before being driven off by a German counterattack. The situation would be vastly different when the main American force resumed its advance on September 5. (The map on the next page shows the Lorraine sector, the principal battlegrounds in Patton's drives for Metz.)

As early as August 24, Adolf Hitler invested Gauleiter Joseph Buerckel with the power to conscript the civilian population to con-

THE LORRAINE SECTOR

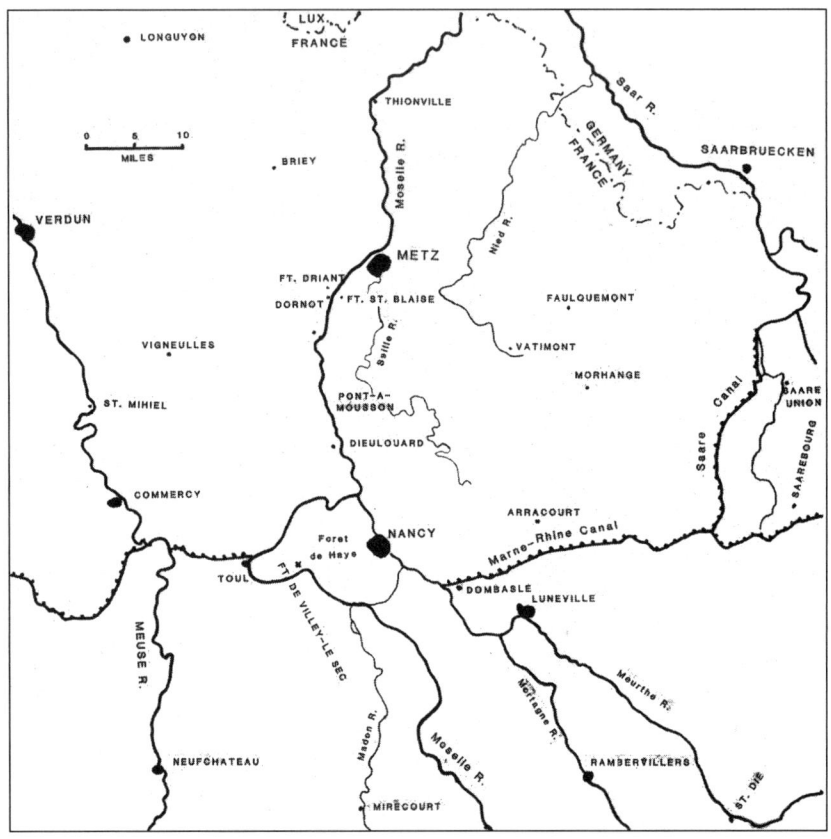

struct defensive works, and in late July, Heinrich Himmler, in his capacity as commander in chief of the Replacement Army, appointed SS Col. Ernst Kemper, the commander of the SS Signal School in Metz, as commandant of the city.[5] Shortly thereafter, the city was declared a fortress, and Kemper was given the task of preparing it for defense.

On July 15, Lt. Gen. Walther Krause succeeded Lt. Gen. Hans von Sommerfeld as commander of the 462nd Replacement Division in Metz.[6] At first, this *Wehrkreis XII* unit controlled nothing but a few military schools and replacement-training units in Lorraine, and its men were convalescents recovering from wounds or were over-age. None of its units were considered fit for combat.

During the third week in August, as Army Group B was being crushed in the Falaise pocket, the 19th Army streamed back from the Riviera, and Patton's tanks roared across France, it became clear that it was time to prepare Metz for defense, and Kemper and Buerckel proved incapable of cooperating with General Krause on almost any issue. It was the typical army-SS feud that seemed almost normal in Nazi Germany and did so much damage to the Third Reich. Buerckel seemed more interested in withdrawing himself, his property, and his staff to Saarbruecken than anything else and decreed that Kemper would take charge of a skeleton civilian staff when he departed. Then, as the field army fell back toward the Franco-German border, both Metz and Thionville came within the zone of Gen. of Artillery Johann Sinnhuber's LXXXII Corps.[7] On September 2, Sinnhuber, a tough East Prussian, appointed Krause commandant of the city. This move obviously did not sit well with the Nazi Party or Führer Headquarters, most notably Martin Bormann. Before the week was out, Sinnhuber was transferred to Fuehrer Reserve and was not employed again until April 1, 1945, when he was named battle commander of the Hamburg-Bremen area. In any event, on September 7, SS Lt. Gen. Hermann Priess's XIII SS Corps took over responsibility for the Metz-Thionville sector but left Krause in charge of Metz's defenses.[8] (Like most of the other SS headquarters formed from the fall of 1944 until the end of the war, the XIII SS Corps—which was formed from the remnants of the army's XXXV Corps—had more army than SS officers. Its chief of staff, for example, was Col. Kurt von Einem, an army officer.)

General Krause went to work and organized a three-regiment, 14,000-man division capable of defending the city. Its major components were the Officer Cadet Regiment, the *Wehrkreis XII* NCO School, the 1010th Security Regiment, and a few replacement-training battalions that were reorganized as infantry units.

The Officer Cadet Regiment (*Fahnenjunkern* Regiment), which was also known as *Kampfgruppe von Siegroth*, was probably the best unit of its size in the world in 1944. It was also very unusual in that it initially had almost no enlisted men. Most of its 1,800 troops were second lieutenants who had earned battlefield commissions on the Eastern Front. In this unit, a man with both grades of the Iron Cross was considered ordinary; the Wounded Badge in Silver and the Close Combat Clasp in Gold were common; the Knight's Cross was not unusual; and German Crosses in Gold flashed all over the place. Its commander, Col. Joachim von Siegroth, was an extremely capable officer,[9] as were all of his battalion, company, and platoon leaders. The regiment was fleshed out by 1,500 experienced replacements, mostly from disbanded infantry units.

The *Wehrkreis XII* NCO School, which was formed into a 1,500-man regiment, consisted of sergeants and corporals attending various military courses in the Lorraine-Weisbaden military district. It was also considered an excellent unit, and its morale was very high. It was commanded by Colonel Wagner. The men of the SS Signal School were also organized into a combat unit, called Battalion Berg after its commander. It was also considered a high-quality formation. Only the 1010th Security, a two-battalion regiment of 500 to 600 over-age men, was rated as poor, and the replacement-training infantry battalions were considered to be of mediocre quality.

Although his infantry was, in general, excellent, Krause's artillery was weak. It consisted of two artillery replacement-training battalions armed with captured 75-millimeter guns of Soviet manufacture. It had no transportation of its own, and the only transport Krause could provide was horses taken from a nearby veterinary hospital. Later, it was reinforced with a single four-gun battery of German 105-millimeter guns.

✠

By September 4, Patton had enough fuel—thanks to engineers who repaired the airfield near Rheins, allowing heavy transport plans to fly supplies to the Third Army—to resume reconnaissance forays. The Battle of Metz began that same day, when the 3rd Cavalry Group, a regiment-size unit, sent strong recon patrols in the direction of the Moselle, both north and south of the city, and ran into the German outpost line, which was manned by the *Fahnenjunker* students. The Americans, who were still engaged in pursuit thinking, expected little or no resistance and had no idea that the Officer Training Regiment even existed. As a result, they fell into a number of well-conducted ambushes. The cavalry group commander was captured in one of these. In another ambush on the Gravelotte road, the officer trainees allowed a strong cavalry detachment to pass; then they blew up the bridge behind it, completely cutting off the cavalrymen, all of whom were subsequently killed or captured. The 3rd Cavalry gained very little information that day, and the American generals were still unaware of the true state of the Metz defenses.

On September 5, Bradley met with Patton and his corps commanders at Chalons-sur-Marne and again assigned the Third Army the tasks of breaching the West Wall, crossing the Rhine, and pushing on to Frankfurt. As soon as the army group commander left, Patton gave General Walker his mission: cross the Moselle, push into Germany, and establish a bridgehead over the Rhine, which was 100 miles east of the Moselle.

Walker's XX Corps consisted of the 5th Infantry Division under Maj. Gen. LeRoy Irwin, the 90th Infantry Division under Brig. Gen. Raymond McClain, and the 7th Armored Division under Maj. Gen. Lindsay McD. Silvester, plus the 3rd Cavalry Group. Walker ordered the 3rd Cavalry to "reconnoiter to the Rhine without delay" and the 7th Armored to "advance east in multiple columns [and] seize crossings over the Rhine," bypassing enemy cities and strongpoints along the way. The 5th was given the task of capturing Metz while the 90th Infantry had the mission of seizing Thionville.[10] Significant resistance was not expected.

As they advanced on September 6, the men of the XX Corps had no detailed maps and were forced to rely on 1:100,000-scale Michelin road maps—the kind used by ordinary civilian motorists. Although they were better educated in history than most present-day Americans, almost none of them had any idea that Metz was a fortified city or that the area west of it was now well defended. Nor were aerial photographs of any help because most of the fortifications were covered by natural vegetation and the Germans were now past masters of the art of camouflaging their positions from aerial observation. The spearheads found the roads blocked and the obstacles defended by determined veterans, equipped with antitank guns and *panzerfausts*. When the Americans got off the roads, they found that the shoulders had been mined and were covered by machine-gun and mortar fire. It was late on September 7 before they pushed the German outposts back across the Moselle, but when they arrived at the river, they found that all the bridges had been blown. They sent back for bridging and assault boats. The stage was set for the Battle of the Dornot Bridgehead.

Dornot was a small, one-street village on the west bank of the Moselle. Maj. Gen. Stafford LeRoy Irwin, the commander of the 5th Infantry Division, planned to cross river here, using his own 11th Infantry Regiment and CCB of the 7th Armored Division. He was unaware that in the hills just beyond the river lay Forts Sommy and St. Blaise, which gave the Germans an excellent view of the entire battlefield. On the other side of the river lay Battalion Voss, a replacement-training unit made up of older-age troops with stomach problems and SS Battalion Berg. Behind them was the 37th SS Panzer Grenadier Regiment of the 17th SS Panzer Grenadier Division. (The Officer Training Regiment was still west of the Moselle, preventing the U.S. 23rd Armored Infantry Battalion from reaching the river north of Dornot.)

The American attack began at 11:15 A.M. and was met by a hail of machine-gun fire. Nevertheless, the 11th Infantry managed to push four companies and two heavy weapons platoons across the river by nightfall. Two companies of the crossing force set out to capture Fort St. Blaise but were surprised to find their path blocked by five rows of barbed wire, a twelve-foot-high iron palisade, and a dry ditch, forty-five feet wide and fifteen feet deep, that surrounded the entire fort. It was a foretaste of things to come. The two companies tried to fall back into the bridgehead but found that the SS had infiltrated behind them, and they were caught on an open hillside by a German crossfire. They suffered heavy casualties and broke up; stragglers were still making their way back to American lines the following morning, and the wounded had to be left behind. That night, the bridgehead was repeatedly attacked by the 37th SS Panzer Grenadier Regiment, which essentially used human-wave tactics. The American infantry showed fire discipline and did not open up until the SS were right on top of their foxholes; then they mowed them down in rows.

Some of the men of the 17th SS Division still had the fanatical determination of their predecessors, but their green replacements lacked the sense of eliteness and tactical skill of the old 17th SS, which had been virtually annihilated in Normandy. There were now too many *Volksdeutsche* and former *Luftwaffe* troops in its ranks. Even so, they took a serious toll on the Americans, who could not be reinforced or resupplied. Seeing his situation as hopeless in the long run, the commander of the 2nd Battalion, 11th Infantry, asked permission to evacuate the bridgehead, but his request was rejected. As a result, the four companies had to endure two more days in the narrow bridgehead, during which they were smashed. Because the Germans held the high ground and could observe the entire battlefield, it proved impossible to build a bridge across the river at that point. Finally, on September 10, General Irwin gave up and allowed them to withdraw. The Dornot bridgehead was evacuated during the night of September 10–11. The assault companies had lost 945 men killed, wounded, or missing, and the 2nd Battalion temporarily ceased to exist.

On September 6, on the northern flank of the U.S. Third Army, the 90th Infantry Division advanced on the Moselle River town of Thionville against Col. Baron Kurt von Muehlen's weak 559th Volksgrenadier Division, which had only two grenadier regiments.[11] Muehlen's rearguard was able to temporarily check the Americans in the small mining town of Briey on the sixth, but it was surrounded the following day and forced to surrender with a loss of almost 500 men.

Despite this victory, the 90th Infantry's northern flank was exposed because it had no real contact with Hodges's First Army. Just to the north, in Luxembourg—unknown to the Americans—lay Col. Karl Britzelmayr's 19th Volksgrenadier Division and the 106th Panzer Brigade "Feldherrnhalle," under the command of Col. Dr. Franz Bäke.[12] This brigade had been formed in late August from the remnants of units smashed on the Eastern Front, mostly from the Panzer Grenadier Division "Feldhernnhalle" and the 11th Panzer Regiment of the 6th Panzer Division. It included a panzer battalion with thirty-nine Panthers and assault guns, a panzer grenadier battalion, an engineer company, and service troops. (This was the standard table of organization and equipment for the new panzer brigades, except the panzer battalion was supposed to have thirty-three Panthers and eleven assault guns. Some of the panzer brigades, however, had two panzer battalions—one Panther battalion with forty-eight PzKw Vs and one tank battalion with forty-eight PzKw IVs—and two panzer grenadier battalions.)

General Knobelsdorf managed to get Berlin's permission to use the 59th Grenadier Regiment—part of the 19th Volksgrenadier—for an attack against the Americans' left flank. Infantry-armor coordination was poor, however, and the panzer brigade went forward alone. During the night of September 7–8, it blundered right between the U.S. 357th and 358th Infantry Regiments and into the town of Mairy—exactly the place were General McClain had set up his command post a few hours before. A wild clash ensued, during which the American general narrowly averted capture and the divisional artillery staff was surrounded. When dawn came, however, the American infantry closed in on the 106th Panzer Brigade, which was soon fighting for its life. It finally made good its escape at 8 P.M. on September 8, having lost 30 tanks, 60 half-tracks, and 100 other vehicles—more than three-quarters of its strength.

The U.S. 90th Infantry spent September 9 awaiting more counterattacks. When none came, it resumed its advance on Thionville and pushed to into the town on the twelfth. The division was preparing to launch an assault crossing over the Moselle at midnight on September 13 when it received new orders from the XX Corps. Cancel the attack and march south, General Walker ordered; the division was needed in the Metz sector.

During the night of September 10–11, while the 90th Division was slowly pushing back the rearguards of the 559th Volksgrenadier, the U.S. 10th Infantry Regiment of the 5th Division launched a crossing of the Moselle near Arnaville, three miles south of Dornot. Supported by thirteen battalions of artillery, the regiment landed in the zone of the 282nd Infantry Battalion, a replacement-training unit that fought with surprising determination. Hill 310, which overlooked the river, had to be taken in heavy fighting which featured hand-in-hand combat with fixed bayonets. By the morning of the eleventh, the 5th Division had three infantry battalions across the river and bridging operations were well underway.

The inevitable German counterattacks, delivered by combat groups from the 17th SS and 3rd Panzer Grenadier Divisions, began at dawn. They were sharp and driven home with great determination but were nevertheless beaten back, thanks largely to the pinpoint close air support of the fighter-bombers. Casualties were heavy on both sides. The 1st and 2nd Battalions of the U.S. 10th Infantry lost half their men but held their perimeter. Shortly after noon the next day, September 12, the U.S. 1103rd Combat Engineer Group completed a treadway bridge across the Moselle, and the tanks of Combat Command B of the the 7th Armored Division began to cross into the bridgehead. Unfortunately for the Americans, a hard, cold rain began to fall that night, and most of the Shermans bogged down.

On September 13, in spite of the rain, General Walker decided to commit the entire 7th Armored Division to the Arnaville bridgehead. He ordered the 90th Infantry Division at Thionville to hand its sector over to the 43rd Cavalry Reconnaissance Squadron and march to the south at once to join the battle west of Metz, while the 5th Infantry and 7th Armored Divisions expanded the bridgehead south of the city. This proved to be easier said than done. It was 3 P.M. on September 16 before the 5th Division could take the vital Hill 396, which at last gave the Americans a firm base from which to drive on Metz. They repulsed a strong German counterattack the following morning in hand-to-hand fighting, but only barely. It had taken the XX Corps ten days to establish one small bridgehead across the Moselle. In the process, the 5th Infantry Division had lost half of its combat strength.

The XX Corps completed its realignment on September 14 and prepared to begin the next phase of the offensive the next day. In accordance with Patton's orders, the 7th Armored Division was to drive east, then south, to come in behind Metz and attack the city from the rear, while the 5th Infantry struck it from the south and the 90th Infantry attacked from the west. It was not Patton's best plan. For one thing, it ignored the fact that the XX Corps was already running seriously short of infantry, especially in the 5th Division. Second, the U.S. XII Corps to the south was tied down in the Nancy area, which did not fall until September 15 and was not completely cleared until September 18, and was in no position to cover the right flank of the 7th Armored; it would therefore have to advance with both flanks exposed. Third, because of the supply situation, he was already running short of tank shells and artillery ammunition. Finally, the 7th Armored would have to cross the Seille and Nied. They were not large rivers, to be sure, but they represented major challenges for an isolated tank division advancing without sufficient infantry support.

On the other side of the line, Knobelsdorf did not believe that Metz could be held against a major attack; he therefore asked Col. Gen. Johannes Blaskowitz for permission to abandon the city. The commander in chief of Army Group G, however, thought the fortress could and should be held, and Adolf Hitler, as usual, agreed with his most optimistic commander. On September 15, he ordered Metz to be held even if the garrison had to let itself be surrounded. The next day, he issued a more sensible order: the 1st Army was to reinforce the flanks of the Metz salient to prevent the garrison from being encircled, which set the stage for the bloodiest fighting of the Lorraine campaign.

On September 18, Knobelsdorf relieved Krause of his command on the grounds that he was not a "strong personality."[13] This may have been true, but in analyzing Kraus's conduct of the Battle of Metz, one finds much to praise and little to criticize. Indeed, he did not remain in Fuehrer Reserve for long. Less than a month later he was named Rear Area Commander of the 6th Army on the Eastern Front, a corps-level position and a definite promotion.[14] He was succeeded in Metz by Lt. Gen. Vollrath Luebbe, a curious choice. His main virtue seems to have been that he was available after the recent disbandment of his 81st Infantry Division. Luebbe, the former commander of the 2nd Panzer Division, was one of the better training officers in the *Wehrmacht*, but his performance as a field commander left much to be desired.[15]

The American advance did not get off to a good start. As the U.S. infantry struggled forward through the rain and mud, SS General Priess, the commander of the XIII SS Corps, soon realized that Walker had stripped his northern flank to add weight to his attacks to the south. He immediately followed suit, reinforced the defenders, and, on September 17, launched a series of counterattacks, mainly with the 17th SS Panzer Grenadier Division, inflicting heavy casualties on the infantry of the 7th Armored Division's CCB. The Americans nevertheless pushed ahead and finally took the village of Marieulles on the third attempt, along with 135 prisoners and a few 88-millimeter flak guns. The American 155-millimeter battalions were already limiting their artillery bombardments to just one minute because of a shortage of shells.

On September 18, the 37th and 38th SS Panzer Grenadier Regiments fell back through the village of Bouxieres, liberally scattering mines behind them, and took up defensive positions west of the Seille in a series of bunkers and obsolete forts dubbed Fortified Group Aisne. (The bunkers had been built by the men of the Imperial Army during the Battle of Verdun in 1916.)

The U.S. 10th Infantry Regiment attacked the left flank of these works on the eighteenth. It advanced without much spirit, which is not surprising, since it had lost 700 men since September 10 and had been in continuous combat for eleven days—mostly in a cold, driving rain. CCR attacked the village of Sillegny in the center of the German line, only to be met by a fury of artillery fire. The Shermans pushed almost to the edge of the village but were forced to withdraw when they ran out of ammunition. That night, they attacked again but were halted on the edge of the village. The following day, the 38th Armored Infantry Battalion joined the battle, and Sillegny became the site of a fierce close-quarter battle. That morning, Lt. Col. W. W. Rosebro, the commander of the 38th, was mortally wounded, and his second in command was killed. Maj. T. H. Wells, the operations officer, took charge of the battalion but was killed before 11 A.M. He was replaced by Lt. Col. Theo T. King, an officer sent from headquarters, but he was wounded that afternoon. By the time the fourth battalion commander received permission to withdraw, the 38th Armored Infantry had lost almost all of its officers and three-fourths of its men. CCR also lost eight commanding officers between September 1 and 22.

Attacking the German perimeter from the west, the U.S. 90th Infantry Division fared no better. Here the fortifications were defended by the 1010th Security Regiment and Officer Training Regiment, whose combat prowess was becoming legendary. The Americans struck with spirit and in places the fighting was hand-to-hand, but in the end, they gained nothing.

General Patton realized very early that the attack on Metz was likely to stall out, so he quickly came up with an alternative plan. He ordered Maj. Gen. Manton Eddy, the commander of the U.S. XII Corps to the south, to break through the West Wall and seize the bridge over the Rhine River at Worms. The Third Army would thus have achieved its breakthrough without taking Metz. It was a bold plan, but Eddy never got the chance to try it out. On September 18, just as he was about to jump off, he was subjected to a surprise attack in the Luneville sector from Gen. of Panzer Troops Baron Hasso von Manteuffel's 5th Panzer Army.

The Luneville offensive was the brainchild of Adolf Hitler. When he conceived it in the second week of September, the Fuehrer intended for Manteuffel to launch a surprise attack with three panzer grenadier divisions and four panzer brigades to halt Patton on the Meuse. Patton pushed his spearheads far beyond this point, however, and had tied down the three panzer grenadier divisions on the Moselle before Manteuffel was ready to strike. Prior to the big offensive, the 106th Panzer Brigade was smashed by the 90th Infantry Division west of Thionville as described above. On September 12, the 112nd Panzer Brigade launched a major preparatory attack against the French 2nd Armored Division at Dompaire, south of Luneville, in the zone of the Allied 6th Army Group. During the first thirty-six hours of this battle, the panzer brigade lost sixty of its ninety-eight tanks. By September 22, it was down to a strength of one Panther and six PzKw IVs and had practically ceased to exist.

Manteuffel nevertheless launched his major offensive on September 18. His forces included the 11th Panzer, 21st Panzer, 15th Panzer Grenadier, and 559th Volksgrenadier Divisions and the 111th, 112th and 113th Panzer Brigades, as well as the Headquarters of Luettwitz's XXXXVII Panzer and Krueger's LVIII Panzer Corps. These forces looked impressive on paper, but Manteuffel actually had little striking power. For example, the 21st Panzer, as General Mellenthin declared, "had virtually no tanks, and was now only a second-rate infantry formation."[16] It was also poorly led by Edgar Feuchtinger, a pleasure-loving Nazi who had recently been promoted to lieutenant general, despite the fact that he was under investigation for having been away from his post on D-Day.[17] The 11th Panzer was not in much better condition; having been "shot to pieces" while covering the 19th Army's withdrawal from southern France, it had only sixteen tanks left[18] and was still en route to the 5th Panzer Army. It was well led by Lt. Gen. Wend von Wietersheim.[19] Eberhard Rodt's 15th Panzer Grenadier Division had suffered heavy casualties in Sicily and Italy, while the 112th Panzer Brigade, which was built around a depleted Panther battalion from the Panzer Lehr Division, was of little combat value.

Manteuffel spearheaded his offensive with the 111th and 113th Panzer Brigades, commanded by Col. Heinrich-Walter Bronsart von Schellendorf and Col. Baron Erich von Seckendorff, respectively.[20] Like the 106th and 112th, these brigades had been created within the last six weeks, and their tanks were brand new—at a time when experienced panzer divisions with a long history of successful armored

THE LORRAINE CAMPAIGN: Fall 1944

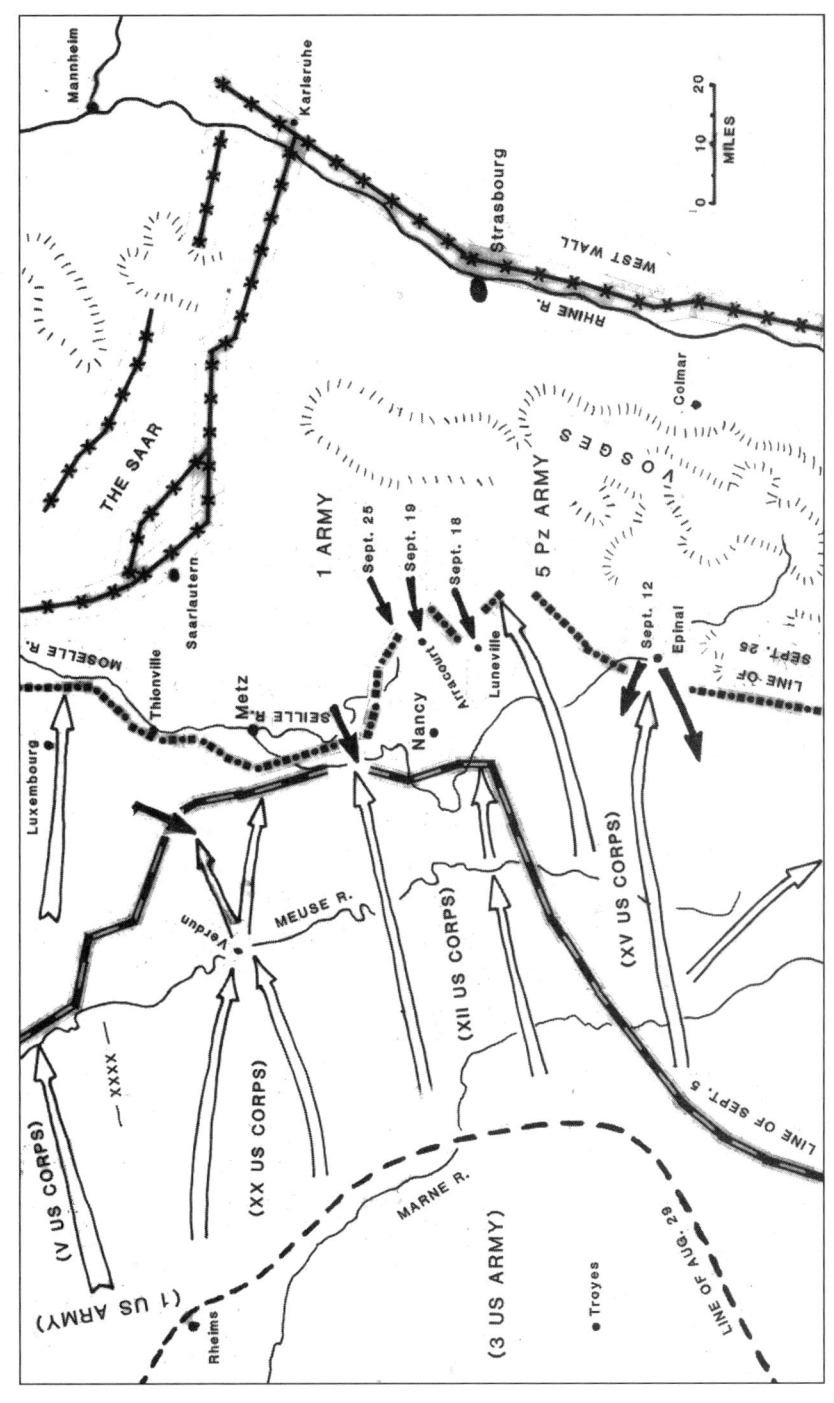

operations could not muster twenty tanks and could not obtain a single replacement. But as in the creation of his new *Volksgrenadier* divisions, Hitler was obsessed with creating new units, which allowed him to delude himself with the illusion of ever-increasing strength—even though many of his old "divisions" now had the combat strength of reduced regiments. The panzer brigades were just another example of Hitler's tendency to deceive himself in the fifth year of the war. (This tendency would increase to the point that during the Battle of Berlin in 1945, he would order into battle armies that did not exist.) Unfortunately for the German Army, the new panzer brigades lacked the skill and teamwork that the men of the older panzer divisions had acquired through many months of working and fighting together. The result was a major German defeat. The offensive took General Eddy by surprise, and the 111th Panzer Brigade and 15th Panzer Grenadier Division took Luneville on the eighteenth, but Eddy and his subordinates reacted so quickly and strongly that they were able to throw the Germans out of the town the same day.

The next day, September 19, Manteuffel tried to reach Nancy by bypassing Luneville to the north, but his 113rd Panzer Brigade ran straight into Maj. Gen. John S. Wood 4th Armored Division at Arracourt north of the Marne-Rhine Canal. In four days of fighting, the 111th Panzer Brigade was all but wiped out, emerging from the battle with only seven tanks and eighty men. The 113th Panzer suffered similar losses, but its exact casualty figures are not known. Combat Command A of the U.S. 4th Armored Division, which bore the brunt of the fighting, lost only twenty-five men killed and eighty-eight wounded, with fourteen Shermans and seven light tanks destroyed. The Germans lost more than 150 panzers, although not all of them were destroyed in battle. Hitler threw the panzer brigades into action so quickly that many of the tanks, fresh from the factories, had not been "run in," and quite a few experienced mechanical failure. The commanders of both the leading panzer brigades had been killed—Bronsart on September 22, Seckendorff the next day—and, during the slaughter, Luettwitz, the veteran commander of the XXXXVII Panzer Corps, became so hysterical that Manfeuffel had to send him to a quiet sector to regain his composure.

Command of the 113th Panzer Brigade devolved on Colonel Burmeister,[21] while Col. Theodor Bohlmann-Combrinck, the commander of the 112th Panzer Brigade, apparently assumed command of the remnants of the 111th Panzer as well. All three brigades were sent to the rear. The 111th was absorbed by the 11th Panzer Division on October 1; the 112th was incorporated into the 21st Panzer Division on or about October 15; and the remnants of the 113th Panzer Brigade were sent to the Eastern Front, where they were absorbed by the Grossdeutschland Panzer Corps.

Thus the panzer brigade experiment ended in failure. Only one other tank brigade was formed—under SS Lt. Col. Otto Skorzeny on November 1. It absorbed Lt. Col. F. H. Musculus's 108th Panzer Brigade. The 150th Panzer was used with limited effectiveness in the Battle of the Bulge and was disbanded in January 1945.

Although German casualties at Luneville were heavy and the American losses were light, the 5th Panzer Army's counterattack did disrupt Patton's timetable. Because of the disastrous supply situation and the fact that the XX Corps was rapidly running out of steam, the delay could not be made good. Patton would probably have tried again had Eisenhower not specifically ordered him to halt all aggressive action. The Third Army was also forced to relinquish the 7th Armored Division and the entire XV Corps, which had only recently been assigned to it and had now come up on Patton's right flank. The 7th Armored was sent north to join the U.S. First Army; the XV Corps was transferred to Dever's 6th Army Group. Heartsick, Patton was forced to go over to the defensive all along the front. In failing to capture Metz, he had suffered his first military defeat.

As a result of the failure of the Luneville attacks, Hitler sacked the politically unreliable and independent thinking Colonel General Blaskowitz, the commander in chief of Army Group G, and his chief of staff, Maj. Gen. Heinz von Gyldenfeldt, who were made scapegoats for the defeat.[22] They were replaced by Gen. of Panzer Troops Hermann Balck and Col. Friedrich-Wilhelm von Mellenthin. Balck, a veteran of dozens of tank battles on the Eastern Front, was described by historian Chester Wilmot as "a notorious optimist with a reputation for ruthless aggression."[23] His appointment was not welcomed by Rundstedt because he had no experience in fighting against the British and Americans. This deficiency was largely offset by Mellenthin, who had spent almost two years serving with Rommel in the desert and who knew as much about fighting the western Allies as anybody.[24]

Balck and his chief of staff were received by the Fuehrer on September 18. Hitler predicted that the Allied offensive would come to a halt along a line from the Scheldt to Metz and that he would use this opportunity to launch a major counteroffensive in November. (This attack—the Ardennes offensive—was eventually delayed until December.) Hitler ordered Balck to continue the 5th Panzer Army's attacks against the U.S. Third Army as quickly as possible. Rundstedt protested this plan on the grounds that the opportunity for a successful tank offensive in Lorraine had passed and that the armor should be moved north into the Aachen sector, which was vulnerable because Model had been forced to commit the bulk of Army Group B's panzer reserves against the British in Holland. Hitler brushed these objections aside.

Manteuffel's second offensive began on September 25. It was directed by Krueger's LVIII Panzer Corps, which now controlled the 11th Panzer, 21st Panzer, and 15th Panzer Grenadier Divisions. These three veteran units could muster only fifty tanks between them. They did not meet with the same kind of disaster that befell the panzer brigades, but they were nevertheless halted after scoring only minor gains in heavy fighting. Then, on September 29, Hitler suddenly became alarmed over the threat to his northern flank and ordered that every tank unit that could be spared be sent north to check the British drive on the Ruhr. The British offensive was checked at Arnhem before even one of these units arrived.

Of the 350 PzKw IVs and Vs Hitler sent to Lorraine in September, more than half had been totally destroyed, and many of the remainder were in the repair shops. It is doubtful that there were 500 operational panzers on the entire Western Front at the end of September, and now Army Group G was particularly deficient in armor. It was also badly in need of a period of rest and reorganization. That is exactly what it got; except for a relatively small-scale attack in the Metz sector, the Americans stopped all along the front.

After the war, Mellenthin wrote: "We now know that the Third Army received categorical orders to stand on the defensive. The rights and wrongs of this strategy do not concern me, but it certainly simplified the problems of our Army Group G. We were given a few weeks' grace to rebuild our battered forces and get ready to meet the next onslaught."[25]

THE BATTLE OF FORT DRIANT

Even though he was forbidden to take aggressive action, Patton did try to take Fort Driant, the key to the whole Metz fortified area west of the Moselle. Built in 1899, it lies southwest of the city and represented major obstacles to any force advancing on Metz from the south. A huge fort, it is about six-tenths of a mile long and 600 to 900 yards wide. Much of it lies below ground. Its artillery included six 100-millimeter guns and six 150-millimeter howitzers. The fort had already played a role in the defeat of the Dornot crossings and had inflicted casualties on the Americans crossing at Arnaville. The American commanders from Patton down felt that it was necessary to eliminate Driant before the fortified salient of Metz could be destroyed. It was defended by the 3rd Battalion of the Officer Training Regiment, which was led by Capt. Rolf Weiler.

A coordinated air and ground attack began on September 21 and was promptly turned back. A regiment of the 90th Division, supported by dozens of batteries, including heavy 8-inch guns and 240-millimeter howitzers, attacked it again on September 27 but was beaten off with heavy casualties. Between September 26 and 30, the fighter-bombers of the XIX Tactical Air Force attacked it with napalm and 1,000-pound bombs, but again without success.

On October 3, supported by all of the XX Corps' artillery, a task force of the 90th Infantry Division attacked again. This time, the engineers succeeded in breaching the southwestern corner of the fort, and two infantry companies rushed in. They tried to overrun the two barracks but were turned back after suffering 50 percent casualties. General Irwin continued to pour troops into the stalemated battle, including a fresh infantry battalion and the 7th Combat Engineer Battalion, but they were soon pinned down in their foxholes. The officer trainees, meanwhile, fought fanatically and beat back every attack. They also took maximum advantage of their tunnels and underground corridors, which enabled them to emerge behind the Americans and ambush them or attack them in the flanks while artillery from nearby forts plastered the Americans. The battle continued until the night of October 12–13 when the American task force finally withdrew. It had suffered 50 percent casualties.

THE FALL OF METZ

After the Battle of Fort Driant, a lull descended on the Metz front. During the lull, the XX Corps was reinforced with the 95th Infantry Division under Maj. Gen. Harry Twaddle, a unit fresh from the United States; the 83rd Infantry Division covering Patton's left flank; and other, smaller forces. On the German side, the Officer Candidate and NCO School Regiments were disbanded because the students were desperately needed to form cadres for the new *Volksgrenadier* divisions. Their former instructors remained at Metz, where they were used to form two new *Volksgrenadier* regiments, although the quality of their men declined markedly. In special recognition of their heroism, the men of the Officer Training Regiment were granted the unusual privilege of wearing a special armband, inscribed "Metz 1944." Siegroth was hailed as a hero of the Third Reich. He was promoted to major general on November 9 and decorated with the Oak Leaves to the Knight's Cross by Hitler himself.

The 462nd Replacement Division was redesignated 462nd Volksgrenadier Division and organized into a three-regiment combat division. Its new organization is shown in Table 5. In addition, it had a strange collection of miscellaneous units, some of which were entering the fortress as late as November 17. They included several static machine-gun and infantry battalions, a Reich Labor Service battalion, a company of former sailors, and a *Volkssturm* battalion. Of these, General Kittel later remarked, "Fighting qualities were equivalent to zero and reliability doubtful, as there were FFI [French Resistance] men in the ranks."[26]

While the 462nd Volksgrenadier completed its reorganzation, General Balck and Colonel Mellenthin prepared for the next offensive, which they expected to come through the historic Lorraine gateway between Metz and the Vosges Mountains. "We estimated that one of the American thrusts would come through Thionville, and we anticipated another big push in the Chateau Salins area, aimed directly at Saarbruecken; the effect of these two drives would be to 'bite out' the fortress of Metz."[27] General Balck allocated 100 of the 140 tanks left in the army group to the 1st Army, which was responsible for the Lorraine gateway. The 19th Army, which defended the Vosges sector, was virtually devoid of armor. Balck had deployed these forces correctly but was unable to make up for his shortages, many of which were caused by the almost constant Allied aerial attack on his supply lines. In addition, much of his artillery consisted of captured guns, and there were only a few shells available for each gun.

TABLE 5: ORGANIZATION OF THE
462ND VOLKSGRENADIER DIVISION, METZ, 1944

Commander, Lt. Gen. Vollrath Luebbe[*]

1215th Volksgrenadier Regiment, Colonel Stoessel[**]; two battalions, made up of the cadres of the Officer Training Regiment and low-grade replacements.

1216th Volksgrenadier Regiment, Colonel Stolz; two battalions, made up of the cadres of the NCO School Regiment and low-grade replacements.

1217th Volksgrenadier Regiment, Lieutenant Colonel Richter; two battalions, made of parts of the former 1010th Security Regiment plus replacement-training battalions.

1010th Security Regiment (reactivated on November 1), Colonel Anton (missing in action on November 17); two battalions

1462nd Artillery Regiment, Colonel Palm; four batteries

1462nd Anti-Tank Battalion, Captain Lautenschlager; three companies

1462nd Fusilier Battalion, Major Voss

1462nd Engineer Battalion, Captain Hasselmann

1462nd Signal Company, Captain Friemel

1462nd Field Replacement Battalion, Captain Gratwohl

---

* Succeeded by Lt. Gen. Heinrich Kittel on November 14.
** Assumed command of the remnants of the division after General Kittel was wounded on November 22.
Source: Kemp, *Metz*, 131.

Meanwhile, the LXXXII Corps, now under the command of Gen. of Infantry Walter Hoernlein, took care of the Thionville-Metz sector.[28] On his northern flank at Thionville was Lt. Gen. Kurt Pflieger's

416th Infantry Division, which had come down from Denmark in early October to replace the 559th Volksgrenadier Division. Its 8,500 troops had had no combat experience since World War I and were made up mostly of elderly men, most of whom were portly or downright fat. For this reason, it was derisively nicknamed the *Schlagsahne* ("Whipped Cream") Division. It was fourth class, fit only for limited defensive roles. To its south lay Col. Karl Britzelmayr's 19th Volksgrenadier Division. Its two infantry regiments had suffered 15 to 20 percent casualties and had received few, if any, replacements. It had only 9,000 men, ten heavy antitank guns and no assault guns to cover a twenty-mile front. South of it lay the 462nd Volksgrenadier, and on its left lay the mediocre 17th SS Panzer Grenadier Division, which was busy absorbing another contingent of green replacements. It was again under the command of SS Maj. Gen. Werner Ostendorff, who had now recovered from the wounds he suffered in Normandy.[29] None of these units was considered fit for offensive operations.

To shore up their weak defenses, the Germans lay mines—20,000 of them in the Thionville sector alone. Balck also stationed five artillery battalions on the border between the 19th Volksgrenadier and 416th Infantry Divisions—in the exact spot the main American attack would strike. On November 1, the 1216th Volksgrenadier Regiment was taken out of Metz and sent north to reinforce the 19th Volksgrenadier Division. It is unclear whether Balck or Hoernlein initiated this move. In any case, to fill the new gap in the defenses, General Luebbe took the old 1010th Security Regiment from the 1217th Volksgrenadier Regiment and reactivated it under the command of Colonel Anton. It consisted of one fortress (i.e., static) heavy machine gun battalion and one static infantry battalion. Both were of low quality and poorly equipped. The only reserve available to the Metz garrison was the 38th SS Panzer Grenadier Regiment, which had been temporarily detached from the 17th SS Division.

As poor as its line-up was, the LXXXII was the strongest corps in the 1st Army's sector. To the south, the XIII SS Corps, now under SS Lt. Gen. Max Simon, had only the 48th Infantry and 559th Volksgrenadier Divisions, and south of them lay Gen. of Infantry Baron Werner von und zu Gilsa's LXXXIX Corps, with the 361st and 553rd Volksgrenadier Divisions. In order to add weight to his Ardennes offensive, Hitler virtually stripped the entire army group of its mobile formations. As of November 5, the only mobile units left in Army Group G were the 21st Panzer with the 19th Army defending against Devers's 6th Army Group to the south and Lt. Gen. Wend von Wietersheim's 11th Panzer Division in reserve behind the 1st Army. In fact, the 11th Panzer was the only division in Army Group G which was not on the front line. Its seven other weak divisions had to defend seventy-five miles of front—a task far beyond its capabilities. In all, Army Group G had 86,000 men. Patton's Third Army alone deployed 250,000 men against it.

On October 18, Eisenhower met with Bradley and Montgomery in Brussels. Once again, he ruled that the offensives north of the Ardennes had priority, but to appease Bradley, he agreed to allow Patton to launch his Saar campaign "when logistics permit."[30] Bradley ordered the Ninth and First Armies north of the Ardennes to begin their attacks on November 4. He told Patton to begin his offensive by November 10. By that time, the 10th Armored Division, which was en route to the front, would have arrived. Patton assigned it to the XX Corps.

Patton planned to start his drive with the XII Corps, which was ordered to seize a bridgehead over the Seille. It was then to send an armored division north to seize the high ground west of Metz while the XX Corps crossed the Moselle north of Thionville and drove east and south, linking up with the XII Corps behind the city: a classic double envelopment—and just what Balck and Mellenthin expected. In all, Walker's XX Corps had thirty infantry battalions, about 500 tanks, and more than 700 guns.

The battle began on November 8 when the U.S. XII Corps attacked to the south. In the XX Corps' sector, only the U.S. 95th Infantry Division attacked on November 8, launching a river crossing over the Moselle in the Uckange area. Its objective was to convince the German generals that the main attack was coming south of Thionville and north of Metz and trick them into committing their reserves prematurely and at the wrong place. This deception did not work, and the 95th was generally contained by the 73rd Volksgrenadier Regiment of the 19th Volksgrenaider Division.

The main XX Corps attack began on November 9 when the veteran 90th Infantry Division crossed the Moselle north of Thionville at the junction of the 416th Infantry and 19th Volksgrenadier Divisions.

Its objective was to secure a bridgehead wide enough to allow Patton to commit the 10th Armored Division. Resistance was fairly stiff from the German infantry, even from the men of the "Whipped Cream" Division.

The critical position in this battle was Fort Koenigsmacker, a pre–World War I structure that dominated the crossing site. It was defended by a 300-man battalion from the 74th Volksgrenadier Regiment of the 19th Division. Fortunately for the Americans, the garrison had no guns in working order, and its defenders were not of the caliber of the Officer Training Regiment. The Americans threw thirty-four-pound satchel charges into every possible opening and poured gasoline down ventilator shafts, igniting it with thermite grenades. By the end of the day, the bridgehead was six miles wide and two miles deep, and seven towns and villages had been cleared. Eight U.S. infantry battalions had crossed the river but had no armor and only a few antitank guns. A determined armored counterattack could still have wiped out the bridgehead, but the Germans had no armor, and a few local counterattacks were ineffective. Balck immediately appealed to Rundstedt for the release of a panzer division, but OKW did not want to release any of the armor earmarked for the Ardennes offensive, even though the generals knew that a successful breakthrough by Patton might endanger the entire operation. Finally, Berlin agreed to release a battle group from the 25th Panzer Grenadier Division, which was refitting near Trier. Because of fuel shortages, however, it could not assemble for the attack until 3 A.M. on November 12. It was still not too late. The American engineers had completed their bridge across the Moselle the day before, but the causeway to it was still flooded and unusable for armor.

The *kampfgruppe* from Trier consisted of the 35th Panzer Grenadier Regiment, augmented by ten tanks and assault guns. It launched its main attack at 6 A.M., overran part of the U.S. 359th Infantry Regiment, and headed straight for the critical bridge. The regiment's reserve battalion ambushed the panzer grenadiers and killed quite a number of them, but still the Germans kept on coming. They pushed to the outskirts of Petite-Hettange, a village only a mile from the bridge. Here they were halted by three American antitank guns and an ad hoc force of cooks, clerks, drivers, and other support troops. They knocked out two of the antitank guns before twenty

American artillery battalions opened up. The battalions were lined up, almost hub to hub, on the west bank of the Moselle and unleashed a devastating bombardment. The panzer grenadiers began to fall back. The retreat was orderly at first; then two American infantry companies struck them in the flank, and the retreat degenerated into a rout. In all, the 35th Panzer Grenadier lost more than 400 men killed and about 150 captured, as well as four tanks and five assault guns. The battle was as good as over. The bridgehead was secure. Later that day, a task force from the 95th Division established a second crossing site at Thionville, and the U.S. 10th Armored Division began to cross the river in force.

Certain German officers, most notably Friedrich-Wilhelm von Mellenthin, had been highly critical of the performance of the 416th and 19th Divisions in this battle—wrongly in my opinion. Considering how poorly armed and equipped they were (the 416th Infantry Division had no assault guns and only captured Russian 122-millimeter guns and a few obsolete fortress pieces) and how large their defensive sectors were (twenty miles for the 19th Volksgrenadier alone), they gave a reasonably good account of themselves. They contained the main American attack for four days, did not surrender in mass, and retreated in good order. The only unit to be routed was the 35th Panzer Grenadier Regiment.

Meanwhile, south of the city, the U.S. 5th Infantry Division began its advance during the night of November 9. Its objective was to advance parallel with the U.S. XII Corps on its right, work its way around the city, and then attack to the north, linking up with the U.S. 90th Infantry Division and completing the encirclement of Metz. To accomplish this task, they would have to cross both the Seille and Nied Rivers.

The task of the 5th was made much easier by the U.S. XII Corps, which defeated the XIII SS Corps (48th Infantry and 559th Volksgrenadier Divisions) on November 8 and forced it back to the west, effectively outflanking the Seille River line. The Americans initially met only light resistance from the rearguards of the 17th SS Panzer Grenadier Division, which was no longer giving a good account of itself. Formerly an elite unit, it had been brought up to full strength after the retreat from France, but the quality of its troops was never the same as before D-Day. Most of its replacements were poorly trained *Volksdeutsche*, and their morale never measured up to the previously high standards of the *Waffen-SS*. It was also woefully short of equipment, having only four PzKw IV tanks and six self-propelled assault guns. As a result, the U.S. 5th Infantry was able to secure a bridgehead across the river by November 10, and the next day, the U.S. 6th Armored Division crossed the Nied and was committed to the battle. That same day, the Germans evacuated German civilians from the city. By nightfall, American artillery was within range of the main road from Metz to Saarbruecken. By November 13, the American engineers had bridged the Nied, and the spearheads of the 5th Division were within three miles of the suburbs of Metz two days later.

Within the fortress-city, General Luebbe suffered a stroke on November 12 and was replaced by Lt. Gen. Heinrich Kittel, the brother of the defender of St. Malo. Kittel was a tough veteran of the Russian front and he had been sent to Metz as an advisor. Probably no one knew more about the defense of fortresses than he. On the Eastern Front, he had been fortress commandant at Rostov, Krivoy Rog, Uman, Tarnopol, and Krakow. Metz, however, was a different matter, and when Kittel officially assumed command of the 462nd Volksgrenadier Division on November 14, he knew he was taking charge of a battle that was already lost. His new command was not particularly awe-inspiring, either. Of the 14,000 men he inherited, he estimated that only 5,500 could be properly classified as combat effectives. He was nevertheless determined to hold out for as long as he could.

That same day, the U.S. 95th Infantry Division joined the battle by attacking the fortifications west of the city. Kittel's single, weak *Volksgrenadier* division was now under attack by three U.S. infantry divisions, which were at or near full strength. Before noon, a regiment of the U.S. 95th broke through the 1217th Volksgrenadier Regiment and pushed behind Forts Driant and Jeanne d'Arc and into the complex of forts and field fortifications called the Seven Dwarves. Kittel at once counterattacked with his only reserve, Major Voss's 462nd Fusilier Battalion, which pushed the Americans out of their foothold among the Seven Dwarves.

Meanwhile, elements of Colonel Richter's 1217th Volksgrenadier emerged from their maze of trenches, bunkers, and tunnels, and cut off two U.S. infantry battalions. It was November 18 before the men of the 95th Division could fight their way through the 1217th to res-

cue them. When they did, however, they had breached the main fortified belt and were able to look down on Metz in the valley below.

To the north, the U.S. 10th Armored and 90th Infantry Divisions
pushed the 19th Volksgrenadier Division to the west, and on November 15, the garrison lost contact with the 1st Army's forces to the
north. Metz was becoming more isolated by the hour. Colonel Stolz's
1216th Volksgrenadier Regiment was cut off from the 19th Volksgrenadier Division by the speed of the American advance, so Stolz led
his regiment back into the fortress, from whence it had come.

The following day, General Balck had a long conversation with his
chief of staff, Colonel Mellenthin, who had one been Rommel's chief
intelligence officer in the African desert. They had a pretty good idea
of Patton's strength, his dispositions, and his actions. They concluded
that they could no longer comply with Hitler's orders to maintain contact with Kittel's forces at Metz. The only way to save the 1st Army was to
retreat to Faulquemont and positions along the Nied in order to block
the American approaches to the Saar and the Siegfried Line. They
issued the appropriate orders to General Knobelsdorf, and on November 17, the 1st Army informed Heinrich Kittel that he was on his own.
Kittel already knew that. On November 15, he had reported to the 1st
Army that he was losing about 15 percent of his effective combat
strength to casualties every day and appealed to Knobelsdorf for help.
All Knobelsdorf could offer was the 38th SS Panzer Grenadier Regiment, a mediocre unit which had been severely depleted in the earlier
fighting. Worse, it was not immediately available; it was locked in combat against the advancing U.S. 5th Infantry Division and would have to
disengage first. Kittel was reduced to shuttling a platoon here or a company there, like a fireman trying to put out fires that were breaking out
all over the place.

On November 16, the local Nazi *Kreisleiter* fled, along with his staff
and a number of Nazi sympathizers and collaborators. Kittel then told
Maj. Gen. of Police Anton Dunkern, the Gestapo chief and Police
President of Metz, to leave the city.[31] Dunkern had already received
orders from Himmler to stay were he was, so Kittel put him in charge
of the straggler assembly points. By late afternoon, the situation had
deteriorated to the point that members of the FFI began appearing
openly in the streets, and some residents were already flying the
French flag. "The German police no longer controlled the situation,"

Kittel recalled later. He ordered the German civilian population evacuated, and eight companies of special military police attempted to do so, but it was already too late.

German resistance was by no means collapsing, however. That same day, the 10th and 11th Infantry Regiments of the U.S. 5th Division were pinned down near the Frescaty airfield by a number of fortress machine gun companies, commanded by SS Lieutenant Colonel Matzdorf. It took an entire American battalion to pin down the 48th Fortress Machine Gun Battalion in two of the Verdun forts. The 11th Infantry suffered 122 casualties that day, indicating that the battle was far from over.

The next day, November 17, the U.S. 5th Infantry Division finally smashed the 38th SS Panzer Grenadier Regiment, and the entire 17th SS Panzer Grenadier Division retreated to the east. It had already received its orders to pull out of the line and withdraw to Germany—Hitler intended to rebuild it and use it in the Ardennes. No one, however, saw fit to aprize General Kittel of this fact. He was under the impression that the 38th SS Panzer Grenadier Regiment, which had been assigned to him by the 1st Army, was still under his command. When the defenders of Fort Queuleu appealed to him for help, Kittel sent orders for the 38th SS to rush to their rescue. It was nowhere to be found. Only later did Kittel learn what had happened. Meanwhile, the U.S. 10th Infantry Regiment surrounded Fort Queuleu and captured Borny, a small town due east of Metz. The jaws were closing. By nightfall, the only road out of Metz was the one through St. Avold to Saarbruecken. The Americans cut it the following morning, and at 10:30 A.M., the U.S. 90th and 5th Infantry Divisions joined hands at Pont Marais, eight miles east of the city. Metz was surrounded.

General Kittel ordered most of the bridges in Metz blown up on November 16. Most of the rest were demolished by the following evening. The last was blown up on November 18, as the Americans were trying to cross it, and several U.S. soldiers were killed. Kittel was well aware that his situation was hopeless, but he intended to kill or tie down as many Americans as he could for as long as possible. He issued his final comprehensive orders on the evening of November 17, assigning his commanders their last positions and instructing them to hold out as long as they could. He intended to force General Walker to take Metz fort by fort and block by block.

The XX Corps began clearing the city on November 18. The 22nd Fortress Infantry Battalion continued to put up stiff resistance inside Fort Queuleu, but a squad from the U.S. 10th Infantry Regiment managed to capture SS General Dunkern, the former police president, who was hiding in a brewery. General Patton allowed himself the pleasure of interrogating him personally, with the help of a Jewish interpreter. He was the first high-ranking SS officer captured by the Third Army.

On November 19, the Americans pushed into the old city and surrounded Colonel Meier, the city commandant, and 700 men from several units in a barracks block. Meier tried to break out that night, but he did not make it and was taken prisoner. By the end of the day, all three U.S. infantry divisions had joined hands and began the slow process of reducing the city and forts. Patton could have used them in his drive on the Saar, but Metz had to be reduced first, so Kittel was accomplishing at least part of his mission.

One by one, the German strongpoints within Metz signed off. Despite sniper fire, the American jaws closed inexorably on the Mudra barracks, the command post of the fortress commander. The Americans assumed they would find him there; Kittel, however, had already concluded that he no longer had any command functions to perform, so he joined the battle and fought like a private soldier. He was wounded in the knee at 11 A.M. on November 22 and was taken to a nearby tobacco factory, which the Germans were using as a hospital and aid station. He signaled Stoessel that he had been wounded, and the colonel assumed command of what was left of the fortress and the division. Shortly thereafter, a captured American medical orderly escaped from the tobacco factory and informed a U.S. infantry detachment of the general's location. They found him on the operating table, under anaesthetic. When he woke up, he was a prisoner of war.

Kittel refused to sign a formal surrender on the grounds that he had already handed command over to Stoessel. He also refused to order the surrender of the outer forts. He was marched away to prison, released in 1947, and died at Ansbach, Middle Franconia, Bavaria, on March 5, 1969. Meanwhile, the Americans finished mopping up the last pockets of resistance in the city the next day.

The U.S. 95th Infantry Division was withdrawn from the battle on November 22 and was sent to the Saar. The 5th Infantry Division was left behind to finish off the remaining forts. It did not waste lives or ammunition in reducing them, but rather let them run out of food and water. Then the forts surrendered on their own, one after another. On December 8, Colonel Richter surrendered the infamous Fort Driant, along with 600 men, to the 5th Division. Then the 5th was summoned to join the rest of the Third Army, which was pushing toward the Saar. By this time, all of the forts had capitulated except one, Jeanne d'Arc, which sheltered the 1462nd Fusilier Battalion and the staff of the 462nd Volksgrenadier Division. The fusilier commander, Major Voss, surrendered the fort to the newly arrived U.S. 87th Infantry Division on December 13, along with 500 men. The Metz area was finally clear.

In all, the Battle of Metz cost the *Wehrmacht* at least 20,000 men— probably more. American casualties were considerably less, but the importance of this battle did not lie solely in its casualties. The defenders of the fortress-city had tied down George Patton's seemingly unbeatable Third Army for almost three full months; one division was occupied until three days before the Battle of the Bulge began. The ad hoc garrison also inflicted on Patton the only defeats he suffered in his military career, proving that he and his army were not invincible. The heroic stand of the 462nd Division did much to restore the morale of the *Wehrmacht,* which seemed to be on the verge of collapse at the end of August. It also prevented the Third Army from breaking the Siegfried Line and doing serious damage to the Third Reich before Hitler could unleash his Ardennes offensive. When the Battle of the Bulge began on December 16, the XX Corps had managed to establish only two bridgeheads across the Saar: one at Saarlautern and one at Dilligen. Both of these had to be abandoned when the Third Army had to be shifted north into the Ardennes. Patton would undoubtedly have done much more damage between September 4 and December 16 had it not been for the defenders of Metz. In fact, it is almost certain that Hitler would have been forced to commit much of his armored reserve to halt Patton, had it not been for Metz. It is quite conceivable that the German Army would not have been able to launch its surprise attack in the Ardennes if not for the Battle of Metz.

THE BATTLE OF ALSACE-LORRAINE

While the 462nd Volksgrenadier Division was sacrificing itself at Metz, the rest of Army Group G—with only two weak armies, Knobelsdorf's 1st and Wiese's 19th—was facing the right flank of Patton's Third Army and the U.S. 6th Army Group (U.S. Seventh and French First Armies, under Generals Patch and de Lattre de Tassigny), which were trying to force their way into Strasbourg and inside the borders of the Reich.

On November 11, the U.S. XX Corps of the American Seventh Army began an offensive in the Baccarat sector, south of the Marne-Rhine Canal. Its objective was to capture the Saverne Gap in the northern Vosges. The American attack struck the 553rd Volksgrenadier, 559th Volksgrenadier, and 708th Infantry Divisions. Maj. Gen. Hans Bruhn's 553rd Volksgrenadier fought well, but the 559th and 708th, which were battered and demoralized, did not. As a result, Army Group G had to commit its only mobile reserve, Wietersheim's 11th Panzer Division, to save the infantry and prevent the Americans from exploiting their success. It arrived just in time and, on November 12, delivered a sharp counterattack against Combat Command A of the U.S. 4th Armored Division. Because of its long experience of fighting in mud and snow on the Eastern Front, the 11th Panzer was able to retake the town of Rodalbe on November 13 and capture an entire American battalion.

Because of the intervention of the 11th Panzer, the 19th Army was able to re-form its broken front and bring up its reserves. On November 14, "The Americans continued to attack stubbornly and with great determination," Mellenthin recalled.[32] The 11th Panzer fell back to the high ground west of Morhange, where Wietersheim made a determined stand. CCB of the U.S. 4th Armored Division and the U.S. 35th Infantry Division attacked the town from the front, while the U.S. 6th Armored Division tried to break through at Faulquemont on the direct road to Saarbruecken. To prevent this, Army Group G moved Feuchtingen's 21st Panzer and Maj. Gen. August Welln's 36th Infantry Divisions into the sector. These divisions were also very weak. The 21st Panzer, for example, had only nineteen tanks and only four panzer grenadier battalions of sixty to seventy men each.[33]

To the south, the French First Army joined the offensive by attacking the left wing of the 19th Army (Lt. Gen. Hellmuth Thumm's LXIV Corps) and driving toward the Belfort Gap and southern Alsace.

Thumm's corps consisted of only Maj. Gen. Hans Oschmann's 338th Infantry Division on the left flank with its back to the Swiss border and Maj. Gen. Heinrich Buercky's 159th Infantry (formerly Reserve) Division on the right flank in the vicinity of the Belfort Gap. That night, strained to the breaking point, the 19th Army withdrew its right wing into the northern Vosges Mountains—a retreat conducted with great skill by the highly competent Wiese.

The next day, the 11th Panzer Division abandoned the ruins of Morhange, but the Americans did not pursue because of difficult terrain and heavy casualties; further, the northern flank of the XII Corps had been exposed as a result of the movements of the U.S. XX Corps, which was in the process of enveloping Metz. Army Group G was therefore able to pull the 48th and 559th Divisions out of the line and combined them into a single *kampfgruppe.*

The French attacks against the left wing of the 19th Army continued. During the night of November 16–17, Wiese withdrew Thumm's LXIV Corps toward the Vosges. Unfortunately, this retreat was mishandled. General Oschmann, the commander of the 338th Infantry Division, had been killed near the Belfort Gap on the first day of the French attack, and his temporary successor, Col. of Reserve Rudolf von Oppen, posted rearguards that were far too weak.[34] As a result, the French armor, advancing with what the chief of staff of Army Group G called "extraordinary dash and elan, reflecting the temperament of the army commander, General de Lattre de Tassigny," was able to break through Wiese's screen.[35] On the eighteenth, the French 1st Armored Division advanced eighteen miles, and the next day, it advanced twenty-five miles, broke into the Upper Alsace, and reached the Rhine River just north of Basel, Switzerland—the first Allied forces to do so. In the process they almost captured General Wiese and invested the town of Belfort. The next day, to the north, the U.S. XV Corps of the Seventh Army continued to push the gallant 553rd Volksgrenadier back toward Sarrebourg. A hundred Shermans broke through Bruhn's lines and surrounded the division at Sarrebourg as evening fell. The 553rd Volksgrenadier seemed doomed but General Bruhn took advantage of a dark night and heavy rain to lead his men through American lines. He made good his escape, but the fall of Sarrebourg had nevertheless driven a wedge between the German 1st and 19th Armies.[36]

General Balck, the commander of Army Group G, realized that the U.S. 6th Army Group was developing a giant pincer, aimed at destroying the 19th Army between the U.S. Seventh Army on the north and the French First Army to the south. The next day, the Americans captured Belfort after a fierce battle, and French tanks entered Mulhouse near the Rhine on the western edge of the Black Forest. Gen. of Cavalry Count Edwin von Rothkirch und Trach, the commander of the LIII Corps, which was responsible for defending southern Alsace, had no mobile reserves but was able to scrap together all sorts of units, including the 30th SS Grenadier Division, an unreliable Russian unit.[37] On November 22, he managed to establish an improvised defensive line between the Vosges and Rhine. That same day, the U.S. XV Corps enveloped Saverne, encircling the 553rd Volksgrenadier and the headquarters of the LXXXIX Corps in the process. The 553rd was able to break out again during the night, along with Gilsa and his corps staff, and reassembled in the Bitche area—without General Bruhn, who was captured by French troops. Once again the Germans were able to stave off disaster by a very thin margin. Almost immediately, however, another catastrophe threatened.

To the north, the southern wing of the U.S. Third Army had been attacking the 11th Panzer Division for days. Wietersheim, as usual, conducted a brilliant retreat, covering the withdrawal of the 1st Army east of Metz. The U.S. 6th Armored Division attacked his left flank, the U.S. 35th Infantry and 26th Infantry Divisions struck his center, and the U.S. 4th Armored Division tried to turn his right. Despite the tremendous odds against them, the veterans of the 11th Panzer were able to prevent a major breakthrough while simultaneously inflicting heavy losses on the Americans. General Wood, the commander of the U.S. 4th Armored Division, tried to solve the dilemma by turning south on November 22. He broke through Col. Alfred Philippi's weak 361st Volksgrenadier Division and headed for the Saar River, which he crossed at Fenetrange on the twenty-fourth. Then he turned north, into the German rear, before Army Group G realized how strong his forces really were.

On November 23, General Leclerc successfully forced the Saverne Gap and reached the plain of Alsace. He drove straight for Strasbourg with his French 2nd Armored Division. All the 1st Army had to bar his path was Col. Gerhard Franz's 256th Volksgrenadier Division, which had just arrived in northern Alsace from the 15th Army in Holland. The understrength 256th was no match for a full-strength armored division, which pushed into Strasbourg on the morning of November 24. Maj. Gen. Franz Vaterrodt, the commandant of the city, surrendered the next day.[38]

For days, General Balck had been begging for another panzer division, but OKW refused because it was still husbanding its armor for the Ardennes offensive. Finally, on November 23, it agreed to loan Balck the Panzer Lehr Division, which was led by Lt. Gen. Fritz Bayerlein. On the afternoon of the twenty-third, even before the entire division had come up, Balck threw it into a counterattack from Phalsbourg toward the Saverne Gap with the objective of cutting off the French 2nd Armored Division. The Panzer Lehr made good progress initially, but on the morning of November 24, it ran into the U.S. XV Corps' covering force—some reconnaissance squadrons and elements of the U.S. 44th Infantry Division—northeast of Sarrebourg. Then Bayerlein was taken in the flank by General Wood's U.S. 4th Armored Division, and a fierce fight developed northeast of Sarrebourg. The Panzer Lehr at that time had only thirty PzKw IVs and thirty-five Panthers, so it was badly outnumbered. By the afternoon of November 25, it had been pushed back and was threatened with envelopment on both flanks. Bayerlein beseeched OKW to call off the attack, but Hitler insisted that the offensive continue. The next day, only the timely arrival of a *kampfgruppe* from Col. Arnold Burmeister's 25th Panzer Grenadier Division prevented the destruction of the left wing of the Panzer Lehr.[39] By November 27, Bayerlein had been pushed back to his original line of departure. That night, the Panzer Lehr Division was withdrawn from the battle and sent north for a hasty rebuilding before the Battle of the Bulge. It was replaced in the line by the 25th Panzer Grenadier.

Although Bayerlein's offensive had certainly not been a German victory, it had forced the U.S. XV Corps to swing north to deal with the Panzer Lehr. This, in turn, forced the Allies to relax their pressure against the 19th Army, which was then able to complete its retreat and firmly establish itself in the Colmar pocket, a bulge on the west bank of the Rhine River north of Mulhouse and south of Strasbourg. Although they attempted an attack in early December, it would be 1945 before the Allies were in a position to launch a major offensive against the pocket.

The Belfort Gap finally fell on November 25. The 19th Army lost much of its right wing, and the 159th, 198th, and 338th Infantry Divisions were decimated. More than 10,000 Germans were captured, and 120 guns and 60 tanks and tank destroyers were destroyed or captured. At the same time, in central Lorraine, in the zone of the German 1st Army, the U.S. XX Corps advanced from Thionville toward the lower Saar. It was initially checked by the 21st Panzer Division in the Orscholz barrier, a naturally strong defensive position which was made even stronger by the construction of antitank ditches and concrete obstacles. It was November 28 before the XX Corps could develop its offensive on Saarlautern. After heavy fighting, the U.S. 95th Infantry Division took the western part of the city on December 1. The 21st Panzer retreated to the eastern bank of the Saar, leaving only one bridgehead on the west bank and only one bridge intact.

Early in the morning of December 3, in a surprise maneuver, American infantrymen and combat engineers took advantage of fog and rain to make an assault crossing of the river. They were able to reach the east bank and take the bridge from the rear before the German engineers, who had already wired it for destruction, could blow it up. The U.S. 379th Infantry Regiment then crossed the bridge and, that evening, captured the first bunkers of the West Wall in that sector.[40]

Adolf Hitler was furious. He and OKW promptly forgot that they had stripped the West Wall of most of its defenses—including obstacles, mines, and telecommunications—and sent them to the Atlantic Wall. Now, of course, scapegoats had to be found. Knobelsdorf, the veteran commander of the 1st Army, had been sacked on November 30 and replaced by Gen. of Infantry Hans Obstfelder.[41] Mellenthin, the chief of staff of Army Group G, was sacked on November 28 for offending a representative of Heinz Guderian, the chief of the General Staff. Guderian also discharged him from the General Staff and placed him under house arrest for insubordination, even though Mellenthin did not utter a word in his own defense. Mellenthin's promotion to major general came through on December 1 while he was still under arrest.[42] He returned to Headquarters, Army Group G, on

December 5, but only long enough to hand his duties to his successor, Maj. Gen. Helmut Staedke, the former chief of staff of the 9th Army on the Eastern Front.[43]

Meanwhile, the U.S. Seventh Army attacked again along a thirty-mile front while the ruins of Saarlautern were finally secured by the U.S. Third Army on December 5. The U.S. 90th Infantry Division established a small bridgehead across the Saar on December 6, but now the Third Army was in some of the thicker sectors of the West Wall, and the U.S. Seventh and French First Armies were being slowed down by mud, snow, pillboxes, lack of air support, and stiffening German resistance. Patton tried to break out of the Saarlautern bridgehead on December 7, and the French launched a series of attacks against the Colmar pocket, but neither was able to make much progress.

They would still be stuck on December 16 when the Battle of the Bulge began. Hermann Balck had accomplished his mission, though he did not get any credit for it. Heinrich Himmler was already angling for a military command, and he had his eye on the Strasbourg-Colmar sector. In mid-December, over Balck's objections, the 19th Army was transferred from Army Group G to the newly created *OB Oberrhein* (Upper Rhine), which was commanded by Himmler. Party interference in military affairs had reached an all-time high. On December 24, Balck fell victim to a Himmler intrigue and was relieved of his command. His successor was Col. Gen. Johannes Blaskowitz, whom he himself had succeeded three months before. There were more changes in the wind.

CHAPTER 10

Clearing the Scheldt

In September 1944, Field Marshal Montgomery had his sights so firmly fixed on the Ruhr and the Rhine that he neglected to clear the Scheldt or cut off Gustav von Zangen's 15th Army's route of retreat across the South Beveland peninsula; both could have been accomplished rather easily. As a result, the port of Antwerp, which had fallen intact and had a potential capacity of 100,000 tons a day[1]—enough to solve all of the Allies' supply problems—was still useless at the beginning of October, and the Allies had already lost several important operational opportunities because of a lack of supplies. Zangen had escaped with the bulk of his army, leaving behind enough men and heavy artillery to keep the sea approaches to Antwerp blocked indefinitely. On the southern shore of the Scheldt, along the Leopold Canal—an excellent defensive position—he left the 64th Infantry Division under the command of Maj. Gen. Kurt Eberding. This area, known as the Breskens pocket, was low, flat, and so boggy that tanks were almost useless here. It also offered almost no protect for advancing infantry. In addition, the 64th Infantry was made up largely of veterans of the Eastern Front who were well supplied with food, artillery, and ammunition left behind by the 15th Army. On Walcheren Island, just north of the Breskens pocket, Zangen left the 8,000 men of Lt. Gen. Wilhelm Daser's 70th Infantry Division. It was not rated as highly as the 64th Infantry; in fact, it was known as the "White Bread" Division because many of its men had stomach ailments and were on special diets. Even men with stomach problems can shoot, and Walcheren provided excellent defensive terrain. Most of the island lies below sea level, and the only land route to it is over the South Beveland peninsula, which is only two miles across at its narrowest point and is easily flooded.

Henry D. G. Crerar's Canadian First Army, which was tied down in the battles for the Channel ports until the beginning of October,[2]

171

CLEARING THE SCHELDT

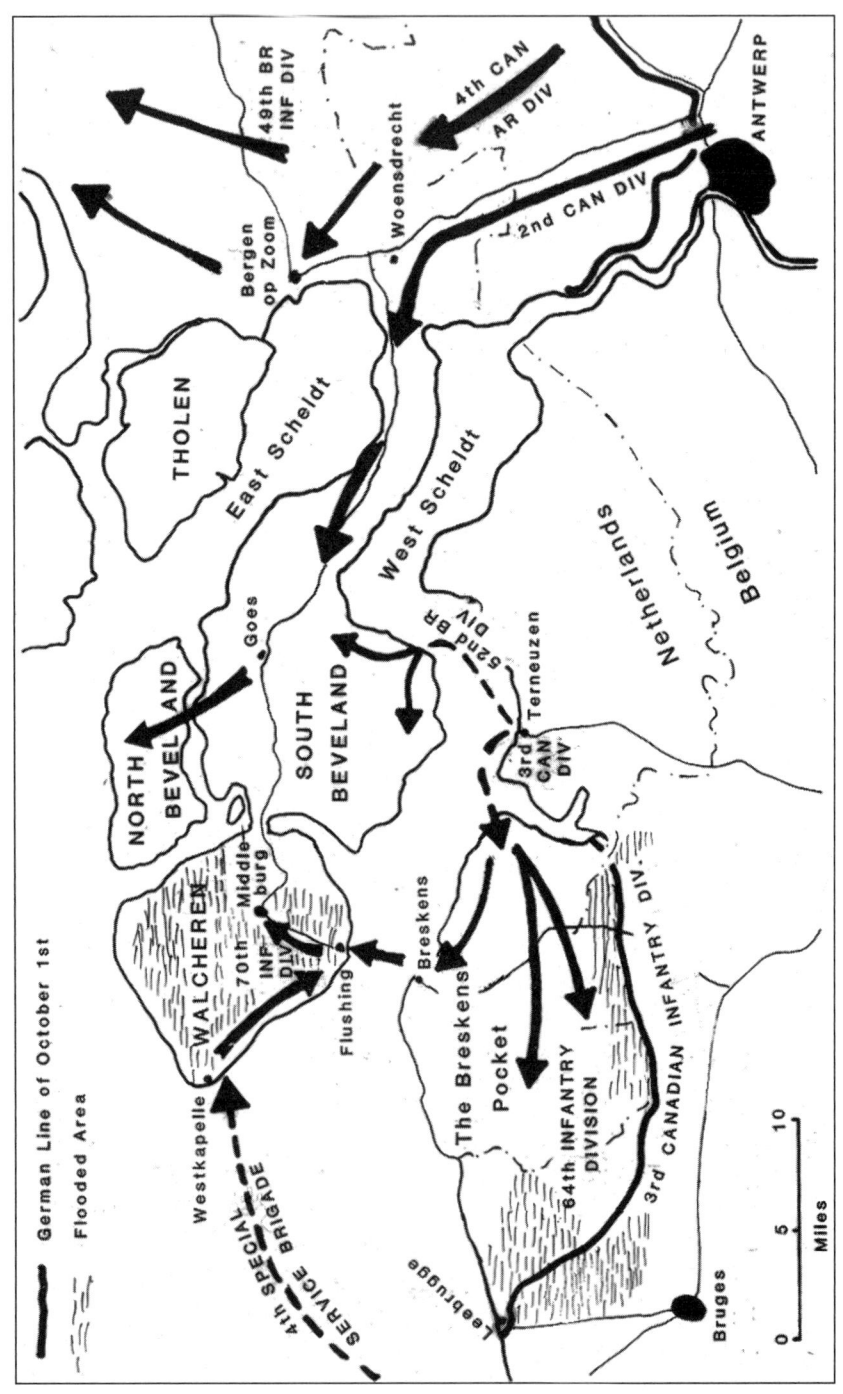

but planning for the clearing of the Scheldt went forward. Early in the planning stage, Lt. Gen. Guy G. Simonds, the commander of the Canadian II Corps, foresaw that left to their own devices, the Germans could use flooding to their own advantage to check and channelize the Allied advance. He suggested that they take this weapon away from the Germans and turn it to their own advantage by using the RAF to blast the dikes on Walcheren Island and let in the sea. This would deny the Germans the use of the roads and isolate their strongpoints on the sand dunes. If the breaches were wide enough, he said, the amphibious vessels could sail across the flooded polders and take the enemy in the rear. It was a very innovative idea, and Crerar rejected it. Montgomery overruled Crerar, however, and approved the plan.

Operations to clear the southern bank of the Scheldt began on October 2. The next day, Bomber Command attacked the West-kapelle Dike with 243 Lancasters, and the North Sea poured into the polders. The Germans could not stop the flooding, and the next week the RAF enlarged the breach and blasted gaps in the dikes at three other points. By the middle of October, 75 percent of the island was flooded, and the German garrison was isolated on three small strips of coastal dunes and in the towns of Flushing and Middelburg.

Crerar fell ill with dysentery during the first week of October and was temporarily replaced as commander of the Canadian First Army by Simonds.[3] On October 6, a brigade of the Canadian 3rd Infantry Division established a precarious bridgehead across the Leopold Canal, and Simonds expected the Breskens pocket would be cleared in three or four days. The German 64th Infantry Division, however, proved to be a tough nut to crack. On October 9, a second Canadian brigade was ferried down the Scheldt and landed in Eberding's rear. Still the defenses did not break. General Eberding made it clear that any premature surrender would be treated as desertion. In an order to his division on October 14, he wrote, "In cases where the names of deserters are ascertained, these will be made known to the civilian population at home, and their next of kin will be looked upon as enemies of the German people."[4] Rather than have their families turned over to the Gestapo, the German infantry fought with great determination. The Canadians had to push them back strongpoint by strongpoint, ditch by ditch. It took the Canadian 3rd Infantry Division two weeks to reach the port of Breskens and cut the pocket in two. Even then the men in the western half of the pocket continued to fight for more than a week. On October 16, no doubt realizing that he had seriously underestimated the amount of time it would require to clear the Scheldt, Montgomery shut down all other offensives in his army group area and assigned the British Second Army to support the Canadian First. Even so, the last of the coastal batteries on the southern bank of the Scheldt estuary were not captured until November 2, and General Eberding was not captured until November 4.[5] The Canadians had cleared the Breskens pocket and taken 12,700 prisoners. The 64th Infantry Division had ceased to exist, but it had delayed the opening of the port of Antwerp for another month.

Meanwhile, the Canadian 2nd Infantry Division advanced eighteen miles from Antwerp and cut the South Beveland peninsula, blocking the escape route of the 70th Infantry Division. By the end of October, in spite of stubborn resistance, the Candians had cleared the peninsula and were preparing for the conquest of Walcheren Island, one of the keys to Antwerp. The battle began on October 31 when the Canadian 2nd Division attacked along the causeway from South Beveland to Walcheren and established a tenuous foothold on the island. General Daser counterattacked the next day and destroyed this bridgehead but, in doing so, played into the Allies' hands, for the main Allied attack was coming from the sea.

During the night of November 1, under the cover of a heavy barrage from the southern shore, the British 4th Commando, which included French and Dutch troops, sailed into Flushing harbor and established a foothold before the surprised German garrison could react. By 10 A.M. the following morning, half of the town was in Allied hands. Meanwhile, following an RAF bombing attack, a second Allied landing force approached Westkapelle but found the coastal batteries still intact. HMS *Warspite* and two monitors attempted to silence the heavy guns but were unsuccessful. When the assault force went in aboard twenty-five landing craft, nine of them were sunk, and eleven were put out of action. While the coastal gunners were busy repulsing this attack, the commandos of the 4th Special Service Brigade landed on the shoulders of the Westkapelle Gap, almost without loss. To the shock of the defenders, several amphibious "Buffaloes" sailed right through the gap and took the village of Westkapelle via an attack from the interior. By nightfall, the commandos had captured the two main coastal batteries on the western side of the island, but the Germans continued to block the eastern causeway until November 4 when amphibious landing craft carrying a brigade from the 52nd Lowland Division landed behind them. Middelburg was captured without a fight on November 6 because the Germans had ceased to resist. General Daser, who was anxious to end the fighting, surrendered to a lieutenant of the Royal Scots, and the last German pocket surrendered on November 10.[6] Like the 64th, the 70th Infantry Division had ceased to exist.

Eliminating the ground resistance was not the same thing as opening the port of Antwerp, for the German Navy had thoroughly mined the Scheldt. It took more than three weeks for 100 Allied minesweepers to clear the seventy-mile channel from the North Sea to the port. The first ship did not dock in Antwerp until November 28. From the time of its capture, the Germans had denied the Allies the use of the harbor for eighty-five critical days. The Allies' supply problems were now solved—but too late for them to win the war in 1944. The days of the heady advances of August and early September were over, and the *Wehrmacht* had regained its balance and recovered. How much it had recovered the Allies would discover in three weeks when Hitler launched his Ardennes offensive and began the Battle of the Bulge.

Notes

CHAPTER 1: THE GREAT WALL OF HITLER

1. The Third Reich was unofficially established on February 28, 1933, when President Paul von Hindenburg suspended the Constitution of the Weimar Republic. This happened the day after an arsonist burned the *Reichstag*.

2. Wilhelm Keitel (1882–1946) wanted to be a farmer, but since he was not in line to inherit the family farm, he joined the army as a *Fahnenjunker* (officer-cadet) in the artillery in 1901. Commissioned the following year, he fought in World War I, where he was seriously wounded by a shell splinter in September 1914. He became a candidate for the General Staff in 1915 and spent the rest of the war in General Staff positions. He briefly served with the *Freikorps* (Free Corps), a loose collection of paramilitary organizations, on the Polish frontier in 1919. Keitel was retained in the *Reichsheer* and spent most of the 1920s and 1930s in General Staff positions, although he commanded a battalion of artillery, spent a year as Infantry Commander III (deputy commander of the 3rd Infantry Division and commander of its infantry components), and commander of the 22nd Infantry Division in Bremen (1934–35). He was named chief of the Armed Forces Office of the Defense Ministry in 1935, an appointment he fought. Hitler advanced him to the post of commander in chief of OKW because he thought—correctly—that Keitel would be easy to control. Wilhelm Keitel was promoted to field marshal on July 19, 1940, and was later hanged at Nuremberg. Like Walter von Brauchitsch, he was greatly influenced by his pro-Nazi wife.

3. Baron Werner von Fritsch was born in 1880 and joined the army as a *Fahnenjunker* in the artillery in 1898. Commissioned in 1900, he had a distinguished career, both as a General Staff officer and as a commander. He led the 2nd Artillery Regiment, 1st Cavalry Division, and 3rd Infantry Division (1931–34) before being named commander in chief of the army on February 1, 1934, an appointment he owed to Hindenburg, not Hitler. When he retired, Fritsch was named honorary colonel of the 12th Artillery. He accompanied this regiment to Poland in 1939 and, on September 22, deliberately exposed himself to enemy machine-gun fire and was killed.

4. For example, Lt. Gen. Viktor von Schwedler (1885–1954), the non-Nazi head of the powerful Army Personnel Office (HPA), was "kicked upstairs." He was promoted to general of infantry in February 1938, transferred to Saxony, and replaced by Wilhelm Keitel's younger brother, Bodewin (1888–1953). Schwedler later commanded the IV Corps in Poland and France and on the Eastern Front.

5. Walter von Brauchitsch (1881–1948) was the son of a Prussian general of cavalry. His older brother, Adolf (1876–1935), retired as a major general in 1929, and his son Bernd became a colonel in the *Luftwaffe* and was an adjutant to Hermann Goering. Walter was educated in the cadet school system and entered the Imperial Army as a lieutenant in 1900. His career followed the path of a Prussian general-in-training, and he was already a major general when Hitler came to power in 1933. In 1937, he became commander of the powerful Army Group 4, which controlled all of Germany's panzer, motorized, and light divisions. Despite his contempt for Brauchitsch, Hitler promoted him to colonel general on February 4, 1938, and to field marshal on July 19, 1940. After he failed to take Moscow, Hitler sacked Brauchitsch on December 19, 1941, and personally replaced him as commander in chief of the army. Brauchitsch, who suffered from heart disease, died in an Allied prison hospital.

6. Baron Hans Seutter von Loetzen, a close personal friend of Adam's, had commanded Army Group 2 from December 1, 1931, until his retirement on September 30, 1933. He resumed his retirement in November 1938 and died on March 20, 1968. He had been born in Stuttgart on October 20, 1875. Curt Liebmann (1881–1960), a native of Coburg and the son of a major general, had previously been chief of staff of Army Group 2, commander of the 5th Infantry Division, and commandant of the War Academy, where General Staff officers were trained. He commanded the 5th Army until his retirement on October 30, 1939.

7. In World War II, the headquarters of German armies were much larger organizations than army group headquarters. An army headquarters was responsible for supply, security, and a wide range of administrative functions. It also included many component units, including a higher artillery headquarters (the *Harko*), which normally controlled several general headquarters artillery battalions, as well as engineer, signal, and other units. The army group, on the other hand, normally had only one function—to control its subordinate armies. In terms of organic units, it generally had a staff company, a signals unit, and little else.

8. Ribbentrop (1893–1946), the former German ambassador to London (1936–38), had succeeded Neurath as foreign minister on February 4, 1938. (Hitler purged the army and the foreign ministry on the same day.) Ribbentrop, who remained in office until April 1945, was hanged at Nuremberg. Neurath (1873–1956), who had been appointed foreign minister in 1932 and later served Hitler as *Reichsprotektor* of Bohemia and Moravia (1939–41), was sentenced to fifteen years' imprisonment in 1946 but was released because of ill health in 1953.

9. Dr. Fritz Todt was born in Pforzheim, Baden-Wuerttemberg, on the northern rim of the Black Forest, in 1891. He served in the infantry and later as an aerial observer in World War I, where he earned the Iron Cross. After the war, he became a civil engineer, earning his doctorate from the University of Karlsruhl in 1931. His dissertation dealt with the sources of defects in tarmac and asphalt road surfaces. Meanwhile, he joined the Nazi Party in early 1922 and was an *Oberfuehrer* in the Brownshirts by 1931. Hitler named him inspector general of German railways in 1933. Later, he was in charge of building the *autobahns* and, in 1938, was placed in charge of the *Organisation Todt* for the construction of

the West Wall. He became Reich Minister for Armaments and Munitions on March 17, 1940. On February 8, 1942, he was killed when his airplane—which he had borrowed from *Luftwaffe* Field Marshal Hugo Sperrle—exploded in midair near Hitler's Rastenburg headquarters. It was speculated that Todt accidentally triggered the self-destruction device on Sperrle's airplane, because the pilot suddenly turned around and was trying to return to base when the airplane blew up. Todt was buried in the Invalidenfriedhof, the German national cemetery, in Berlin. He was replaced by Albert Speer.

10. War Office, Great Britain, *The Trials of German Major War Criminals*, vol. 28 (1978), 378–79 (ND 1780-PS) (hereafter cited as *TGMWC*).

    Gustav von Wietersheim (1884–1974) was born in Breslau, Silesia (now Wroclaw, Poland), and was a product of the cadet schools. During World War II, he commanded the XIV Motorized (later Panzer) Corps (1938–1942) and proved to be an excellent commander of motorized infantry. Hitler sacked him on September 15, 1942, because he opposed one of the Fuehrer's senseless orders during the Stalingrad campaign. He ended the war as a private in the *Volkssturm*.

11. Halder was deputy chief of the General Staff under Beck. He was eventually replaced by Gen. of Infantry Kurt Zeitzler (September 24, 1942), Col. Gen. Heinz Guderian (July 21, 1944), and Gen. of Infantry Hans Krebs (March 28, 1945). Halder (1884–1972) ended the war in a concentration camp.

12. David Irving, *The War Path: Hitler's Germany, 1933–1939* (New York: Viking Press, 1979), 134.

13. *TGMWC*, vol. 20, 606 (Manstein's testimony).

14. Ludwig Beck, who was deeply involved in the attempt to overthrow Adolf Hitler, was executed after he botched a suicide attempt on July 20, 1944. Gen. Wilhelm Adam had a peaceful retirement in Garmisch, Bavaria, and died on April 8, 1949, having outlived Adolf Hitler by almost four years.

CHAPTER 2: THE RETREAT

1. The original OB West (1940–42) was Field Marshal Erwin von Witzleben. Hitler forced him into involuntary retirement in March 1942. He was deeply involved in the plot to assassinate the Fuehrer on July 20, 1944. He was arrested the next day, tried quickly, and hanged on August 6.

2. The British alone landed 900 tanks in three armored brigades on D-Day.

3. J. F. C. Fuller, *The Second World War, 1939–1945: A Strategical and Tactical History* (New York: Duell, Sloan and Pearce, 1949), 294; Gordon A. Harrison, *Cross-Channel Attack* (Washington, DC: Office of the Chief of Military History, Department of the Army, 1951), 225, 267, 228–30; Charles B. MacDonald and Martin Blumenson, "Recovery of France," in Vincent J. Esposito, ed., *A Concise History of World War II* (New York: Praeger, 1964), 80; Alfred C. Mierzejewski, "Railroads," in David G. Chandler and James L. Collins, eds., *The D-Day Encyclopedia* (New York: Simon & Schuster, 1994), 448; Friedrich Ruge, "The Invasion of Normandy," in H. A. Jacobsen and J. Rohwer, eds., *Decisive Battles of World War II: The German View* (New York: Putnam, 1965): 323–29; Hans Speidel, *Invasion 1944: Rommel and the Normandy Campaign* (Chicago: Regnery, 1950), 46–47; John Toland, *Adolf Hitler* (Garden City, NY: Doubleday, 1976), 1,071.

4. Bernard Law Montgomery, The Viscount of Alamein, *Normandy to the Baltic* (Boston: Houghton Mifflin, 1948), 54; also see Samuel W. Mitcham, Jr., *Desert Fox in Normandy* (Westport, CT: Praeger, 1997), 130–32.

5. Joseph Lawton Collins was born in New Orleans, Louisiana, in 1896. He graduated from West Point in 1917 and was assistant chief of staff of U.S. occupation forces in Germany in 1920–21. He later served as an instructor at West Point, the Infantry School at Fort Benning, Georgia, and the Army War College, Carlisle Barracks, Pennsylvania, and did tours of duty in the Philippines and at the Artillery School at Fort Sill. He was a colonel and chief of staff of the Hawaiian Department when Pearl Harbor was attacked on December 7, 1941. He led the U.S. 25th Infantry Division in the Pacific (1942) and earned his nickname, Lightning Joe, on Guadalcanal. He led the VII Corps in France and Germany and was considered the best American corps commander in the European theater of operations. He was named deputy commander of Army Ground Forces in August 1945 and was chief of staff of the U.S. Army (1949–53) during the Korean War. Later, he was U.S. representative to NATO. He retired in 1956 and died in 1987.

6. Schlieben was born in Eisenach, the birthplace of Bach, in 1894. He entered the Imperial Army when World War I began, served in the *Reichsheer*, and was a lieutenant colonel when the war started. During World War II, he had served as a staff officer and had commanded the 108th Rifle Regiment, 4th Rifle Brigade, and 18th Panzer Division in Russia (1941–43). Here he had broken out of an encirclement without orders, apparently earning the censure of the Nazis. He was forced to give up command of the 18th Panzer in September 1943, and after three months' unemployment, he was given command of the 709th Infantry Division in France—a definite demotion. After he surrendered, Hitler denounced him as the worst kind of German general, and Schlieben was fortunate that he was out of Hitler's reach. He died in 1964.

7. Robert Sattler (1891–1978) served in the infantry in World War I and in the *Reichswehr*. He commanded the East Prussian 176th Infantry Regiment in Poland, Belgium (where it was involved in the capture of Dunkirk), and in the northern sector of the Eastern Front. He was apparently wounded or fell ill on April 19, 1942; in any case, he did not return to active duty until early 1943 and was never given another field command. Promoted to major general on October 1, 1943, he was unemployed from December 1943 until April 1944, when he was named commandant of Cherbourg. Wolf Keilig, *Die Generale des Heeres: Truppenoffiziere, Sanitätsoffiziere im Generalstrang, Waffenoffiziere im Generalstrang, Offiziere d. Kraftfahrparktruppe im Generalstrang, Ingenieur-Offiziere im Generalstrang, Wehrmachtsrichter im Generalstrang, Verwaltungsoffiziere im Generalstrang, Veterinäroffiziere im Generalstrang* (Friedberg, Germany: Podzun-Pallas-Verlag, 1983), 291.

8. Maj. Gen. Rudolf Stegmann, the commander of the 77th Infantry Division, and Lt. Gen. Heinz Hellmich, the commander of the 243rd Infantry Division, were both killed in action by fighter-bombers.

9. Harrison, *Cross-Channel Attack*, 441, 447. Also see William B. Breuer, *Hitler's Fortress Cherbourg: The Conquest of a Bastion* (New York: Stein and Day, 1984), 252.

10. Harrison, *Cross-Channel Attack*, 441–47; Ruge, "The Invasion of Normandy," 343.

11. Walter Hennecke was born in Bethelm, Hanover, in 1898. He joined the navy as a war volunteer in 1915 and was commissioned ensign the following year. He spent most of his career aboard ships of the line and commanded the obsolete

battleship *Schleswig-Holstein* (May–October 1941). He spent most of his World War II career as commander of the Ship Artillery School. He was named Naval Commander of Normandy on May 6, 1943, and was promoted to rear admiral on March 1, 1944. He was released from captivity on April 18, 1947, and died on New Year's Day, 1984. Hans H. Hildebrand and Ernst Henriot, *Deutschlands Admirale, 1849–1945: Die Militärischen Werdegänge der See-, Ingenieur-, Sanitäts-, Waffen- und Verwaltungsoffiziere im Admiralsrang*, 3 vols. (Osnabrück, Germany: Biblio, 1988–96), 2: 59–60.

12. Ruge, "The Invasion of Normandy," 343.
13. Guenther Hans von Kluge was born in Posen, Prussia (now Poznan, Poland), on October 30, 1882. He attended cadet schools, joined the Imperial Army as a *Faehnrich* (senior officer cadet) in 1900, and was commissioned in the 46th Field Artillery Regiment in 1901. A first lieutenant and battalion adjutant by 1910, he was sent to the War Academy to complete General Staff training and, after graduating, was sent to war in 1914 as adjutant of the XXI Corps. He later led a battalion on the Western Front (November 1915–April 1916) before returning to General Staff assignments with the 89th Infantry Division. He was seriously wounded at Verdun in 1918. After the war, he served on the staff of the 3rd Infantry Division in Berlin (1921–23) and the Defense Ministry (1923–26), as commander of the V Battalion of the 3rd Artillery Regiment at Sagan (1926–28), and as chief of staff of the 1st Cavalry Division at Frankfurt/Oder (1928–30). In 1930, he became commander of the 2nd Artillery Regiment and the following year became Artillery Commander III (*Artilleriefuehrer III*) and deputy commander of the 3rd Infantry Division. In February 1933, he was promoted to major general and named Inspector of Signal Troops. The next year, he was promoted to lieutenant general and became commander of the 6th Infantry Division in Muenster. He continued his rapid advancement in the fall of 1934, when he was given command of *Wehrkreis VI* (Military District VI, a corps-level headquarters), also in Muenster. He was promoted to general of artillery in 1936. He was firmly on the side of Werner von Fritsch, the commander in chief of the army, during the crisis of early 1938, but for once, he had miscalculated politically. He was on Hitler's list to be retired when the dictator replaced Fritsch with Walter von Brauchitsch. He was, however, brought out of retirement in the fall of 1938 during the Sudetenland crisis as commander of Army Group 6. In August 1939, just before the war began, Army Group 6 became the 4th Army. Kluge was not Hitler's first choice for this post, but for once, the Nazi leader allowed himself to be overruled, although it was made clear to Kluge that he was on probation. To Hitler's surprise, Kluge led his army very well in Poland, before he was severely injured in an airplane crash near the end of the campaign. Hitler nevertheless promoted him to colonel general, effective October 1, 1939. Kluge returned to the command of the 4th Army and led it in the western (French) campaign of 1940. As a result, Hitler promoted him to field marshal on July 19, 1940. The following year, Kluge led the 4th Army in Operation Barbarossa, the invasion of the Soviet Union. Here he proved a much better commander of infantry than armor, earning him the censure of both Hermann Hoth, the commander of the 3rd Panzer Army, and Heinz Guderian, the commander of the 2nd Panzer Army. When the German Army stalled before Moscow, Kluge was given command of Army Group Center on December 18, 1941, replacing Fedor von Bock. Here

he demonstrated a talent for political survival, escaping blame for disasters, and finding scapegoats. Among others, he fired Col. Gen. Adolf Strauss, the commander of the 9th Army; Col. Gen. Erich Hoepner, the commander of the 4th Panzer Army; and Gen. of Mountain Troops Ludwig Kuebler, who had succeeded him as commander of the 4th Army. Most notably, he secured the dismissal of his old enemy, Col. Gen. Heinz Guderian, the "father" of the blitzkrieg, who commanded the 2nd Panzer Army in Russia and who was relieved on December 25, 1941. (Guderian had once challenged Kluge to a duel.)

Kluge led the 4th Army until October 28, 1943, when his car skidded on some ice and he was seriously injured. He did not return to active duty for eight months. Earmarked for a command on the Western Front, he spent several days at the Fuehrer's Headquarters in Berchtesgaden, during which time he acquired an overly optimistic view of the situation in Normandy. On July 2, 1944, he succeeded Gerd von Rundstedt as OB West. When Rommel was wounded on July 17, Kluge assumed the post of commander in chief of Army Group B himself.

14. Baron Leo Geyr von Schweppenburg, called "von Geyr," was born in Potsdam on February 2, 1886, the son of an old military family. He entered the service as a *Fahnenjunker* (officer cadet) in 1904 and was commissioned in the family regiment, the 26th Light Dragoons (2nd Wuerttemberg Dragoons) in 1905. He was appointed to the War Academy in 1911 and spent most of World War I in General Staff positions, although he did briefly command a battalion in 1917. A sophisticated and urbane person, bright, articulate and well-educated, and with great social skills, Geyr represented Germany as military attaché in London, Brussels, and The Hague in the 1930s and was an excellent military diplomat. Seeing that the future belonged to the panzer branch, he befriended Heinz Guderian and transferred to the tank arm in 1937. He commanded the 3rd Panzer Division (1937–40), XXIV Panzer Corps (1940–42), XXXX Panzer Corps (1942), and LVIII Reserve Panzer Corps (1942–43) before being assigned to OB West in July 1943 as commander-designate of Panzer Group West, which was formed in October 1943. An aristocratic snob, he found it difficult to get along with Erwin Rommel, the "Desert Fox," who was the son and grandson of school teachers. Geyr's forced retirement lasted only a few weeks. On July 21, 1944, the day after the unsuccessful attempt on Hitler's life, his friend Guderian became the new chief of the General Staff of the Army. The following month, Guderian managed to get Geyr installed as his successor as inspector general of panzer troops. Captured by the Americans at the end of the war, Geyr was a prolific writer about military affairs. Until the end of his life, Geyr maintained that he was right and Rommel was wrong concerning the use of German strategic reserves in Normandy. It is difficult to follow his logic, however. Despite his strong anti-Nazi sympathies, Geyr refused to join the anti-Hitler conspirators, who approached him as early as 1938. He died at Irschenhausen on January 27, 1974.

15. Breuer, *Hitler's Fortress Cherbourg*, 256.

16. Rommel survived his wounds, but after the Gestapo discovered his involvement in the anti-Hitler plot, which ended in the failed July 20 assassination attempt, the Desert Fox was forced to commit suicide on October 14, 1944.

17. David Mason, *Breakout: The Drive to the Seine* (New York: Ballantine Books, 1969), 45.

18. William B. Breuer, *Death of a Nazi Army: The Falaise Pocket* New York: Stein and Day, 1985), 157.

19. Model was born in Genthin, Saxony-Anhalt, on January 24, 1891, the son of a music teacher of very modest means. He joined the army in 1909 as a *Fahnenjunker* in the 52nd Infantry Regiment and almost quit because of the harshness of the training. Sent to the Western Front with his regiment in World War I, he became adjutant of the I Battalion before he was severely wounded near Arras in May 1915. (He would be wounded four times during the war, one bullet passing through his body without striking a vital organ.) Promoted to first lieutenant in 1915, Model took part in the early stages of the Battle of Verdun before being sent to an abbreviated General Staff course in 1916. He served on the staff of the 5th Infantry Division, where he fought at Verdun again (late 1916) and in the Vosges and Champagne districts (1917), where the 5th was lightly engaged. Model was promoted to captain in November 1917 and served on the staff of the Guards Replacement Division during the summer offensive of 1918. He ended the war with the 36th Reserve Division in the Somme sector.

After the war, Model was engaged in putting down Communist insurrections in the Ruhr. It was here that he met Herta Huyssen, his future wife. She gave him three children: Christa, Hella, and Hansgeorg, a future West German general.

Captain Model was selected for the *Reichsheer* in 1919 and first established a reputation for himself by writing a small book about Prussian Field Marshal August Gneisenau (1760–1831). Later he became known as an expert on technical and training matters. He was physically tough, shorter than average, somewhat thickset, with a close-cropped "whitewall" haircut, and he sported a monocle, which he wore constantly.

Model was assigned to the 2nd Infantry Regiment (1920), where he commanded a company, and the 3rd Infantry Division (1925). He progressively was a General Staff tactics instructor (1928); chief of the training branch at the *Truppenamt*, the clandestine General Staff (1930); a battalion commander at Allenstein, East Prussia (1932); and chief of the technical office (late 1933). A pro-Nazi, he annoyed General Beck during the Sudetenland Crisis of 1938 by constructing duplicates of Czech fortifications and then proving that German forces could successfully attack them. He was promoted to major (1929), lieutenant colonel (1932), colonel (1934), and major general (March 1, 1938). Humorless and with few friends, he was blunt, outspoken, an uncomfortable subordinate and a very difficult superior, especially to his officers, many of whom hated him. He meddled in the affairs of his subordinate commanders to the point that he entered the army's slang. "To Model" was the equivalent of an American fruit basket turnover. To "de-Model" was to restore calm and order. He was an odd man, a complicated man, and also a very private man. He hated war stories, for example, and did not allow people to tell them in his home.

Model was chief of staff of the IV Corps during the Polish campaign and of the 16th Army during the French campaign of 1940. Promoted to lieutenant general on April 1, 1940, he led the 3rd Panzer Division with great distinction in Russia until October 1, 1941, when he was promoted to general of panzer troops and became commander of the XXXXI Panzer Corps. Then, on January

12, 1942, he was given command of the 9th Army, which was nearly surrounded at Rzhev, just west of Moscow. Model saved the 9th Army and later conducted a skillful withdrawal from the Rzhev salient. Meanwhile, he was seriously wounded on September 1, 1942, when a Soviet bullet cut his pulmonary artery while he was on a reconnaissance flight. He returned to duty in January 1943 and led the 9th Army in the Battle of Kursk, where his strategy was largely responsible for the German defeat. Nevertheless, he was given command of the 2nd Panzer Army while simultanouesly leading the 9th and withdrew in good order, inflicting heavy losses on the Red Army in the process. On March 31, 1944, he was given command of Army Group North. Later, he commanded Army Groups South (later North Ukraine) and Center, before being sent to the Western Front. Known as "the Fuehrer's Fireman," he was given only the most difficult and demanding assignments, and he usually mastered them. He was promoted to field marshal on March 1, 1944.

 20. Charles Whiting, *Ghost Front: The Ardennes before the Battle of the Bulge* (Cambridge, Mass.: Da Capo, 2002), 41–42.

CHAPTER 3: THE RETREAT ENDS

 1. Count Christoph zu Stolberg-Stolberg (1898–1968) was born in Westheim, Westphalia. He joined the army as a *Fahnenjunker* in the Guards Rifle Battalion in October 1914, fought in World War I, served in the *Reichswehr*, and was a lieutenant colonel commanding the II Battalion of the 60th Infantry Regiment in 1937. Later, he was promoted to colonel (March 1, 1940) and major general (September 1, 1943). When World War II began, he was given command of the 159th Infantry Regiment, which he led in the Norwegian campaign (1940) and on the Eastern Front (spring 1943). He briefly commanded the 160th Replacement Division in Denmark (July 1–31, 1943) and then was named commander of the 721st Eastern Troops Unit. He became commander, Eastern Troops, 7th Army, in November 1943; commander, Division Sector Dinant-Brittany (January 1944); and commander, Division Sector Antwerp-Scheldemuendung (June 4, 1944). Surprised both by the speed of the British advance into Belgium and by a partisan uprising, he was captured by partisans in Antwerp on September 4, 1944, and totally failed to defend the city or destroy the harbor. He resided in Arnsberg, Westphalia, after the war.

 2. Known as "Div. Nr. 176," it was not upgraded to the 176th Infantry Division until November 2. It did, however, have a strength of 10,637 men; see Georg Tessin, *Verbände und Truppen der deutschen Wehrmacht und Waffen SS im Zweiten Weltkrieg 1939–1945*, 17 vols. (Frankfurt am Main, Germany: Mittler, 1966–2002), 7: 186–87. It was commanded by Maj. Gen. Berthold Stumm (1892–1972), who was replaced by Col. Christian-Johannes Landau (1897–1952) on November 1. Landau, who was promoted to major general on January 1, 1945, had previously commanded the 36th and 248th Artillery Regiments on the Eastern Front.

 3. Kurt Student was a Prussian, born in Neumark, Brandenburg, on May 12, 1890. He was educated in the Royal Prussian Cadet School at Potsdam and at Gross Lichterfelde Academy, Germany's West Point. He entered the service as a *Faehnrich* in the 1st Jaeger Battalion in 1910 but then underwent pilot training in 1913 and spent World War I as an aviator. He flew reconnaissance airplanes, fighters, and bombers on the Eastern and Western Fronts, where he was severely wounded in May 1917. He also shot down six French airplanes. He was

selected for the *Reichswehr*, became a member of the secret General Staff, and spent most of the Weimar era in aviation-related assignments. Always interested in innovation, he managed to secure an appointment as commander of the 7th Air Division, which was then forming in Muenster in 1938. Here he became father of the German parachute branch. He served as commander of the 7th Air (which became a parachute unit) and inspector of parachute and airborne forces until 1940. After playing a major role in the conquest of the Netherlands, he was accidentally shot in the head by SS troops during the Battle of Rotterdam (May 1940) and was incapacitated until January 1941, when he became commander of the XI Air Corps, which he commanded in the airborne invasion of Crete. It was successful, but the paratroopers suffered such heavy losses that Hitler resolved to never again launch a major airborne operation, and he never did. Student, meanwhile, was promoted to major general (April 1, 1938), lieutenant general (January 1, 1940), general of fliers (later general of paratroopers) (May 29, 1940), and colonel general (July 13, 1944), and he commanded the 1st Parachute Army (1943–44) and Army Group H (1944–45) on the Western Front. He was named commander in chief of Army Group Vistula on April 29, 1945, but because the front had collapsed, he never actually took command. His only child was a fighter pilot who was killed in action in 1944. He surrendered to the British in Schleswig-Holstein at the war and was tried for war crimes in Crete. He was convicted and sentenced to five years' imprisonment, but the sentence was never confirmed. His happy marriage ended when his wife died, and his son and only child, a fighter pilot, was killed in action in 1944. Without the family he so dearly loved, the airborne pioneer retired at Lemgo (Lippe District), North Rhine-Westphalia, and died a lonely old man on July 1, 1978, at the age of eighty-eight.

4. Roland Friesler was born in Celle on October 30, 1893. He served in the Imperial Army during World War I and was captured on the Russian Front. When he returned to Germany, he promptly joined the Communist Party but became disillusioned with it. In 1925, he joined the Nazi Party. Meanwhile, he attended law school and became a prosecuting attorney in Kassel. When Hitler came to power in 1933, Friesler became chief personnel officer of the ministry of justice. The next year, he became state secretary of the Prussian ministry of justice; later, he held the same office in the Reich ministry of justice. He became president of the infamous People's Court in August 1942.

5. Charles Whiting, *Siegfried: The Nazis' Last Stand* (New York: Stein and Day, 1982), 14.

6. Hans Speidel was born in Metzingen, Wuerttemberg, on October 28, 1897. He joined the army as an infantry officer-cadet in 123rd Grenadier Regiment in late 1914. He fought on the Western Front in World War I, served in the *Reichsheer*, and was Ia of the 33rd Infantry Division (1937–39), IX Corps (1939–40), and Army Group B (1940); and chief of staff to the Military Governor of France (1940–42), of the V Corps (1942–43), to the German General with the Italian 8th Army (1943), of the 8th Army (1943–44); and of Army Group B (April 15–September 9, 1944). A lieutenant colonel when World War II began, he was promoted to colonel (1941), major general (January 1, 1943), and lieutenant general (January 1, 1944). During Rommel's absence on D-Day, Speidel performed poorly. He was nevertheless retained as chief of staff by Rommel, Kluge, and Model. Despite Field Marshal Model's efforts to protect

him, Speidel was arrested on suspicion of being involved in the anti-Hitler conspiracy, but the Court of Honor did not expel him from the army; he therefore could not be executed, but he did spend the rest of the war in prison. In 1955, he became a lieutenant general (the equivalent of a three-star general in the U.S. Army under the new rank structure) in the West German Army and held high positions in NATO. Speidel retired on March 31, 1964, and died at Bad Honnef on November 28, 1984.

Hans Krebs (1898–1945) was born in Helmstedt, Lower Saxony. He joined the army as a war volunteer in August 1914 and spent most of his World War I service with the 78th Infantry Regiment, fighting in France (1914), Russia (1915), France again (1915–16), Russia again (1916), and France (1917–18), where he saw action at Picardy and on the Somme. Meanwhile, Krebs was promoted to *Fahnenjunker* in December 1914, attended a ninety-day officer training course at Doeberitz in the winter of 1914–15, and was commissioned in June 1915. He rejoined the 78th in March 1915 but was severely wounded on June 2. He received his commission in the hospital. Later, he served as a machine-gun company commander and an infantry company commander and spent the last thirteen months of the war as the regimental adjutant. Krebs was selected for the *Reichsheer* and served in a variety of infantry, staff, and artillery assignments between 1919 and 1930. He began his General Staff training in 1930 and also studied Russian, a language in which he was fluent. He served in the foreign armies section of the Troop Office and was assistant to the military attaché in Moscow from 1933 to 1934.

After spending a year as a company commander, Krebs was Ia of the 24th Infantry Division (1935–37), chief of operations of the training department of the High Command of the Army (OKH) (1937–38), and chief of OKH's training department (1938–late 1939). He was named chief of staff of the VII Corps (December 1939–1940) before going to Moscow as German military attaché (1940–41). After Hitler invaded Russia, Krebs was named chief of staff of the 9th Army on January 14, 1942. This began a long association with the 9th's commander, Walter Model. Krebs became chief of staff of Army Group Center on March 1, 1943, and chief of staff of Army Group B on September 5, 1944. He was named chief of operations of OKH on February 17, 1945, but was wounded by a U.S. Air Force bombing attack on Zossen on March 15. He nevertheless accepted an appointment as acting chief of the General Staff of the Army on April 1. At 9:30 P.M. on May 1, 1945, with the Red Army in control of most of Berlin, Hans Krebs shot himself in the head in the Fuehrer Bunker. Krebs was promoted to first lieutenant (1925), captain (1931), major (1936), lieutenant colonel (1939), colonel (1940), major general (February 1, 1942), lieutenant general (April 1, 1943), and general of infantry (August 1, 1944).

7. Siegfried Westphal (1902–1982) was born at Leipzig. He entered the service as a sixteen-year-old cavalry *Fahnenjunker* the day before World War I ended. Commissioned in the 11th Cavalry Regiment in 1922, he spent most of his pre–World War II career in that branch. A General Staff officer, he spent virtually the entire war in General Staff appointments, serving as Ia of the 58th Infantry Division (1939–40), XXVII Corps (1940), and Panzer Group Afrika (later Panzer Army Afrika). Severely wounded on May 31, 1942, he did not return to duty until the end of August. He became chief of staff of Rommel's Panzer Army Afrika in October and, from December 1 to 29, 1942, commanded the 164th Light Afrika

Division. Westphal reported himself sick at the end of the year. After he returned to duty in 1943, he was named chief of staff of OB South (later Southwest), the German command in Italy. He collapsed from stress, overwork, and exhaustion during the Battle of Rome on June 5, 1944. After he recovered, he was named chief of staff of OB West on September 9, 1944, a post he held until the end of the war. An excellent General Staff officer, he was promoted rapidly in World War II, from major at the beginning to lieutenant colonel (1941), colonel (1942), major general (1943), lieutenant general (1944), and general of cavalry (1945). He lived in Dortmund and Celle after the war.

Bodo Zimmermann (1886–1963) was born in Metz (then part of Germany) and was educated in the cadet school system. He entered the Imperial Army as a *Faehnrich* in the 145th Infantry Regiment in 1906. He became a member of the General Staff, fought in World War I, and was discharged as a major in 1920. Unlike many of his peers, Zimmermann had no desire to resume his military career during Hitler's peacetime expansion and in fact did not return to the service until December 1939 when, as a lieutenant colonel, he was appointed to the operations staff of the 1st Army. He became Ia of Army Group D (later OB West) in October 1940 and held this post for the rest of the war, serving under Erwin von Witzleben, Gerd von Rundstedt, Guenther von Kluge, Walter Model, Rundstedt again, and Field Marshal Albert Kesselring. He was promoted to colonel (December 1, 1942), major general (December 1, 1944), and lieutenant general (May 1, 1945). He lived in Bonn after the war.

8. This estimate was wrong. Eisenhower actually had only forty-nine divisions on the European mainland at this time.

9. Chester Wilmot, *The Struggle for Europe* (New York: Harper, 1952), 481. Figures are for PzKw IVs, Panthers, Tigers, and 75-millimeter StuG assault guns. They do not include obsolete tanks and light tanks of foreign manufacture.

10. Tony Foster, *Meeting of Generals* (Toronto: Lorevan Publishing, 1986), 397.

11. Martin Blumenson, *Breakout and Pursuit* (Washington, DC: Office of the Chief of Military History, Department of the Army, 1961), 695.

12. Hans von Salmuth was born in Metz, then a German garrison town, in 1888. He entered the service as an officer-cadet in 1907 and was commissioned in the 3rd Grenadier Guards Regiment in 1909. During World War I, he served as a battalion executive officer and then as a General Staff officer. He served during the *Reichsheer* era and was chief of staff of Army Group North (later B) during the invasions of Poland and France. He was promoted to general of infantry in 1940 and commanded XXX Corps (1941), 17th Army (1942), 4th Army (1942), 2nd Army (1943–43), 4th Army again (1943), and 15th Army (1943–44). Promoted to colonel general on January 1, 1943, he was relieved of his command on August 25, 1944, when it was determined that he had been approached by the conspirators of July 20 and had not reported them. He was tried as a war criminal by the U.S. Military Tribunal at Nuremberg and was sentenced to twenty years' imprisonment in 1948 for assisting SS murder squads (*Einsatzgruppen*) in murdering Jews; however, he secured an early release in 1953. Salmuth retired to Wiesbaden and died in Heidelburg during the night of December 31, 1961–January 1, 1962.

Gustav-Adolf von Zangen was born in Darmstadt in 1892. He entered the Imperial Army as an officer-cadet in 1910 and was commissioned in the infantry. After World War I, he was discharged from the army, so he joined the police. Zangen reentered the army as a lieutenant colonel in 1935 and rose rapidly, commanding the 88th Infantry Regiment (1938–41), 17th Infantry Division (1941–43), LXXXIV Corps (1943), LXXXVII Corps (1943), Army Detachment von Zangen in northern Italy (1943–43), and 15th Army on the Western Front. Zangen was promoted to colonel (1938), major general (1942), lieutenant general (January 1, 1943), and general of infantry (June 1, 1943). A talented commander, he was nevertheless forced to surrender the 15th Army to the Americans at the end of the Battle of the Ruhr Pocket on April 18, 1945. He lived in Hanau/Main after the war and died there in 1964.

13. Ruediger von Heyking was born in Rastenburg, East Prussia (now Ketzyrn, Poland), in 1894 and entered the service as a *Fahnenjunker* in March 1914. Commissioned later that year, he served for two years as a platoon leader and company commander in the 85th Infantry Regiment, fighting in Belgium and France, including the Battles of the Marne and Somme. From September 1917 to January 1918, he trained as an aerial observer. On January 31, after only a few days back at the front, he was wounded, shot down, and captured by the French. Released in the summer of 1920, he was selected for the *Reichsheer* and spent the years from 1920 to 1929 in the 4th Motor Transport Battalion. He officially retired in 1929 but actually underwent secret flight training. He returned to the 4th Motor from 1931 to 1934 as a company commander and then transferred to the *Luftwaffe* as a flight instructor. From 1938 to 1940, he commanded the 21st Flight Training Wing and then the 2nd Transport Wing (1940–41) and the Flight Training Division (1941). He led the 1st Air Landing Wing of the XI Air Corps on the Eastern Front from 1941 to late 1942. Heyking assumed command of the 6th Luftwaffe Field Division in central Russia (November 1942), was on the staff of the XI Air Corps (November 1943), and commanded the 6th Parachute Division from May 1, 1944, the day it was formed in Amiens, France. General Heyking was captured by the British on September 4, 1944. He was released from the POW camps in June 1947 and moved to Bad Godesburg in the Rhineland, where he died on February 18, 1956. Heyking was promoted to first lieutenant (1924), captain (1929), major (1934), lieutenant colonel (1936), colonel (1939), major general (November 1, 1941), and lieutenant general (July 1, 1943).

14. Walter Wadehn (1886–1949) was born in Wilhelmshaven and entered the army as a war volunteer with a supply unit in 1914. In 1915, he was promoted four times: to corporal, sergeant, *Faehnrich*, and second lieutenant. He began training as an aerial observer in late 1916 and spent the last two years of the war as an aerial observer. He was discharged as an honorary first lieutenant in 1920. Fourteen years later, he entered the *Luftwaffe* as a captain. From 1934 to 1939, Wadehn was a bomber and instrument flight instructor. On September 13, 1939, he became commander of the 3rd Group of 77th Bomber Wing (KG 77). After the Polish campaign, he was chief of a *Luftwaffe* officer selection staff (late 1939 to March 1942) and then served as commander of the 72nd Flight Training Wing. Next, Wadehn commanded three divisions: the 10th Luftwaffe Field Division (September 25, 1942), 3rd Parachute Division (September 1, 1943), and 8th Parachute Division (January 6, 1945). Wadehn was promoted to major (1937), lieutenant colonel (1941), colonel (September 1, 1942), and major general (September 1, 1943). He surrendered to the British on May 5, 1945. Released from the POW camps in February 1948, he settled in Hanover.

Joachim von Tresckow (1894–1958) was born in Danzig, West Prussia (now Gdansk, Poland). He attended cadet schools and joined the army as a *Faehnrich* in 1912. He was commissioned in the 73rd Fusilier Regiment in 1915 and fought on both the Eastern and Western Fronts. Selected for the Reichsheer, he was named commander of the III Battalion of the 58th Infantry Regiment in 1938 and led it in the Saar. He assumed command of the regiment itself in December 1939 and directed it in the French campaign and on the central sector of the Russian Front, including the Battle of Moscow and the winter battles of 1941–42. On March 3, 1942, he assumed command of the 328th Infantry Division on Russian Front. The division was sent back to the west in the fall and took part in the occupation of Vichy France in November 1942. It was posted to Marseilles, where it was rebuilt, and it returned to Russia in 1943, where it fought in the Battles of Kursk and Kharkov, among others. The division was downgraded on November 2, 1943, and its remnants were attached to the 306th Infantry Division. Tresckow, meanwhile, returned to Germany as inspector of Italian units in the Reich. On February 1, 1944, he was named commander of the 18th Luftwaffe Field Division, which he led until October. In 1945, he briefly served as acting commander of the LIX Corps on the Eastern Front. Tresckow was promoted to lieutenant colonel (1937), colonel (1940), major general (June 1, 1942), and lieutenant general (March 1, 1943). He lived in Bueckeburg after the war.

15. Ernst-Guenther Kraetschmer, *Die Ritterkreuztraeger der Waffen-SS* (Preussisch Oldendorf, Germany: KW Schutz, 1982), 1 ff.

16. Kurt Meyer, *Grenadiers: The Story of Waffen SS General Kurt "Panzer" Meyer* (Mechanicsburg, PA: Stackpole Books, 2005), 303–8.

17. Blumenson, *Breakout and Pursuit*, 694.

18. Albert Seaton, *The German Army, 1933–45* (New York: New American Library, 1985), 238.

19. Charles B. MacDonald, *The Mighty Endeavor: American Armed Forces in the European Theater in World War II* (New York: Oxford University Press, 1969), 359.

20. Lanham (1902–1978) later became a major general and commanded the 1st Infantry Division (1953–54).

21. Whiting, *Ghost Front*, p. 42.

22. Ibid., 48–49.

23. MacDonald, *The Siegfried Line Campaign* (Washington, DC: Office of the Chief of Military History, Department of the Army, 1963), 51.

24. Whiting, *Ghost Front*, 57–58.

25. Dr. Jur. Franz Beyer was born in Bautzen in eastern Saxony in 1892 and joined the navy as a *Seekadett* in 1911. He served in the navy in World War I, fought aboard the *Westphalia* and in Finland, and was discharged as a lieutenant in 1919. He then received a fine legal education and joined the police. He entered the army in 1935 with the relatively high rank of lieutenant colonel. He was made a battalion commander on April 1, 1935—the day he joined the army—despite the fact that his only previous military experience had been in the navy. Beyer nevertheless proved to be a very capable infantry leader. He commanded the II Battalion of the 66th Infantry Regiment (1935–39), 131st Infantry Regiment (1939–late 1941), and the 331st Infantry Division (December 1941–February 1943), and fought in Poland, France, and the Russian Front. He led the 44th Infantry Division *Hoch und Deutschmeister* in Italy

(March–late December 1943). He was then assigned to Army Group A as a supplementary officer, used to serve as an acting commander to fill temporary vacancies. In this capacity, between February and August 1944, he served as acting commander of the XVII, LVII Panzer, V, and XXXXIX Mountain Corps, all on the Eastern Front. Transferred to the Western Front, he assumed command of the LXXX Corps on August 7, 1944—his fifth corps in six months. This time, however, it was a permanent appointment, and he led the LXXX until the end of the war. He surrendered on May 8, 1945, and was discharged from the POW camps in 1947. He settled in Bad Wiessee, a spa town on Lake Tegernsee in Upper Bavaria, where he died in 1968.

26. MacDonald, *Siegfried Line Campaign*, 64–65.
27. Siegfried Westphal, *The German Army in the West* (London: Cassell, 1951), 174.
28. MacDonald, *Siegfried Line Campaign*, 64–65.
29. Whiting, *Ghost Front*, 67–68.
30. Fromm, who commanded the Replacement Army from 1939 to 1944, knew about the plot to assassinate Hitler but did nothing to stop it. After it failed, however, he had five witnesses executed, including Col. Count von Stauffenberg, his own chief of staff, and Ludwig Beck, the former chief of the General Staff. Fromm was arrested on July 21, 1944. Since the Nazis did not have enough witnesses to convict Fromm of treason, Hitler had him shot for cowardice on March 19, 1945.
31. Tessin, *Verbände und Truppen*, 1: 89–93.
32. Alfred D. Chandler, Jr., ed., *The Papers of Dwight D. Eisenhower*, vol. 4, *The War Years* (Baltimore: Johns Hopkins Press, 1970), 2,121.
33. Gerhard von Schwerin was born in Hanover on June 23, 1899. He was educated in various cadet schools and became a *Faehnrich* in the 2nd Guards Regiment in 1914. He fought on the Western and Eastern Fronts in World War I. He was discharged as a lieutenant in 1920. He re-entered the service in 1922 as a lieutenant in the East Prussian 1st Infantry Regiment and was on the staff of OKH when the next world war began. Count von Schwerin commanded the I Battalion of the elite Grossdeutschland Motorized Infantry Regiment, the 86th Rifle Regiment, the Grossdeutschland Regiment itself, and the 200th Special Purposes Regiment (1939–41) before taking charge of the 76th Infantry Regiment (1941–42) on the Eastern Front. After briefly serving as acting commander of the 254th Infantry Division (April–May 1942), he was acting commander of the 8th Jaeger Division (summer 1942) and commander of the 16th Panzer Grenadier Division (November 13, 1942–August 23, 1944), which was upgraded to the 116th Panzer Division in the spring of 1944. Sacked during the Battle of Aachen, his friends on the General Staff saved his career and secured for him the command of the 90th Panzer Grenadier Division in Italy (December 1, 1944). From April 1 to 25, 1945, Schwerin commanded the LXXVI Panzer Corps in Italy and surrendered it to the Allies. He was promoted to major general (October 1, 1942), lieutenant general (June 1, 1943), and general of panzer troops (April 1, 1945). He lived in Bonn for a time but died in Rottach-Egern, Upper Bavaria, in 1980 at the age of eighty-one.
34. Rudolf Schmeer was an early Nazi. He was deputy *gauleiter* of Cologne-Aachen (1931–32) and a lieutenant general in the Brownshirts (*SA Gruppenfuehrer*). After Hitler took power, he became a *kreisleiter* in Aachen. His brother Eduard was an SS general.

35. Gerhard Mueller, a native of Breslau, was born in 1896. He entered the service as a *Fahnenjunker* in 1915, was commissioned in the 154th Infantry Regiment in 1916, and fought on the Western Front. Like many officers not selected for the *Reichsheer*, he joined the police in 1920 and returned to the army as a captain in 1935. He commanded the 33rd Anti-Tank Battalion (1938–41) and the I Battalion of the 33rd Panzer Regiment, which he led into Russia on June 22, 1941. Seven days later, he lost an arm in battle. He returned to active duty on February 1, 1942, as commander of the 5th Panzer Regiment, which he led with some distinction in the Gazala Line–Tobruk battles in North Africa. Transferred back to Berlin, Mueller was a branch chief at OKH before assuming temporary command of the 116th Panzer Division (August 23, 1944). The staff, however, revolted against him, and he was temporarily replaced by Col. Heinrich Voigtsberger. He was given permanent command of the 9th Panzer Division on September 1, 1944. (This division, however, had suffered so many casualties in the Normandy/Falaise battles that it had been temporarily merged with the 2nd Panzer Division for tactical purposes.) His performance as a divisional commander left much to be desired, however, and General Brandenburger, the commander of the 7th Army, relieved him of his command on September 18. Although he had just been promoted to major general on September 1, 1944, he held no further important assignments. At the end of the war, he was deputy commandant of Pilsen. He died in Landau in 1977.

36. Paul Mahlmann (1892–1963) was born in Gispersieben and, after attending various cadet schools, entered the service as a second lieutenant in the 98th Infantry Regiment in 1914. He fought on the Western Front in World War I, served in the *Reichsheer*, and assumed command of the 181st Infantry Regiment upon mobilization in August 1939. He led this regiment in the Saar (1939) and France (1940) and on the central sector of the Russian Front (1941–42). He was acting commander of the 137th Infantry Division from February to May 1942 (also in central Russia), and after a brief tour of staff duty in Germany, he assumed command of the 147th Reserve Division (December 25, 1942–July 31, 1943). Sent back to the Eastern Front, he commanded the 39th Infantry Division in the retreat to the Dniepr (1943) before assuming command of the 353rd on November 30, 1943, as it was in the process of forming in Brittany. He led it until February 15, 1945, fighting in Normandy, in the Falaise breakout, and in the Siegfried Line battles, and distinguishing himself in the Battle of the Huertgen Forest. He was relieved of his command in February 1945 for reasons not disclosed by the available records. His division was destroyed in the Ruhr Pocket two months later. He was promoted to colonel (1939), major general (January 1, 1943), and lieutenant general (June 1, 1944).

37. The 526th Replacement Division had been formed on December 20, 1941, from *Landesschuetzen* (older-age men) units in the Cologne-Aachen area. In September 1944, it had 12,711 men, organized into three grenadier regiments. It had only one artillery battalion (instead of the usual regiment) and lacked signal equipment. Its commander, Lt. Gen. Kurt Schmidt, would be killed in Holland on March 3, 1945.

38. Gerhard Engel was born in Guben, Brandenburg, in 1906. (The eastern half of Guben became Gibin, Poland, after the war.) He joined the *Reichsheer* as a *Fahnenjunker* in 1925 and was commissioned second lieutenant in the Wuerttemberger 5th Infantry Regiment in 1930. He was promoted to captain in 1937 and

was appointed Hitler's adjutant on March 10, 1938, after Hitler fired Col. Friedrich Hossbach for disobeying his orders during the Fritsch crisis. Engel held his post until the fall of 1943. Then he became so inspired by one of Hitler's speeches that he volunteered for frontline duty. He was given command of the 27th Infantry Regiment of the 12th Infantry Division on October 1, 1943. This division was largely destroyed in the Battle of Minsk-Vitebsk on the Eastern Front in the summer of 1944. The divisional commander, Lieutenant General Bamler, was captured on June 27, and Engel, who had been promoted to full colonel on May 1, succeeded him.

Engel managed to escape the destruction of Army Group Center, and when the 12th Infantry Division was rebuilt as a *Volksgrenadier* unit, he retained command. The rebuilt division was sent to the Western Front, where Engel distinguished himself in the Battle of Aachen. He would be absent twice: in November 1944 and January–February 1945, during which time he was recovering from wounds. He was promoted to major general on November 1, 1944, and was named commander of the newly formed Division Ulrich von Hutten on April 12, 1945. He surrendered this command to the Americans at the end of the war. Released from the POW camps in December 1947, he resided in Dusseldorf and Soecking after the war. He died in 1976.

39. Heinrich Voigtsberger was born in Gera, Thuringia (forty miles south of Leipzig), on February 10, 1903. He entered the *Reichsheer* as a *Fahnenjunker* in 1922, but because of a lack of officer positions available in the "Treaty Army," he was not commissioned until 1926. He nevertheless advanced rapidly and, by 1935, was a captain commanding a company in the 2nd Machine Gun Battalion. In December 1939, he was promoted to commander of this battalion. By now a major, he would be advanced to lieutenant colonel (1942) and colonel (August 1, 1943). Meanwhile, he assumed command of the 60th Panzer Grenadier Regiment of the Greyhound Division on May 14, 1942, and served on the southern sector of the Russian Front.

40. After proving more loyal to General Schwerin than to orders from Berlin, Colonel Voigtsberger could no longer remain in the 116th Panzer Division, so he was sent to a division commanders' course in October. After a leave, he assumed command of the 309th Infantry Division (later Infantry Division Berlin) on the Eastern Front. He was promoted to major general on April 1, 1945. His division was destroyed in the Halbe Pocket on or about April 29, 1945. Voigtsberger, however, seems to have been one of the few to escape. He settled in Wittlich, Rhineland/Westphalia, after the war and died in Munich on March 17, 1959.

41. Siegfried von Waldenburg was born in Gross Leipe, near Breslau, Silesia, in 1898. Also a professional soldier, he entered the army in 1916 and was commissioned second lieutenant in the 1st Guards Grenadier Regiment in August 1917. He fought on the Eastern and Western Fronts, was selected for the *Reichsheer*, and was a major and chief of operations of the 6th Infantry Division when World War II broke out. After serving in the Saar and French campaigns, he was chief of staff of the XIII Corps (1940–41) and fought on the Russian Front before being sent to Italy as deputy military attaché and chief of staff to the German General in the Headquarters of the High Command of the Italian Armed Forces (1941–44). He commanded the 26th Panzer Grenadier Regi-

ment in southern Russia and the Ukraine (April–September 1944) before being given command of the battered 116th Panzer Division on September 14, 1944. He was promoted to major general on December 1, 1944. General Waldenburg led the 116th Panzer for the rest of the war and died in Hanover in 1973.

42. Baron Harald von Elverfeldt was born in Hildesheim, Lower Saxony, in 1900. After being educated in cadet schools, he joined the 1st Guards Regiment of Foot as a *Faehnrich* in the spring of 1918. He fought on the Western Front in World War I, served in the *Reichsheer*, and was Ia (chief of operations) of the 3rd Light (later 8th Panzer) Division during the Polish campaign. Later, he served as Ia of the XV Panzer Corps (1940–1941) and as chief of staff of the LVI Panzer Corps (1941–43), 9th Army (1943), and 17th Army (1943). After distinguishing himself on the Russian Front for two and a half years, he was given command of the 9th Panzer Division on September 16, 1944. A captain at the beginning of 1937, he was promoted to major general on September 1, 1944. He proved to be as good a commander as he was a General Staff officer. Harald von Elverfeldt was killed during the Battle of Cologne on March 6, 1945. He was so highly thought of at Fuehrer Headquarters that a posthumous promotion to lieutenant general followed.

43. Friedrich Koechling was born in Ahaus (on the Dutch border in North Rhine–Westphalia) on June 22, 1893. He joined the army as a *Fahnenjunker* in the 159th Infantry Regiment in 1912 and was commissioned the following year. He served with the 159th virtually throughout World War I, fighting in Belgium, on the Aisne, and at Verdun, Champagne, and Laon, among other battles, during which he was wounded three times. In the process, he was a battalion adjutant, company commander, regimental adjutant, and, briefly, a battalion commander. He was promoted to first lieutenant in 1916. Koechling served in the *Freikorps* in 1919 and joined the *Reichsheer* later that year. He spent the entire 1919–1935 period in the 16th Infantry Regiment, which headquartered at Oldenburg, not far from his home town. He commanded a battalion in the 16th (1934–35) before being transferred to Herford, Westphalia, where he commanded the III Battalion of the 58th Infantry Regiment (1935–38). When Germany mobilized on August 26, 1939, Koechling was given command of the 287th Infantry Regiment, which he led on the Upper Rhine, in the invasion of France, and in the northern sector of the Russian Front (1939–1942). On April 10, he assumed command of the 254th Infantry Division, which was defending a sector of the line south of Leningrad. He apparently fell ill (there is no record of his being wounded) and was placed in Fuehrer Reserve on September 5, 1942. Although he received an unusually rapid promotion to lieutenant general, he was not re-employed until October 15, 1943, when he assumed command of the XXXXII Corps in the Crimea. Later, he took command of four other corps: the XXXXIV (December 1, 1943), XXXXIX Mountain (February 15, 1944), X (June 25, 1944), and LXXXI (September 21, 1944). In the process, he fought in the Dnieper withdrawal, in the Nikopol Bridgehead, in the retreat across Latvia, and in the first battles of the Courland Pocket. He led the LXXXI Corps at Aachen, in the Siegfried Line, and in the Ruhr Pocket. He surrendered on April 13, 1945, and was released from captivity in 1947. Friedrich Koechling was promoted to captain (1924), major (1933), lieutenant

colonel (1936), colonel (1939), major general (June 1, 1942), lieutenant general (January 1, 1943), and general of infantry (February 1, 1944). He died in Coesfeld, Muensterland, not far from where he was born, on June 6, 1970.

44. Seyss-Inquart, a prominent Nazi attorney, played a major role in the Nazi annexation of Austria in 1938. He was *Reichkommissar* of the Netherlands from May 1940 until the end of the war. A strong anti-Semite, Seyss-Inquart did all he could to exterminate the Dutch Jewry. He was hanged at Nuremberg as a major war criminal on October 16, 1946. He was fifty-four years old. Shortly before his suicide, Adolf Hitler appointed Seyss-Inquart foreign minister in the new Doenitz government.

Anton Mussett, the brutal leader of the Dutch Nazi Party, was also convicted of war crimes in 1946. He was executed by a Dutch firing squad on May 7 of that year.

45. Cornelius Ryan, *A Bridge Too Far* (New York: Simon and Schuster, 1974), 23.
46. Ibid., 23n.
47. Milton Shulman, *Defeat in the West* (New York: Dutton, 1948), 278.
48. Kurt Chill (1895–1976) was born in Thorn, West Prussia (now Torun, Poland), and enlisted in the army in 1913. He was promoted to corporal that same year and to sergeant in 1914. Commissioned in the 61st Infantry Regiment in 1915, he fought in East Prussia, Russia, and France as a platoon leader, company commander, and battalion adjutant. He attended the Aerial Observation School at Thorn in 1917 and served in aviation units until the end of the war. He joined the police service in 1919 and rose to the rank of major of police. He re-entered the army as a major in 1935, commanded a company in the 65th Infantry Regiment (1935–36), and then spent a year on the staff of the 30th Infantry Division at Luebeck before assuming command of the I Battalion of the 1st Infantry Regiment at Koenigsberg (1937–40), which he led in Poland. In Fuehrer Reserve from February to late December 1940, he commanded the East Prussian 45th Infantry Regiment in the northern sector of the Eastern Front (1941–September 1942). He then commanded the 122th Infantry Division (1942–44) in northern Russia, the 85th Infantry Division on the Western Front (February 10–December 7, 1944), and the LV Corps in East Prussia (February 6–May 12, 1945) at the end of the war. He neverthess seems to have managed to surrender to the western Allies, possibly escaping on the last boat. Released from prison in 1947, he settled in Groemitz, Holstein (on Luebeck Bay), where he died on July 5, 1976.

Kurt Chill was promoted to lieutenant colonel (1938), colonel (March 1, 1941), major general (December 1, 1942), and lieutenant general (June 1, 1943).

49. Parachute Training Division Erdmann became the 7th Parachute Division on September 10, 1944.
50. B. H. Liddell Hart, *History of the Second World War* (New York: Putnam, 1970), 565.
51. Brian Horrocks, *A Full Life* (London: L. Cooper, 1974).
52. Felix Schwalbe (1892–1974) was born at Kleinpriessligk, Saxony, near Leipzig. He entered the service as a volunteer in 1912 and was commissioned second lieutenant in the 102nd Infantry Regiment in late 1914. Meanwhile, he fought in Belgium, at the Battle of the Marne, and in France. Selected for the *Reich-*

swehr, he assumed command of the 461st Infantry Regiment when Germany mobilized in August 1939. He led the regiment in Poland (1939) and France (1940) and was then given command of the 109th Infantry Regiment in Belgium in early 1941. He fought on the central sector of the Russian Front (1941–42). Apparently, his health gave way during the Russian winter of 1941–42 because he spent the period from February to September 1942 in Fuehrer Reserve. In any case, he assumed command of the 344th Infantry Division at Bordeaux, France, on September 27 and led it until August 1944, fighting in Normandy and in the retreat across France (to Aachen) in the process. He was given command of the 719th Infantry Division in Antwerp in September and assumed command of the LXXXVIII Corps in the Netherlands on December 22, 1944. He led it until the end of the war. Schwalbe retired to Bielefeld in eastern Westphalia. He was promoted to lieutenant colonel (1937), colonel (1940), major general (October 1, 1942), lieutenant general (October 1, 1943), and general of infantry (March 1, 1945).

53. Ryan, *Bridge Too Far,* 115. Walter Poppe (1892–1968) was born in Kassel, was educated in cadet schools, and joined the army as a second lieutenant in the infantry in 1914. He fought in World War I, served in the *Reichswehr,* and was a colonel commanding the 465th Infantry Regiment when World War II began. He was promoted to major general (April 1, 1942) and lieutenant general (January 1, 1943). Meanwhile, he led the 465th Infantry Regiment of the Saxon-Sudeten 255th Infantry Division (August 26, 1939–January 12, 1942) in the conquests of the Low Countries, on occupation duty in France and Poland, and in the central sector of the Eastern Front. Poppe then led the division itself (January 12, 1942–October 1943) until it had suffered such heavy casualties that it had to be downgraded and absorbed by another division. Poppe, meanwhile, briefly commanded the 217th Infantry Division on the Eastern Front (October–November 1943) and then the 364th (later 77th) Infantry Division in Poland and France (November 1943–April 1944). He assumed command of the 59th Infantry Division when it was formed in the summer of 1944 and led it until February 1945, serving on the Western Front. He resided in Herford, Westphalia, after the end of the war.

54. Albert Seaton, *The Fall of Fortress Europe, 1943–1945* (New York: Holmes and Meier Publishers, 1981), 156.

CHAPTER 4: ARNHEM

1. Wilhelm Bittrich (1894–1979) was born in Wernigerode am Harz, the son of a German trade representative. He joined the 19th Reserve Jaeger Battalion when World War I broke out but transferred to the air service in the fall of 1914. Here he was wounded twice and ended the conflict as a second lieutenant and a fighter pilot. He was a member of the *Freikorps von Huelsen* in the early 1920s and fought against the Poles in the eastern marshlands. He joined the *Reichsheer* as a pilot in 1923 and trained German aviators in Russia in the 1920s. Later, he was a civilian employee of the *Luftwaffe,* working as an instructor pilot, and was involved in training aviators at the secret German airbase in Russia. He joined the Nazi Party in 1932 and entered the SS in July 1933. A member of the SS-VT (*SS-Verfügungstruppe*), the forerunner of the Waffen-SS, Bittrich was soon given command of a battalion (the I Battalion of the SS "Ger-

mania" Regiment) because of his solid and varied military background, and was an SS colonel commanding the SS-Regiment Deutschland in late 1940. He took charge of the 2nd SS Panzer Division after Paul Hausser was wounded in late 1941 but had to give it up after he fell ill in early January 1942. In May 1942, Bittrich assumed command of the 8th SS Cavalry Division "Florian Geyer," which he led against partisans in the Balkans until December. On February 15, 1943, he assumed command of the 9th SS Panzer Division "Hohenstaufen," which was just being formed. Bittrich assumed command of the II SS Panzer Corps when Hausser was promoted to the command of the 7th Army. Promoted to *SS-Obergruppenführer und General der Waffen-SS* on August 1, 1944, he made a number of unguarded, derogatory remarks about Himmler and the Nazi leadership. Also, in direct defiance of SS policy, he allowed church services to be held in his command. Himmler ordered him recalled to Berlin, but this move was blocked by Field Marshal Model, who protected him.

A brave and talented commander who was highly respected by his men, Bittrich led the II SS in the Battles of Arnhem and the Bulge (1944) and in Hungary (1945). He surrendered to the Americans, who handed him over to the French. Bittrich was kept in jail until 1954, when he was finally released. He held the Knight's Cross with Oak Leaves and Swords (which was awarded on May 6, 1945, a week after Hitler's suicide and several days after Himmler had been stripped of his posts). He was then tried for war crimes committed in Bordeaux but was acquitted. He died in Wolfratshausen, Upper Bavaria, on April 19, 1979. See Jost W. Schneider, *Verleihung Genehmigt!*, Winder McConnell, ed. and trans. (San Jose, CA: R. James Bender Publishing, 1977), 35–37; Kraetschmer, *Die Ritterkreuztraeger der Waffen-SS*, 220–23; and Nikolaus von Preradovich, *Die Generale der Waffen-SS* (Berg am See, Germany: Vowinckel-Verlag, 1985), 21–22.

2. Ryan, *Bridge Too Far*, 46.
3. James M. Gavin, *Airborne Warfare* (Washington, DC: Infantry Journal Press, 1947), 81.
4. Ryan, *Bridge Too Far*, 329.
5. The affable Harmel had been a member of the "Youth Group" of the notorious Rossbach *Freikorps* before he joined the *Reichsheer* in 1926. He joined the SS as a sergeant in the "Germania" *Standarte* in 1935 and succeeded Bittrich as commander of the "Deutschland" SS Motorized Regiment during the Battle of Moscow in December 1941.
6. Scarfaced Walter Harzer was only an acting divisional commander. He had joined the *Reichsheer* in 1931 at age nineteen. After spending three years in the 13th Infantry Regiment, he joined the *SS-Verfügungstruppe* (the forerunner of the *Waffen-SS*) in 1934 and attended the *Junkerschule* (officer training school) at Bad Toelz in 1935 and 1936. He began his troop service as a platoon leader in the "Deutschland" SS Regiment in 1938 and was a company commander in the Polish campaign. After a tour of duty as a tactics instructor at the *Junkerschule* in Brunswick, he assumed command of the II Battalion of the 4th SS Infantry Regiment. He later served a General Staff apprenticeship under Col. Walter Wenck, the chief of staff of the LVII Panzer Corps, and with the 23rd Panzer Division before returning to the SS as Ib (chief supply officer) of the 10th SS Panzer Division. In May 1943, he became Ia (chief operations officer) of the 9th SS Panzer, which was commanded by Bittrich. When Bittrich assumed com-

mand of the II SS Panzer Corps on June 28, he was replaced by *SS-Oberführer* Sylvester Stadler. SS Col. Thomas Mueller was acting divisional commander from July 10 to 15 while Stadler was hospitalized with his wounds. Stadler then led the 9th SS until July 31, when he was wounded again and temporarily replaced by *SS-Oberführer* Friedrich Wilhelm Bock, the former artillery commander of the 4th SS Panzer Grenadier Division "Police." After receiving his Oak Leaves on September 2, Bock became the commander of the II SS Panzer Corps Artillery and was succeeded by Harzer. See Herbert Fürbringer, *9. SS-Panzer-Division "Hohenstaufen"* (Heimdal, Germany: Editions Heimdal, 1984), 425–27.

7. Ryan, *Bridge Too Far*, 152.
8. Johann Baptist Albin Rauter was born in Klagenfurt, Carinthia (southern Austria), in 1895. An engineering student in 1914, he joined an Austro-Hungarian mountain infantry regiment and fought in World War I. Discharged as a first lieutenant, he joined the *Freikorps* and fought the Poles in Upper Silesia. He met Adolf Hitler in 1929, promptly became a Nazi, joined the SS in 1935, and became leader of the SS Southeast Department at Breslau. In May 1940, he became Higher SS and Police Leader of the Netherlands, a post he held until he was seriously wounded by the Dutch Resistance on March 6, 1945. Ironically, Rauter was not the target of the ambush; rather, the starving Dutch were trying to hijack a German Army truck carrying meat, and Rauter's Mercedes got in the way. The Dutch nevertheless shot everyone in the car, and Rauter escaped only by playing dead. He was still in the hospital when the British arrested him at the end of the war. During World War II, Rauter deported 110,000 Dutch Jews to concentration or extermination camps. Six thousand of these survived. After being convicted for war crimes, he was shot by a Dutch firing squad at Scheveningen in 1949.
9. Ryan, *Bridge Too Far*, 152–53.
10. Friedrich Kussin was an engineer officer. Born in Aurich, Lower Saxony, on the German-Dutch border in 1895, he joined the army in 1913 and was commissioned a lieutenant in the 2nd Railroad Regiment in 1914. He spent virtually his entire career in railroad units or in staff assignments. Promoted to lieutenant colonel in 1937, he led the 80th Engineer Battalion of the Austrian 44th Infantry Division in France. Promoted to colonel in 1939 and major general on April 1, 1943, he commanded the 5th Railroad Engineer Regiment (1940) and the 8th Railroad Engineer Regiment in the East (1942–43). He apparently fell ill in late March 1943 because he was without an assignment for eighteen months. He was named commander of the 642nd Field Administrative Headquarters at Arnhem on September 2, 1944.
11. Ryan, *Bridge Too Far*, 329.
12. Ibid., 250.
13. Fürbringer, *9. SS-Panzer-Division "Hohenstaufen"*, 425–27. Spinder was acting commander of the 9th SS Panzer Artillery Regiment.
14. Ibid., 427.
15. Shan Hackett (1910–97) was later deputy chief of the Imperial General Staff (1963–66) and general officer commanding of the British Army of the Rhine (1966–68). After his retirement in 1968, he wrote a bestselling novel about World War III.

16. A tough veteran, Euling had joined the SS in 1938 as a private in the old SS-VT. He volunteered for officer's training in 1939 and graduated from the SS *Junkerschule* at Braunschweig in 1940. He had served as a platoon leader, orderly officer, and regimental adjutant before undergoing General Staff training in 1943. He served on the staff of the II SS Panzer Corps on both the Eastern and Western Fronts until the fall of 1944, when he took charge of the I Battalion of the 22nd SS Panzer Grenadier Regiment.
17. Ryan, *Bridge Too Far*, 434.
18. Ibid., 437.
19. J. L. Moulton, *The Battle for Antwerp: The Liberation of the City and the Opening of the Scheldt* (London: I. Allan, 1978), 61.
20. Ryan, *Bridge Too Far*, 479.
21. Ibid., 503.

CHAPTER 5: AACHEN

1. Moulton, *Battle for Antwerp*, 74.
2. John S. D. Eisenhower, *The Bitter Woods* (New York: Putnam, 1969), 76.
3. Robert Goralski, *World War II Almanac, 1931–1945: A Political and Military Record* (New York: Putnam, 1981), 346–47; Keilig, *Die Generale des Heeres*, 133.
4. Ferdinand Heim was born in Reutlingen in the Swabian district of south Wuerttemberg, in 1895. He entered the Imperial Army as an officer-cadet with the 13th Field Artillery Regiment in June 1914 and fought in Belgium and France. Commissioned in early 1915, he was promoted to first lieutenant in October 1918. He would later he promoted to captain (1928), major (1934), lieutenant colonel (1937), colonel (August 1, 1939), major general (February 1, 1942), and lieutenant general (November 1, 1942). Selected for retention in the *Reichswehr*, Heim spent most of the 1919–27 period with the 5th Artillery Regiment at Stuttgart. Here he took his *Wehrkreis* examination and scored in the upper 15 percent, qualifying for secret General Staff training. He began this process in 1923, trained in Berlin for a year (1927–28), and became a probationary member of the General Staff. He was employed in the Troop Office and Defense Ministry in Berlin (1928–32) before spending a year as a battery commander with the 9th Artillery Regiment. He then became an instructor at the Infantry School at Doeberitz (1933–34) and the War Academy (1934–37). He then joined the staff of the XVI Motorized Corps in Berlin (1937), becoming its chief of operations (1938) and then chief of staff (1939–40). After fighting in Poland (1939), Heim became a branch chief at OKW (1940) and was chief of staff of the 6th Army (September 1940–1942) before taking over the 14th Panzer Division on July 1, 1942. After being involved in the street fighting in Stalingrad, he was named commander of the XXXXVIII Panzer Corps on November 1, 1942. The corps was a technical disaster. Ordered to prevent the encirclement of Stalingrad, most of Heim's tanks broke down almost immediately, and the corps itself barely escaped encirclement. An enraged Hitler ordered Heim arrested on November 26. He was placed in solitary confinement at the notorious Moabit Prison in Berlin. His health broke under the strain, and he was in the hospital from April to June 1943. He was subsequently discharged from the army in August 1943. Finally released, Heim was on the retired list for a year. He was recalled to active duty on August 5, 1944, and

named commandant of Boulogne. He surrendered it to the Canadians on September 23, 1944.

5. Ferdinand Heim was released from prison in February 1948. He subsequently lived in Ulm and died there on November 14, 1977.

6. Goralski, *World War II Almanac*, 348–49; Moulton says Calais fell on September 30. *Battle for Antwerp*, 77.

7. MacDonald, *Siegfried Line Campaign*, 271–72. The U.S. 3rd Armored Division (along with the 1st and 2nd) was one of the three "heavy" U.S. armored divisions, having a strength of 232 tanks. Later American armored divisions had only 168 tanks.

8. Friedrich Koechling assumed command of the LXXXI Corps on September 21.

9. MacDonald, *Siegfried Line Campaign*, 290.

10. Whiting, *Bloody Aachen* (New York: Stein and Day, 1976), 114–15.

11. Ibid., 177; MacDonald, *Siegfried Line Campaign*, 290.

12. Charles Whiting, *Bloody Aachen*, 110–11. Colonel Leyherr was killed in action in the spring of 1945.

13. Leland S. Hobbs (1892–1966) was the former chief of staff of the U.S. Third Army. He later commanded the III Corps (1946), 2nd Armored Division (1947), the IX Corps (1949), and was deputy commander of the U.S. Third and First Armies (1947–49 and 1951–53, respectively). He retired in 1953.

Clarence R. Huebner (1888–1972) was the former director of training of the Army General Staff. After commanding the V Corps in northwestern Europe (1945), he was chief of staff and then deputy commander of the U.S. European Command. He retired in 1950.

14. Georg Keppler (1884–1966) was born in Mainz, the son of an army colonel. Keppler followed in his father's footsteps and joined the army as a *Fahnenjunker* in 1913. Commissioned in the 73rd Fusilier Regiment in June 1914, he was wounded in action at St. Quentin on August 29. Following his recovery, he served on the staffs of the 39th Infantry Brigade and the 19th Reserve Division and was wounded twice more. Not selected for the *Reichsheer*, he joined the State Police in Hanover in 1920. Keppler joined the NSDAP in 1930 and the SS-VT (the armed SS) as an SS major in the fall of 1935. He commanded a battalion in the Deutschland Regiment before becoming the first commander of the "Der Fuehrer" Regiment in Vienna in 1938. After leading it in the western campaign of 1940 and in the early stages of the Russian campaign, Keppler became acting commander of the "Totenkopf" SS Division on July 15, 1941. After the division's permanent commander recovered from his wounds and returned, Keppler was named temporary commander the "Nord" SS Division, but he fell ill with a brain tumor. He was not able to return to duty until the spring of 1942, when he assumed command of the 2nd SS Panzer Grenadier Division "Das Reich," which was rebuilding in France. Keppler's tumor flaired up again, and he was hospitalized or on medical leave from February until the end of August 1943. When he returned to active duty, Keppler was named commander of the Waffen-SS District Bohemia and Moravia. From April to September 1944, he was commander of the Waffen-SS in Hungary. Meanwhile, he was promoted to SS lieutenant general (April 1, 1942) and general of Waffen-SS (June 21, 1944).

Keppler temporarily replaced Sepp Dietrich as commander of the I SS Panzer Corps in France from August 16 to October 24, 1944. He then led the

III (*germanisches*) SS Panzer Corps on the Eastern Front from October 30, 1944, to February 4, 1945. He assumed command of the XVIII SS Corps on February 12 and led it until the end of the war, surrendering to the Americans on May 22, 1945. A POW until April 1948, he settled in Hamburg, where he ran a chemist shop. He died in Hamburg on June 16, 1966.

15. Whiting, *Bloody Aachen*, 115.

16. MacDonald, *Siegfried Line Campaign*, 290.

17. Walter Denkert (1897–1982) was born in Kiel and entered in the service as a war volunteer in 1914. He served on the Eastern Front and was promoted to corporal and sergeant, underwent officer training, and received a commission as a reserve second lieutenant in the 23rd (Landwehr) Infantry Regiment in 1915. He transferred to the 379th Landwehr Infantry Regiment in October 1915 and became a platoon leader and company commander. In October 1917, he transferred again, this time to the 86th Fusilier Regiment on the Western Front, where he led a platoon in a machine-gun company, commanded a mortar company, and temporarily served as regimental adjutant. He was also wounded in action on March 22, 1918, and spent a month in the hospital. He served in the *Freikorps* in 1919 and was discharged from the army later that year. A Hamburg policeman for the next sixteen years, Denkert rejoined the army as a major in 1935. He successively commanded the 13th Battalion of the 65th Infantry Regiment (1935–38), 52nd Machine Gun Battalion (1938–39), and the II Battalion of the 27th Infantry Regiment (1939–40). He served on the staff of OKH (1941), where he specialized in army flak units, and commanded 47th Infantry Regiment (1941) and 8th Infantry Regiment (1941–42). Apparently, he fell ill in September 1942. Denkert held no further appointments until June 11, 1943, when he became commandant of the Army Weapons School for Panzer Troops at Kharkov. On March 12, 1944, he became acting commander of the 6th Panzer Division. Later, he briefly commanded the 19th Panzer (March 28–June 16, 1944) before being given command of the 3rd Panzer Grenadier Division on October 3, 1944. He was promoted to lieutenant general on April 20, 1945. Earlier promotions included major of police (1934), major (1935), lieutenant colonel (1939), colonel (February 1, 1942), and major general (June 1, 1944). He surrendered his division on May 8, 1945, and was released from the POW camps in 1947. He died in the city of his birth on July 9, 1982.

18. Wilck had not had a brilliant career. He joined the Imperial Army in 1916 but was still a major in 1940. Promoted to lieutenant colonel later that year, he had spent three years commanding an occupation regiment, which was spread out over 600 miles of Norway. He was sent to Russia in 1943 and, after surviving a year on the Eastern Front, was given command of the 246th Volkgrenadier Division in the fall of 1944. It was not an elite unit. The original 246th Infantry Division had fought in France and on the Russian Front, but it had been destroyed at Vitebsk when Army Group Center was slaughtered. The 246th Volksgrenadier had been activated in *Wehrkreis XIII* on September 15 when it absorbed the partially formed 565th Grenadier Division. The new division consisted of the 352nd, 404th, and 689th Grenadier Regiments, each with two battalions, and the 246th Artillery Regiment of four battalions. It had a strength of 8,000 men, mostly ex-sailors, former *Luftwaffe* ground crewmen, and new recruits; very few had more than four weeks of infantry training.

19. Whiting, *Bloody Aachen*, 151.
20. Ibid., 120.
21. Ibid., 149–50.
22. Ibid., 151.
23. Ibid., 177.

CHAPTER 6: THE BATTLE OF THE HUERTGEN FOREST (PART 1)

1. Charles Whiting, *The Battle of the Hurtgen Forest: The Untold Story of a Disastrous Campaign* (New York: Orion Books, 1989), 14–16.
2. The 89th Infantry Division (the "Horseshoe Division") had been formed from reinforced infantry regiments in the Replacement Army in January 1944. (In the German Army in World War II, a "reinforced infantry regiment," if it referred to a specific unit, had an artillery battalion.) The division had been sent to Norway, where a divisional artillery regiment had been formed from the artillery battalions of its infantry regiments, which lost their guns. The division was sent to Normandy in late June and had collapsed under heavy British air and ground attacks. It was later encircled at Falaise, where both of its grenadier regiments were destroyed. It had been hastily rebuilt, using Landwehr (older-age men) and replacement and training battalions. Both Rundstedt and Model recommended that it be dissolved, but Hitler refused to allow it.

   Colonel Roesler was replaced by Maj. Gen. Walter Bruns on September 15, 1944.
3. Paul Mahlmann was relieved of his command on February 15, 1945, and was never re-employed. Since his hometown of Erfurt was now behind what became known as the Iron Curtain, he settled in Munich. He died in 1963.
4. Charles MacDonald, *The Battle of the Huertgen Forest* (Philadelphia: Lippincott, 1963), 63.
5. Helmut Becker (1898–1971) was born in Gruen, County Vogtland, Saxony, on June 2, 1898. (Today, Vogtland is in the Free State of Saxony, in extreme east-central Germany.) He joined the army as a *Fahnenjunker* in the 182nd (6th Royal Saxon) Infantry Regiment in June 1915, was commissioned in 1916, and fought on the Western Front as a platoon leader, signal officer, and battalion adjutant. He left the army after the armistice but returned to active duty in 1934. When Germany mobilized on August 26, 1939, he was given command of the 1st Battalion of the 173rd Infantry Regiment, which he led in Poland, France, and central Russia. He assumed command of the 173rd Regiment itself on January 6, 1942, and led it until March 29, 1943, when he fell ill and was placed in Fuehrer Reserve. He returned to the front on October 15, 1943, when he assumed command of the 504th Grenadier Regiment, which he led in several difficult battles. He was sent to the Western Front in the fall of 1944 and was acting commander of the 275th Infantry Division during the Battle of the Huertgen Forest from October 11 to November 22. He assumed command of the 85th Infantry Division (also in the Huertgen) on November 22, but was seriously wounded on December 7. He remained in various hospitals until June 1945. Meanwhile, he was promoted to major general on January 30, 1945.

   Bechler was in the Reserve Hospital in Koenigstein in the Taunus Mountains when it was captured by the Red Army in the spring of 1945. In 1948, however, he escaped from a Soviet prison camp and fled to the West, which he reached in June. He settled in Kassel, northern Hesse, on the Fulda River and died there on January 9, 1971.

6. William Hood Simpson was born in Weatherford, Texas, in 1888. He graduated from the U.S. Military Academy at West Point, served in the Philippines, the Mexican Punitive Expedition (1916), and World War I, where he received temporary promotions to major and lieutenant colonel. By 1940, Simpson was a colonel (permanent rank) commanding the 9th Infantry Regiment. Later, he commanded the 35th Infantry Division at Camp Robinson, Arkansas. He took command of the Ninth Army in May 1944, which was in charge of the forces that captured Brest.

    After the fall of Berlin, Simpson commanded the U.S. Second Army, which headquartered in Memphis, Tennessee. He retired in late 1946 and was later promoted to full (four-star) general on the retired list. He died in 1980 and is buried in Arlington National Cemetery.

7. MacDonald, *Battle of the Huertgen Forest*, 97–98.

8. Siegfried von Waldenburg was born in Gross Leipe near Breslau, Silesia, in 1898. A professional soldier, he entered the army in 1916 and was commissioned second lieutenant in the 1st Guards Grenadier Regiment on August 2, 1917. He fought on the Eastern and Western Fronts, was selected for the *Reichsheer*, and was a major and chief of operations of the 6th Infantry Division when World War II broke out. After serving in the Saar and French campaigns, he was chief of staff of the XIII Corps (1940–41) and fought on the Russian Front before being sent to Italy as deputy military attaché and chief of staff to the German General in the Headquarters of the High Command of the Italian Armed Forces (1941–44). He commanded the 26th Panzer Grenadier Regiment in southern Russia and the Ukraine (April–September 1944) before being given command of the battered 116th Panzer Division on September 14, 1944. He led it with a great deal of skill, which led to his promotion to major general on December 1, 1944. Waldenburg led the 116th Panzer for the rest of the war and surrendered to the western Allies in May 1945. He died in Hanover in 1973.

CHAPTER 7

1. Hasso von Manteuffel was born in Potsdam in 1897. His distinguished ancestry included several Prussian generals and a prime minister. He was educated in cadet schools, entered the service as a *Faehnrich* in the 3rd Hussars Regiment in 1916, fought in World War I, served in the *Freikorps*, and was selected for the *Reichsheer*. When World War II began, he was on the staff of the Panzer Troop School (1939–40). He commanded the 3rd Motorcycle Battalion (1940), the I Battalion of the 7th Rifle Regiment, the 6th Rifle Regiment, and the 7th Panzer Grenadier Brigade (1941–42)—all except the 3rd on the Eastern Front. He continued his advancement in 1943 when he was given command of the ad hoc Division von Manteuffel in Tunisia. He was wounded and flown out of the pocket in the spring of 1943, just before Army Group Afrika collapsed. After he recovered, he assumed command of his old unit, the 7th Panzer Division, in Russia on August 1, 1943. He was given command of the Grossdeutschland Panzer Grenadier Division on February 1, 1944. On September 1, 1944, he was promoted to general of panzer troops and given command of the 5th Panzer Army, skipping the corps level of command altogether. He had earlier been

promoted to lieutenant colonel (1939), colonel (1941), major general (May 1, 1943), and lieutenant general (February 1, 1944).

Manteuffel led the 5th Panzer Army on the Western Front until February 28, 1945, when he again reported to Fuehrer Headquarters in Berlin. He was given command of the 3rd Panzer Army on the Eastern Front. Unable to halt the last Soviet offensive, he surrendered to the British at Hagenow on May 3 and was released from prison shortly before Christmas 1946. He went to work for the Oppenheim Bank in Cologne, where he was joined by his wife, who had been living in a refugee camp near Hamburg. Later, he went to work for a manufacturing firm, was elected to the town council of Neuss-on-the-Rhine, and was a member of the West German Parliament from 1953 to 1957. He later retired to Diessen on Lake Ammersee, Bavaria, where he died in 1978.

2. Gustav-Adolf von Zangen was born in Darmstadt in 1892. He entered the Imperial Army as an officer-cadet in 1910 and was commissioned in the infantry. After World War I, he was discharged from the service, so he joined the police. Zangen reentered the army as a lieutenant colonel in 1935 and rose rapidly, commanding the 88th Infantry Regiment (1938–41), 17th Infantry Division (1941–43), LXXXIV Corps (1943), LXXXVII Corps (1943), Army Detachment von Zangen in northern Italy (1943–43), and 15th Army. Zangen was promoted to colonel (1938), major general (1942), lieutenant general (1943), and general of infantry. A talented commander, he was nevertheless forced to surrender the 15th Army to the Americans at the end of the Battle of the Ruhr Pocket on April 18, 1945. He lived in Hanau/Main after the war and died there in 1964.

3. MacDonald, *Siegfried Line Campaign*, 409.

4. Peter Koerte was born in Berlin on June 26, 1896. He joined the 3rd Foot Guards Regiment in December 1914 as a war volunteer but soon transferred to the 53rd Reserve Infantry Division, where he was awarded a direct battlefield commission as a reserve officer on November 4, 1915. Koerte spent the entire balance of the war on the Western Front as a platoon leader and company commander. During the civil unrest following the armistice, he served in the *Freikorps von Loewenfeld*, putting down Communist insurrections. He was discharged from the army in 1920 and joined the police but returned to active duty on October 15, 1935. He commanded a company in the Prussian 5th Infantry Regiment in Stettin (1935–36), another company in the 25th Infantry Regiment at Stargard (1936–37), and the I Battalion of the 96th Infantry Regiment (1938–41), which he led in Poland, Belgium, France, and Russia (northern sector). On October 31, 1941, he assumed command of the 26th Infantry Regiment, which he commanded until March 1944, fighting in the Lake Ilmen, Demyansk, and Starya Russa sectors. He apparently became ill in early 1944 because he was placed in Fuehrer Reserve and was not recalled to active duty until October 9, 1944. He assumed command of the 246th Volksgrenadier Division on the Western Front on November 7 and fought in the Aachen sector and in the Ardennes. Promoted to major general on January 1, 1945, he reported himself ill the following day and spent the rest of the war in hospitals. The British captured him when they overran Hamburg on May 5, 1945. Released from POW hospitals in August 1946, Peter Koerte settled in Bielefeld, Westphalia, where he had once been a police officer. His health continued to deteriorate, and he died on January 13, 1947.

5. The original 12th Infantry Division had been largely destroyed on the Eastern Front in the summer of 1944. It was rebuilt in East Prussia as the 12th Volksgrenadier. It had a strength of 14,800 men in the autumn of 1944. The division ended up in the Ruhr Pocket and surrendered to the U.S. Army.

6. Max Bork was born in Forsthaus Lasdehnen in the Pillkallen District of East Prussia (now Dobrowolsk, Russia) on January 1, 1899. He joined the army in July 1916 as a *Fahnenjunker* in the 176th Infantry Regiment and served on the Western Front. He was wounded in early 1918 and ended the war as a company commander. Accepted into the *Reichsheer,* he spent the period from 1921 to 1930 in the 3rd Infantry Regiment at Deutsch-Eylau, East Prussia (now Ilawa, Poland). He passed his *Wehrkreis* examination and began his General Staff training in 1930. After completing the program, he spent a year as a company commander in the 23rd Infantry Regiment at Rastenburg, East Prussia (now Ketrzyn, Poland) (1935–36), before becoming Ia of the 9th Infantry Division at Giessen in Hesse (west-central Germany) (1936–38) and the 45th Infantry Division in Linz, Austria (1938). He was assigned to the transport department of the General Staff at OKH at Zossen in late 1938. From January 15, 1940, to January 19, 1942, Bork (a colonel from August 1, 1941) was chief of staff of the LIII Corps in the central sector of the Eastern Front. He became chief of staff of the rebuilt 6th Army in the southern sector of the Russian Front on March 10, 1943, and on April 1 was promoted to major general. He was named chief of staff of Wehrkreis General-Government (formerly Poland) on April 20, 1944. A promotion to lieutenant general followed on July 1. He assumed command of the 47th Volksgrenadier (formerly Infantry) Division in northern Jutland, Denmark, on September 18. He led this division in the Aachen sector and in the Rhineland until March 1945, when he took charge of the XIII Corps. His last assignment was the command of the ad hoc Corps Bork, which he directed in Thueringia and Saxony from April 15 to June 26, 1945. He surrendered to the western Allies and was in POW camps until 1948. Finally released, he moved to Brunswick in Western Germany and died in Hollern-Twielenfleth, Lower Saxony, on July 4, 1973.

7. MacDonald, *Battle for the Huertgen Forest,* 130.

8. MacDonald, *Siegfried Line Campaign,* 414.

9. Baron Heinrich von Luettwitz was born on the family estate at Krumpach, East Prussia, in 1896. Unable to secure his father's permission to enter the service when World War I began, Heinrich ran away from home, joined the army as a private, and went to the Western Front at age seventeen. His mother used her influence to have Heinrich breveted second lieutenant two days before his eighteenth birthday. Luettwitz distinguished himself in the trench fighting in France in 1917, during which he was severely wounded. He was accepted into the *Reichsheer* as a cavalry officer but was converted to the concept of motorized warfare in 1929 and commanded the 3rd Motorized Battalion in 1936–37. He led a reconnaissance battalion in Poland, where he was severely wounded, and commanded the 59th Rifle Regiment of the 20th Panzer Division in Russia (1941–42). After Stalin's winter offensive was checked, Luettwitz commanded the 20th Rifle Brigade (1942), 13th Panzer Division (1942–43), and 2nd Panzer Division (1944), which was later transferred to France. After the Normandy campaign, he was given command of the XXXXVII Panzer Corps in September 1944. He was a very good divisional commander but was less successful com-

manding a corps, especially in the Battle of the Bulge. In the Battle of the Ruhr Pocket, Luettwitz did not try to offer fanatical resistance, and together with Bayerlein (now commander of the LIII Corps) and General of Infantry Erich Abraham (commander of the LXIII Corps), he surrendered to the Americans on April 16, 1945. He was released from prison in 1946 and retired to Neuberg in Bavaria, where he again cultivated his horsemanship and acquired a stable from funds saved from his old estates, which were now lost. He died at Neuburg on October 9, 1969 at the age of seventy-three. His widow, two sons, and a daughter survived him. He was promoted to lieutenant general on June 1, 1943, and to general of panzer troops on November 1, 1944.

10. Eberhard Rodt was born in Munich in 1895. He joined the Bavarian 2nd Ulam Regiment as a war volunteer in 1914 and was commissioned the following year. He served in the *Reichsheer* and later commanded the I Battalion of the 18th Cavalry Regiment (1936–39), 7th Cavalry Regiment (1939), 25th Reconnaissance Battalion (1939–40), 66th Panzer Grenadier Regiment (1942), and 22nd Panzer Division (November 8, 1942–March 1943) on the Eastern Front. Sent to Italy to recouperate with the remnants of his staff, Rodt was promoted to major general on March 1, 1943. Despite the fact that he had basically failed as a panzer division commander in Russia, Rodt was charged with forming the 15th Panzer Grenadier Division in Sicily out of the survivors of the 15th Panzer Division of the Afrika Korps, plus assorted miscellaneous units. In effect, he was given a second chance, and Rodt took full advantage of this opportunity by performing brilliantly as a divisional commander in Sicily and Italy and on the Western Front, fully justifying the confidence his superiors had in him, despite his previous failure in the East. He was promoted to lieutenant general in 1944 and led the 15th Panzer Grenadier until mid-January 1945, when the was wounded by an Allied fighter-bomber. He was still recovering at the end of the war. He died in the city of his birth in 1979, just after his eighty-forth birthday.

11. Whiting, *Siegfried*, 79.

12. Hubert Essame, *The Battle for Germany* (New York: Scribner, 1969), 87.

13. Whiting, *Siegfried*, 79.

14. Ibid., 82.

15. Blumentritt was an army officer. He was formerly Rundstedt's chief of staff. The XII SS Corps was formed on August 1, 1944, from the remnants of the LIII Corps, which had been largely destroyed in Russia. It was mainly made up on army personnel.

16. Theodor Tolsdorff was born in Lehnarten, East Prussia, on November 3, 1909. He volunteered for the service in 1934 and was commissioned in the 22nd Infantry Regiment at Gumbinnen, East Prussia (now Gusev, Russia), in 1936. He was still in the 22nd on November 1, 1943, when he assumed command of the regiment. From 1939 to 1945, he rose from a lieutenant commanding a company to a lieutenant general commanding a corps. In the meantime, he earned the Knight's Cross with Oak Leaves, Swords, and Diamonds—mostly on the Eastern Front. He was wounded fourteen times. Tolsdorff assumed command of the 340th Volksgrenadier Division on September 1, 1944, and fought in the Siegfried Line battles. He took charge of the LXXXII Corps on April 1, 1945. After the war, he lived in Wuppertal-Barmen and died in Dortmund on May 5, 1978.

17. Truman E. Boudinot (1895–1945) was previously the executive officer of the U.S. Army's Armored Training Center at Fort Knox, Kentucky (1941–42) and commander of the 32nd Armored Regiment (1942–43). Later, he commanded the 3rd Armored and 7th Armored Divisions.
18. MacDonald, *Siegfried Line Campaign*, 424.
19. Whiting, *Siegfried*, 82.

CHAPTER 8: THE BATTLE OF THE HUERTGEN FOREST (PART 2)

1. Raymond O. Barton (born 1889) was one of the best of the American division commanders. He graduated from West Point in 1913, served in France, and commanded the 1st Battalion of the 8th Infantry Regiment in Germany until 1923. His unit was the last American occupation force to leave Germany after World War I. Barton commanded the 4th Infantry Division from July 1943 to December 26, 1944, when he stepped down for medical reasons. Barton retired soon after and died on February 9, 1963. He is buried in Augusta, Georgia.
2. Georg Kossmala was born in Myslowitz, Silesia (now Myslowice, Poland), on October 22, 1896. He joined the Upper Silesian 63rd Infantry Regiment as a war volunteer in September 1914 and fought in France and Russia. From 1920 to 1935, he was a police officer before rejoining the army as a captain. He commanded the III Battalion of the 38th Infantry Regiment (1938–late 1939) and the I Battalion of the 222nd Infantry Regiment (later the I Battalion of the 570th Infantry) (1941–42). He fought in Poland, Belgium, and France before assuming command of the 3rd Security Regiment in March 1941 and the 6th Infantry Regiment in July 1942. Kossmala led the 6th Infantry in several difficult battles on the Eastern Front. He was named acting commander of the 32nd Infantry Division in Russia in August 1944. Sent to the Western Front, he took charge of the 272nd Volksgrenadier Division on September 15, 1944, and led it in the Siegfried Line battles until December 16, when he took charge of the 344th Volksgrenadier Division. This unit was sent to the Eastern Front in January 1945. Kossmala, who was promoted to major general on January 1, 1945, fought his last battles in his native Silesia. He was missing in action near Oberglogau on February 28, 1945.
3. Hans Schmidt was born in Bayreuth, Upper Franconia—the home of Richard Wagner— on March 14, 1895. He joined the army when World War I broke out as a *Fahnenjunker* in the Bavarian 7th Infantry Regiment and fought on the Western Front. Selected for the *Reichsheer,* he was commanding the III Battalion of the 41st Infantry Regiment as a major in 1935. (This unit was based at Amberg, Upper Palatinate, not far from Bayreuth.) Later, he was promoted to lieutenant colonel (1938), colonel (late 1940), major general (April 1, 1943), and lieutenant general (October 1, 1943). He led the III Battalion of the 41st in Poland, commanded the 245th Infantry Regiment in France and southern Russia (1940–43), and assumed command of the 68th Infantry Division in the southern sector of the Eastern Front on January 24, 1943. He led it until November 1943, when he returned to Germany. He assumed command of the 275th Infantry Division on December 10, 1943, and led it for the rest of the war. Part of the division was at Flensburg when the Third Reich fell, although part of it was destroyed in the Halbe Pocket on the Eastern Front. After the war, Schmidt lived in Weiden, Upper Westphalia. He died on November 28, 1971.
4. MacDonald, *Battle of the Huertgen Forest,* 168.

5. Ibid., 171.
6. Ibid., 177.
7. Ibid., 177–78.

CHAPTER 9

1. John C. H. Lee (1887–1958) was the former commandant of Fort Mason, California, Port of Embarkation (1940–41) and commander of the 2nd Infantry Division (1941–42). Later, he was deputy commander in chief of U.S. Forces in the European theater of operations (1945) and commander in chief of U.S. Forces in the Mediterranean theater of operations (1945–47). He retired in 1947. Lee, who was very active in the Episcopal Church, was a West Point graduate and held the Distinguished Service Medal and the Silver Star from World War I.

2. Anthony Kemp, *The Unknown Battle, Metz, 1944* (New York: Stein and Day, 1981), 5.

3. Ibid., 41.

4. F. W. von Mellenthin, *Panzer Battles: A Study of the Employment of Armor in the Second World War* (Norman, OK: University of Oklahoma Press, 1956), 375.

5. Joseph Buerckel was born on March 30, 1895, in Lingenfeld, in the Germersheim District of the Palatinate. A schoolteacher, Buerckel was a Nazi Party organizer in the Saar-Palatinate as early as 1925 and rose to *gauleiter* of the region in 1934. He later served as *gauleiter* of Vienna and *Reichsstatthalter* (governor) of Austria (1939–40). Later, he was civil administrator of Lothringen (formerly Lorraine, France) (1940–44) and *gauleiter* and governor of the Bavarian Palatinate and Prussian Saar (1941–44). He and his wife apparently killed themselves at Neustadt an der Weinstrasse, Rhineland-Palatinate, on September 28, 1944.

6. Walter Krause (1890–1960) was born in Schweidnitz, Silesia, and joined the army as a *Fahnenjunker* in the Silesian 156th Infantry Regiment in early 1909. Commissioned the following year, he was a platoon leader, battalion adjutant, company commander, mortar company commander, and brigade adjutant on the Western Front during World War I. He was wounded twice and spent the period from November 1914 to March 1916 in hospitals or convalescing in a replacement battalion.

   After the war, Krause served in the *Freikorps* (1919–21), joined the *Reichsheer*, and was in the 17th Infantry Regiment at Brunswick from 1921 to 1930 before being detached to the defense ministry. After spending the period from 1932 to October 1935 as the transport officer of the 3rd Cavalry Division, Krause assumed command of the I Battalion of the 66th Infantry Regiment at Magdeburg in October 1935. He took command of the regiment itself in October 1938 and led it in the Polish campaign. Krause was commander of the Infantry School at Doeberitz from October 1939 to October 1942, but he was detached on temporary duty long enough to command the 243rd Infantry Division during the second phase of the French campaign (1940). After commanding the 900th Motorized Lehr Brigade (1941–42), he led the Saxon 14th Motorized Division in the Rzhev salient from October 1, 1942, to January 1, 1943. He was then given command of the 170th Infantry Division, which he led during the siege of Leningrad and in the retreat to Narva. (The 170th was a definite step down from commanding the 14th Motorized.) Promoted to first lieutenant (1915), captain (1922), major (1932), lieutenant colonel (1935), colonel (1938), major general (January 1, 1942), and lieutenant general (September 1, 1943), Krause took command of the 462nd Replacement Division at Metz on July 15, 1944. Sacked on October 15, he was immediately given command of the 593rd Rear Army Area—a definite promotion. He led the 593rd until the end of the war and surrendered to the U.S. Army. Released in June 1947, he died in Goettingen, Lower Saxony, West Germany, on October 25, 1960.

Hans von Sommerfeld was born in Magdeburg, Saxony-Anhalt, on January 1, 1888. He was educated in cadet schools and joined the army as a *Faehnrich* in the infantry in 1906. He fought in World War I, served in the *Reichsheer*, and was promoted to colonel and named commander of the 33rd Infantry Regiment in 1935. He was commander of the 9th Frontier Guard Command during the invasion of Poland and assumed command of three divisions during World War II: the 526th Infantry (October 1939); the 306th Infantry (November 1940); and the 462nd Replacement (December 24, 1942–July 15, 1944). He was given a territorial command on the Rhine River in October 1944. Promoted to major general (October 1, 1939) and lieutenant general (September 1, 1941), Sommerfeld lived in Rheine, North Rhine-Westphalia, after the war. He died on January 10, 1961.

7. Johann Sinnhuber was born in Wilkoschen, East Prussia, in 1887, joined the army as a *Fahnenjunker* in April 1907, and was commissioned in the 52nd Field Artillery Regiment in 1908. He fought in World War I, served in the *Reichsheer*, and was a lieutenant colonel commanding the 21st Artillery Regiment at Elbing, West Prussia (now Elblag, Poland), in 1934. He was later promoted to colonel (1935), major general (1939), lieutenant general (April 1, 1941), and general of artillery (October 1, 1943). He was named commander of *Arko 18* in 1938 and led it in Poland (1939) and France (1940). On May 21, 1940, Sinnhuber was given command of the 28th Infantry Division, which he led in Belgium, France, and the drive on Moscow. The division suffered such heavy casualties that it had to be withdrawn to France, where it was rebuilt as a light (later *jäger*) division. It was sent back to the Eastern Front in 1942 and was involved in the storming of the Soviet naval base of Sevastopol in the Crimea and in the siege of Leningrad. Sinnhuber led the division until May 1943. After a furlough, he assumed command of the LXXXII Corps in northern France on July 10, 1943. He led it in the retreat across France and was relieved of his command on September 1. On April 1, 1945, he was recalled to active duty and commanded a battle group in the Hamburg-Bremen sector until mid-April. He retired to Augsburg, in the Swabian District of Bavaria, where he died in 1974.

8. Hermann Priess (1901–85) was born in Marnitz, near Mecklenburg, the son of a butcher. He joined the army as a war volunteer in the 18th Dragoon Regiment in 1919, even though World War I was already over. Germany, however, was in the throes of a civil war, and Priess first saw action as a member of the *Freikorps*. He served in the Baltic States, where he fought against the Communists and was wounded at Riga. He returned to Germany and was assigned to the 14th Cavalry Regiment at Ludwigslust but was discharged in 1920. Priess joined the Nazi Party and the SS in 1933 and became an SS lieutenant in 1935. He was an SS captain when the war broke out. He commanded the II Battalion of the 2nd SS Artillery Regiment in Poland and then transferred to the infa-

mous "Totenkopf" (Death's Head) Division. He commanded the II Battalion of the 3rd SS Artillery Regiment in France and the 3rd SS Artillery Regiment in Operation Barbarossa. In February 1943, he was named commander of the SS Panzer Grenadier Division "Totenkopf" (later redesignated 3rd SS Panzer Division "Totenkopf"). Promoted to *SS Gruppenfuehrer und Generalleutnant der Waffen-SS*, he led the "Death's Head" Division on the Eastern Front until August 1944, when he assumed command of the XIII SS Corps (August 7–October 24, 1944). He was named commander of the I SS Panzer Corps on November 9, 1944. Priess led the corps for the rest of the war. He surrendered to the U.S. Army on May 8, 1945. On July 16, 1946, he was sentenced to twenty years' imprisonment for the Malmedy Massacre, but he was released from prison in October 1954. He retired to Ahrensburg, Schleswig-Holstein, where he died on February 2, 1985. The best book yet written about the senior SS commanders is Mark C. Yeager, *Waffen-SS Commanders*, 2 vols. (Atglen, PA: Schiffer, 1999).

9.   Joachim von Siegroth was born in Oberlobendau, Sudetenland, on December 25, 1896. Educated in cadet schools, he joined the army as a *Fahnenjunker* in the 33rd Fusilier Regiment in 1914 and fought in Russia and on the Western Front. He was discharged from the service in 1919 and joined the police. Siegroth rejoined the army as a major in 1935 and was assigned to the staff of the War School at Dresden. When Germany mobilized in August 1939, he was named commander of a battalion in the 122nd Infantry Regiment, and he fought in Poland and France. He commanded an infantry regiment (1940–44), mainly on the Eastern Front, and was named commander of the VI Officer Training School on July 1, 1944. He fought at Metz and was promoted to major general on November 9, 1944. He was missing in action on the Eastern Front in April 1945. Siegroth had been promoted to lieutenant colonel in 1939 and colonel on February 1, 1942.

10. Kemp, *The Unknown Battle, Metz, 1944*, 41.

11. Baron Kurt von Muehlen (1905–71) was born in Ulm, Wuerttemberg, on January 22, 1905. He joined the *Reichsheer* as a *Fahnenjunker* in the 5th Engineer Battalion in Ulm in 1923. Later, he transferred to the 13th Infantry Regiment at Ludwigsburg, where he was promoted to second lieutenant in 1927. By 1936, he was a company commander in the 75th Infantry Regiment at Freiburg, near Ulm, which he led on the Upper Rhine after the war broke out in 1939. In 1940, Muehlen commanded the I Battalion of the 75th Infantry Regiment in the French campaign. In June, he became adjutant of the 5th Infantry (later *Jäger*) Division, of which the 75th was a part. He was given command of the 5th Machine Gun Battalion (October 1941) during the Russian campaign, and he assumed command of the 75th Infantry Regiment in June 1942. Muehlen led his regiment until June 1944, fighting in the northern sector of the Eastern Front. On June 11, he assumed command of the 559th Grenadier (later Volksgrenadier) Division, which he led in the Siegfried Line battles, in Lorraine and the Saar, on the Mosel, in the retreat to and from the Rhine, and in the retreat across southern Germany. He surrendered the remnants of his division to the western Allies at the end of the war. Muehlen was promoted to lieutenant colonel (1942), colonel (1943), major general (November 9, 1944), and lieutenant general (April 20, 1945). He died at Kressbornn, Baden-Wuerttemberg.

12. Karl Britzelmayr was born in Passau, Lower Bavaria, in 1894. He joined the Bavarian Army as a *Fahnenjunker* in 1913 and was commissioned second lieu-

tenant in the Bavarian 16th Infantry Regiment in October 1914. Meanwhile, he fought in Lorraine, when he was seriously wounded on August 27, 1914. He was not discharged from the hospital until late April 1915. He returned to the Western Front as a battalion adjutant in October; later, he commanded a company in the Bavarian 26th Infantry Regiment in Romania (1916–17). Next, he was a machine-gun officer with the I Bavarian Corps, and from February to December 1918, he was personal orderly officer to Prince Oskar of Prussia. Promoted to first lieutenant in 1918, he was discharged from the service in 1919 but returned as a captain in 1934. From 1934 to 1938, Britzelmayr commanded a company in the 62nd Infantry Regiment at Landshut; then he was on the regimental staff until February 1939. On August 26, 1939, when the Third Reich mobilized and Britzelmayr assumed command of the III Battalion of the 179th Infantry Regiment, which he led in Poland and France. He led the 217th Infantry Regiment in the northern sector of the Eastern Front from October 1941 to August 1943, taking part in the siege of Leningrad. He also temporarily commanded the 57th Infantry Division (December 1942–January 1943). After heading the Company Commanders' School in Sissonne, France (April 1943–January 1944), Britzelmayr attended a five-week divisional commanders' course and was assigned to OB West for use as a division commander. He remained with OB West from early June to September 10, 1944, when he was finally given temporary command of the remnants of the 347th Infantry Division. He was made permanent commander of the 19th Volksgrenadier Division on November 23, 1944, and led it in the Saar, the Rhineland battles, and the retreat into Franconia. Meanwhile, he was promoted to major (1937), lieutenant colonel (December 1940), colonel (January 1, 1942), and major general (December 1, 1944). He was captured by the Americans on April 30, 1945. Released in June 1947, he returned to Landshut, where he died in 1968.

Franz Bäke, a Franconian, was a dentist by profession. He was born in Schwarzenfels, Fulda County, Hesse, in 1898. He entered the service as a war volunteer in the 53rd Infantry Regiment in 1915, fought on the Western Front, and was discharged as a sergeant in 1919. He served in *Freikorps von Epp* after the war and then studied dentistry in Hagen, Westphalia. Returning to active duty as a second lieutenant of reserves in the 6th Reconnaissance Battalion (1937), he was promoted to lieutenant of reserves (1939), captain of reserves (1941), major of reserves (1942), lieutenant colonel of reserves (1943), colonel of reserves (1944), and major general of reserves (April 20, 1945). His posts included commander of the 1st Company, 6th Reconnaissance Battalion (1940–41); Ia of the 11th Panzer Regiment (1941–42); commander of the I Battalion, 11th Panzer Regiment (1941–42); commander of the II Battalion, 11th Panzer Regiment (1942–43); commander of the 11th Panzer Regiment (1943); commander of Heavy Panzer Regiment Bäke (1943–44); and commander of the 106th Panzer Brigade "Feldherrnhalle" (May 1, 1944). Bäke formally assumed command of the remnants of the 13th Panzer Division (Panzer Division Feldherrnhalle 2) on March 9, 1945, when it was virtually certain that his predecessor, General Schmidhuber, was dead. An incredibly brave officer, Bäke personally knocked out at least three Soviet tanks in close combat, using infantry weapons. He held the Knight's Cross with Oak Leaves and Swords. He was promoted to major general on April 1, 1945. Released from the POW camps in 1950, he resumed the practice of dentistry. Ironically, he died in

Hagen, Westphalia, on December 12, 1978, as the result of injuries suffered in a traffic accident.

13. Hugh M. Cole, *The Lorraine Campaign* (Washington, DC: Historical Division, Department of the Army, 1950), 234.

14. After being relieved of his command by General Knobelsdorff, General Krause was given command of the 593rd Rear Army Area, a corps-level command. He directed the 593rd until the end of the war and surrendered to the U.S. Army. Released in June 1947, he died in Goettingen, Lower Saxony, West Germany, on October 25, 1960.

15. Vollrath Luebbe was born in Klein-Lunow, Mecklenburg, in 1894. He joined the Saxon 103rd Infantry Regiment as a *Fahnenjunker* in 1912 and fought with his unit throughout World War I, serving exclusively on the Western Front, where he was wounded at least once. Commissioned in 1914 and promoted to first lieutenant in 1917, he was selected for the *Reichsheer*. He spent five years with the 10th Infantry Regiment in Dresden (1920–25) and ten years as a company commander in the 9th Infantry Regiment in Potsdam (1925–35). After serving two and a half years as a tactics instructor at the War School at Dresden (1935–37), Luebbe was transferred to Ohrdruf (also in Saxony) as a battalion commander in the 103rd Infantry Regiment. In the fall of 1938, he switched to the motorized branch and became commander of the 13th Rifle Regiment of the 5th Panzer Division, which he led in Poland, Belgium, France, and Greece. On August 1, 1941, he became commander of the 2nd Rifle Brigade of the 2nd Panzer Division. He took command of the division itself on September 5, 1942, and led it on the central sector of the Russian Front. Apparently, Luebbe's handling of the 2nd Panzer left something to be desired, for—after years of commanding motorized and armored formations—he was transferred back to the infantry in early 1944. He led the 81st Infantry Division in northern Russia from April 5 to July 1, 1944, when he fell ill. He returned to active duty on October 9 as commander of the 462nd Replacement Division but suffered a mild stroke on October 23 and had to be relieved. Luebbe briefly commanded the 49th Infantry Division in the West (November–December 1944), before assuming command of the 433rd Replacement Division at Kuestrin, Pomerania, on December 27. This unit was soon under attack from the Red Army. Luebbe was captured on February 1, 1945, and remained in Soviet prison camps until 1955. He settled in Bad Bramstedt, Schleswig-Holstein, where he died on April 25, 1969. Luebbe was promoted to major general on October 1, 1942, and to lieutenant general exactly one year later.

16. Mellenthin, *Panzer Battles*, 377, 380.

17. Feuchtinger was promoted to lieutenant general on August 1, 1944.

18. Wilmot, *The Struggle for Europe*, 538.

19. Wend von Wietershein was born in Neuland, Landkreis Loewenberg, Lower Silesia, on April 8, 1900. He was educated in cadet schools and joined the Imperial Army as a *Faehnrich* in the 4th Hussars on August 6, 1918. He was commissioned the following year and was chosen for the *Reichsheer*. A convert to the mobile branch, he was a major and adjutant of the 3rd Panzer Division when the war began. He moved progressive up the promotion chain, assuming command of the 3rd Motorcycle Battalion (March 5, 1940), 113th Panzer Grenadier Regiment (July 20, 1941), and 11th Panzer Division (August 10, 1943). In the process, he was promoted to lieutenant colonel (1941), colonel

(1943), major general (November 1, 1943), and lieutenant general (July 1, 1944). He was also very highly decorated, earning the Knight's Cross with Oak Leaves and Swords. He died on September 19, 1975, at Bad Honnef, near Bonn, in the Rhineland.

20. Heinrich-Walter Bronsart von Schellendorff was born in Neustrelitz, Mecklenburg-Vorpommern (in the northeast part of present-day Germany) on September 21, 1906. He joined the *Reichsheer* as a *Fahnenjunker* in 1924 and was commissioned in 1928. He spent the entire 1924–39 period in the 6th Cavalry Regiment at Pasewalk, reaching the ranks of first lieutenant (1932) and captain of cavalry in 1935. When World War II began, he was named commander of the mounted squadron of the 179th Reconnaissance Battalion and served in the Saar . He became commander of the 36th Motorized Reconnaissance Battalion in November 1939 and led it in France (1940), the conquest of the Baltic States (1941), and northern Russia (1941–42). He was promoted to major in January 1940 and given command of the 36th Motorcycle Battalion in March 1942, which he led in northern Russia. On February 1, 1943, he was promoted to lieutenant colonel and given command of the 13th Panzer Grenadier Regiment of the 5th Panzer Division on the Eastern Front. Bronsart was recalled to Germany in the spring of 1944 and was attached to the staff of OKH. In early August 1944, he was sent to Hirschberg to attend a division commanders course, and on September 4, 1944, he assumed command of the 111th Panzer Brigade on the Western Front. He was killed in action at Dieuze, near Metz, on September 22. A colonel since April 1, 1944, he was posthumously promoted to major general.

   Baron Erich von Seckendorff was born in Goerz in 1897. (Apparently, this refers to Greifswald am Goerz, near the shore of the Baltic Sea, north of Neubrandenburg.) He joined the army as a *Fahnenjunker* on August 2, 1914, when World War I began, and was commissioned in the 5th Dragoon Regiment, which fought on the Eastern Front. He served in the *Reichsheer* and was a major commanding the IV Battalion of the 4th Cavalry Regiment in 1937. Promoted to lieutenant colonel in March 1939, he assumed command of the 6th Motorcycle Battalion in May and led it Poland, Belgium, and France. On July 25, 1940, he took command of the 114th Rifle (later Panzer Grenadier) Regiment of the 6th Panzer Division. He fought on the Eastern Front and (except for a period when his regiment was sent to France to rebuild) remained there until the spring of 1943, when he returned to Germany to take charge of the XI Panzer Command of the Replacement Army. He was promoted to colonel on February 1, 1942. Seckendorff assumed command of the 113th Panzer Brigade in the fall of 1944 and was killed in action at Lagarde, west of Metz, on September 23, 1944. He was posthumously promoted to major general.

21. This was apparently Col. (later Lt. Gen.) Arnold Burmeister, the commander of the 25th Panzer Grenadier Division.

22. After the fall of France, Blaskowitz was placed in Fuehrer Reserve on September 21, 1944, he was recalled to active duty and led Army Group G again from December 24, 1944, to January 28, 1945. He led Army Group H in the Netherlands from January 28 to April 7, 1945, and was commander in chief of OB Netherlands when Germany surrendered. Arrested as a war criminal because he had blown up some Dutch dikes to delay the Allied advance (a militarily prudent act), he was broken in spirit and committed suicide in Nuremberg on February 5, 1948.

23. Wilmot, *Struggle for Europe*, 538. Hermann Balck (1893–1982), a Prussian from Danzig, entered the army as an infantry *Fahnenjunker* in 1913. He fought in World War I (where he was wounded three times), served in the *Reichswehr*, and distinguished himself as commander of the 1st Rifle Regiment in France in 1940. Later, he commanded the 3rd Panzer Regiment (1940–41) and the 2nd Panzer Brigade (1941). After a tour of duty with the Office of Mobile Troops at OKH, he led the 11th Panzer Division on the Eastern Front (1942–43), was acting commander of the elite Grossdeutschland Panzer Grenadier Division (1943), and commanded the XIV Panzer Corps in Italy until he was injured in an airplane crash. After he recovered, he served as commander of the XXXX Panzer Corps (1943), XXXXVIII Panzer Corps (1943–44), 4th Panzer Army (late 1944) (all in Russia), Army Group G on the Western Front (1944), and 6th Army in the East (late 1944 to the end of the war). He was awarded the Knight's Cross with Oak Leaves, Swords, and Diamonds and was promoted to lieutenant general on January 1, 1943, and to general of panzer troops on November 1, 1944. He moved to Stuttgart after the war and died in Erbenbach-Rockenau a week before his eighty-ninth birthday.

24. Friedrich Wilhelm von Mellenthin was born in Breslau, Silesia (now Wroclaw, Poland), in 1904. He came from a long line of professional soldiers and servants of Prussia. His father, a lieutenant colonel, was killed in action on the Western Front in 1918. F. W. joined the "Treaty" army as a private in 1924, became a *Fahnenjunker*, and was commissioned in the 7th Cavalry in 1928. An outstanding equestrian even into his eighties, he remained with his regiment until 1935, when he began his General Staff training. In the fall of 1937, he became Ic of *Wehrkreis III*, which took the field as the III Corps in 1939. He was Ia of the 197th Infantry Division in the French campaign (1940) and Ic of the 1st Army in occupied France (1940–41). Mellenthin became Ic of the 2nd Army in the Balkans campaign (1941), German liaison officer to the Italian 2nd Army (1941), Ic of Panzer Army Afrika and its forerunners (1941–42), and acting Ia of the panzer army at El Alamein. He fell ill with amoebic dysentery and was medically evacuated back to Europe in September 1942. After he recovered, he served on the southern sector of the Eastern Front from November 29, 1942, to September 14, 1944, under Knobelsdorff and Balck, as chief of staff of the XXXXVIII Panzer Corps, acting commander of the 8th Panzer Division, and chief of staff of the 4th Panzer Army. Sent to the Western Front, he was chief of staff of Army Group G from September to November 29, 1944.

25. Mellenthin, *Panzer Battles*, 382.

26. Kemp, *The Unknown Battle, Metz, 1944*, 151.

27. Mellenthin, *Panzer Battles*, 383–84.

28. Walter Hoernlein was born in Bluethen, near Karstaedt, in the Westpriegnitz District of Mecklenburg-Vorpommern (which is also called Mecklenburg–Western Pomerania). He joined the Imperial Army as a *Fahnenjunker* in the 140th Infantry Regiment on November 27, 1912. His World War I career was brief: he was wounded and captured by the French on October 5, 1914, and spent the next five years in captivity. Released in 1919, he was nevertheless selected for the *Reichswehr* and spent the Weimar years in the infantry. He commanded a machine-gun company in the 4th Infantry Regiment at Deutsch Krone for seven and a half years (1926–34). After commanding a training battalion at Luebeck (1934–35), Hoernlein was transferred to Hamburg and led

the I Battalion of the 69th Infantry Regiment from October 1935 to November 1, 1939, including the Polish campaign. He was then given command of the 80th Infantry Regiment, which he directed in Luxembourg, France, Belguim, and Russia. He was given command of the elite Grossdeutschland Infantry Regiment on August 1, 1941, and continued to command it after it was expanded into a division in the spring of 1942. Hoernlein remained in command until January 30, 1944. (Balck and Strachwitz temporarily commanded the division when Hoernlein was on leave in 1943). He apparently fell ill because he did not have another assignment until August 1, 1944, when he assumed temporary leadership of the LXIV Corps during the retreat across southwestern France. On September 2, he took command of the LXXXII Corps, fighting on the Loire and in Champagne and Saargebeit. Placed in Fuehrer Reserve on December 1, 1944, he commanded *Wehrkreis II* (the Pomeranian Military District) from February 1 to April 28, 1945. Unable to prevent the Soviets from overrunning his home district, Hoernlein was given command of the XXVII Corps, which was in OKH Reserve on the Eastern Front. He surrendered it to the western Allies on May 3, 1945. Released from the POW camps in 1947, he retired to Cologne, where he died in 1961. He was promoted to first lieutenant (1919), captain (1927), major (1934), lieutenant colonel (1937), colonel (1940), major general (April 1, 1942), lieutenant general (January 1, 1943), and general of infantry (November 9, 1944).

29. Werner Ostendorff was born in Koenigsberg on August 15, 1903 and joined the *Freikorps* at age fifteen, helping put down Communist insurrections in his native East Prussia. He joined the East Prussian 1st Infantry Regiment as a private in 1925 and entered a promotion to second lieutenant in 1930. He transferred to the *Luftwaffe* as a first lieutenant in 1934 and trained as a pilot and aerial observer. He transferred again—this time to the SS—in 1935 and was an instructor (apparently in aerial photo interpretation) until 1938. He then commanded a company in the SS Regiment "Der Fuehrer" and became the commander of the SS-VT's antiaircraft battalion during the Polish campaign of 1939. In the meantime, he impressed Paul Hausser, who made him the first Ia of the SS Division "Das Reich" (later 2nd SS Panzer) in October 1939. He held this position in the French and Russian campaigns (1940–42) and became chief of staff of the SS Panzer Corps (again under Hausser) in June 1942. This unit was redesignated II SS Panzer Corps in June 1943. He distinguished himself in the Battle of Kharkov in March 1943 and, as a result, was given command of the 17th SS Panzer Grenadier Division "Goetz von Berlichingen" in January 1944. He led this command in the Battle of Normandy from D-Day to June 15, when he was seriously wounded near Carentan. He returned to duty on October 21, but he left again in December to become chief of staff of Himmler's Army Group Upper Rhine. Ostendorff assumed command of the 2nd SS Panzer Division on the Eastern Front on February 10, 1945, and led it until March 9, when he was critically wounded by an incendiary shell during the fighting in Hungary. He died in the hospital at Bad Aussee on May 4, 1945. Ostendorff, who was a highly capable and well-liked officer, was one of the few SS officers to refuse to renounce his Christian faith. He had been promoted to SS captain (1936), major (1939), lieutenant colonel (late 1940), colonel (1942), Oberfuehrer (April 20, 1943), major general (April 20, 1944), and lieutenant general (December 1, 1944). He left behind a wife, a son, and a daughter.

30. Cole, *Lorraine Campaign,* 299.
31. Anton Dunckern was the first Gestapo chief in the Saarland after it returned to Germany in 1935. He left the Saarland in 1935. Dunckern survived the war and later practiced law in Munich. He died on December 9, 1981. See Andreas Schulz, *Die Generale der Waffen-SS und der Polizei,* 3 vols. (Bissendorf, Germany: Biblio Verlag, 2003), vol. 1.
32. Mellenthin, *Panzer Battles,* 391.
33. The 21st Panzer Division had 12,350 men, 127 tanks, and 40 assault guns when the Battle of Normandy began. It ended the campaign with 300 combat effectives and a weak battalion of tanks. It absorbed the 112th Panzer Brigade in September and October.
34. Hans Oschmann was born on December 24, 1894, in Schoenberg, a suburb of Berlin. He joined the Kaiser's army as a *Fahnenjunker* in the fall of 1913 and became a second lieutenant in the 1st Telegraph Battalion in June 1914. He served in World War I and the *Reichsheer* and was a lieutenant colonel and commander of the VII Signal Troop Command in 1938. A signals officer most of his career, Oschmann was promoted to colonel (February 1, 1940) and major general (August 1, 1943). He directed the XIII and V Signal Troop Commands (late 1939–1941), the 666th Signal Interception Regiment (1941–42), and the 3rd Signal Reconnaissance Command (1942–early 1943). He assumed command of the 741st Infantry Regiment on March 31, 1943, and led it until the end of July. Then he became commander of the 704th Eastern Troops Unit (August 1, 1943) and the 286th Security Division (November 1, 1943), which he led until August 5, 1944. During this period, the 286th was largely destroyed (along with most of Army Group Center) on the Eastern Front. After a leave, Hans Oschmann assumed command of the 338th Infantry Division of Army Group G. He was killed in action at Faunbe in southeastern France on November 14, 1944. He was posthumously promoted to lieutenant general.

    Rudolf von Oppen was born in Koblenz in the Rhineland-Palatinate on October 25, 1887. He was educated in the cadet schools and joined the army as a *Fahnenjunker* in the 1st Guards Regiment in 1905. He fought in World War I and was discharged in 1920 with the honorary rank of major. He returned to active duty as a major of reserves in 1936 and was promoted to major general of reserves on January 1, 1945. In the meantime, he commanded a replacement battalion (1939) and the 23rd Replacement Regiment (1940). He became Ia of the LX Corps, Ia of the LXXXIV Corps (1940), chief of staff of the LXXXIII Corps (1942–43), chief of staff of the LXXXV Corps (October 1943–March 1944), commander of Fortress Brigade Belford (November 1944), and commander of the 338th Infantry Division (1944). He commanded the 352nd Volksgrenadier Division, the 805th Replacement Division, and the 352nd Volksgrenadier again (1945). He was captured on April 29, 1945. After being released from prison, Oppen settled at Hugstetten, Baden, and died in 1954.
35. Mellenthin, *Panzer Battles,* 396.
36. Cole, *Lorraine Campaign,* 464.
37. Edwin von Rothkirch und Trach was born in Militsch, Lower Silesia (now Milicz, Poland), on November 1, 1888. He was educated in cadet schools, joined the army as a second lieutenant in the 17th Dragoon Regiment in 1908, fought in World War I, and was accepted into the *Reichsheer.* In 1934, he became commander of the 15th (Prussian) Cavalry Regiment in Paderborn, North

Rhine–Westphalia. He was given command of the 2nd Rifle Brigade of the 2nd Panzer Division in Meiningen, southern Thuringia, in March 1938, but Rothkirch did not seem suited to the armored branch. In any case, he was given a sector command near Breslau, Silesia, in late 1938, which was a definite step down. Upon mobilization, he became chief of staff of the XXXIV Corps Command (not quite a corps level headquarters), with which he served in Poland (1939). He then assumed command of the 442nd Landsschützen Division, made up mainly of men forty-five years of age and older, which was posted on the Dutch frontier in 1940. After the fall of Paris, Rothkirch returned to Poland was chief of the 365th Higher Field Administrative Command (*Oberfeldkommandantur 365*) in Warsaw (1940–42). On January 5, 1942, he was given command of the 330th Infantry Division of the 3rd Panzer Army on the central sector of the Eastern Front. Rothkirch was rear area commander for Army Group Center from September 1943 until the end of the year; then he commanded an ad hoc corps. On November 3, 1944, he assumed command of the LIII Corps on the Western Front. He had made a nice professional recovery since his unsuccessful command of the 2nd Rifle Brigade in 1938. Rothkirch was captured just east of the Rhine by the Americans in March 1945. Meanwhile, he had been promoted to colonel (1936), major general (March 1, 1940), lieutenant general (March 1, 1942), and general of cavalry (January 1, 1944). He lived in Oberurff, Hesse, West Germany, after the war and died on July 29, 1980.

38. Franz Vaterrodt was born in Diedenhofen, Lothringen (now Thionville, Lorraine, France), in 1890. He joined the army as an infantry *Fahnenjunker* in 1909 and had a rather undistinguished career. Discharged in 1920, he joined the Baden Police and rose to the rank of colonel. He rejoined the army as a lieutenant colonel in 1934 and was commandant of Strassburg from March 3, 1941, until its surrender. He was promoted to major general on March 1, 1941.

39. Arnold Burmeister was born in Norburg, on Alsen Island, a Danish island in the Baltic Sea, in 1899. He joined the army as a private in the 24th Infantry Regiment on June 7, 1916, rose to the rank of *Faehnrich*, and was captured by the French on October 25, 1917. He returned to Germany in late 1919 and was discharged as an honorary lieutenant in 1920. He re-enlisted in the *Reichsheer* as a corporal in 1922 and was finally promoted to second lieutenant in 1924. He spent the years from 1922 to 1939 in the *Preussisch-Mecklenburgisches* 14th Cavalry Regiment at Ludwigslust, eventually becoming a battalion commander. In February 1939, however, he transferred to the armored branch and joined the staff of the 6th Panzer Regiment at Zossen. He led the II Battalion in Poland, Holland, Belgium, and France. In May 1941, he was transferred to the Panzer Troop Branch of OKH, and in late October, he assumed a similiar post with the Replacement Army. He was given command of the 201st Panzer Regiment, a unit equipped with captured French tanks, in Paris in July 1942. He returned to the Eastern Front as commander of the 23rd Panzer Grenadier Brigade of the 23rd Panzer Division in October 1942, but it was dissolved on November 11, 1942, and Burgmeister returned to Germany as commander of the 202nd Panzer Regiment (also equipped with French tanks) at Stuttgart later that month. In January 1943, Burmeister was sent back to France to command the 26th Panzer Regiment at Amiens. He was then given command of the 21st Panzer Brigade of the 20th Panzer Division on the Eastern Front. He led it from March 18 to July 18, 1943, when he was critically wounded during the Bat-

tle of Kursk. He remained in various hospitals until the spring of 1944, when he returned to active duty at Wuensdorf as a department chief in the Instruction Office of the Panzer Inspectorate.

Arnold Burmeister returned to the battlefield on October 9, 1944, as commander of the 25th Panzer Grenadier Division on the Western Front. It fought in the Siegfried Line and in the Saar. Later, in early 1945, it was transferred to the 9th Army on the Oder sector. On April 25, 1945, as the 9th Army was being destroyed, Burmeister was ordered to assume command of the XXX Corps of the 25th Army in the Netherlands. He thus escaped Soviet captivity but was unable to reach his new command. He was captured by the British on May 3, 1945, and was a POW until February 1947.

Burmeister was promoted to first lieutenant (1928), captain of cavalry (1933), major (1936), lieutenant colonel (1940), colonel (April 1, 1942), and major general (January 1, 1945). He received an accelerated promotion to lieutenant general on April 20, 1945. He died in 1988 in Stuehlingen, Baden-Wurttemberg, on the Swiss border.

40. The U.S. 379th Infantry Regiment captured the first bunkers of the West Wall.
41. Hans von Obstfelder was born in Steinbach-Hallenberg, Hessen-Nassau, in 1886. He entered the service as a *Fahnenjunker* in the Bavarian 5th Field Artillery Regiment in 1905 and was promoted to colonel on March 1, 1933, a month after Hitler took power. Promotions to major general (1936), lieutenant general (1938), and general of infantry (June 1, 1940) followed. Obstfelder commanded the 28th Infantry Division (1936–40), XXIX Corps (1940–43), LXXXVI Corps (1943–late 1944), 1st Army (December 1, 1944–February 28, 1945), and 19th Army (March 1–28, 1945). Despite his pro-Nazi political convictions, he was sacked by Hitler near the end of the war. After being released from the POW camps, Obstfelder resided in Kassel, Hessen, where he died in late 1976, at the age of ninety.
42. After he was released from house arrest, Mellenthin commanded a regiment in the 9th Panzer Division during the last stages of the Battle of the Bulge. He became chief of staff of the 5th Panzer Army on March 5, 1945, during the Battle of the Ruhr Pocket. He was captured by the Americans on May 3. After being released from the POW camps, the homeless and penniless Mellenthin emigrated to South Africa, founded an airline, and died a millionaire in Johannesburg on June 28, 1997, at the age of ninety-two.
43. Helmut Staedke was born in Munich, Bavaria, in 1905. He entered the *Reichsheer* as a *Fahnenjunker* on April 24, 1924, and was commissioned in the 7th Artillery Regiment in Munich in late 1927. He underwent General Staff training in the 1930s and in 1938 was a General Staff officer with the 4th Panzer Division. After fighting in Poland (1939), he was named chief of operations (Ia) of the 6th Panzer Division, with which he saw action in Belgium and France (1940). After a short stint on the staff of the War Academy (1940–41), he was attached to the staff of Army Group North for the invasion of the Soviet Union (1941). In August of that year, however, he was named Ia of the 20th Panzer Division, also on the Eastern Front. He held this post until October 1942, when he was attached to the operations branch of the General Staff. In January 1943, he became chief of staff of the XXXV Corps on the central sector of the Russian Front. In September, he was promoted again, this time to chief of staff of the 9th Army, also in central Russia. The 9th Army was crushed in July

1944 and XXXV Corps was forced to surrender; Staedke, however, was promoted again on November 29, 1944, when he was selected to replace F. W. von Mellenthin as chief of staff of Army Group G on the southern sector of the Western Front. He gave up his post in February 1945 to attend a division commanders' course and, on April 26, assumed command of the 198th Infantry Division on the southern sector of the Western Front. Meanwhile, he was promoted to lieutenant general on April 1, 1945. Earlier he had been promoted to lieutenant colonel (1942), colonel (1943), and major general (April 1, 1944). He surrendered to the Americans in May 1945. After being discharged from the POW camps, he resided in Tuebingen and died on September 3, 1974.

CHAPTER 10

1. Moulton, *Battle for Antwerp*, 77. The maximum daily capacities of other ports included Dieppe (7,000 tons), LeHavre (5,000 tons), Boulogne (11,000 tons), Calais (personnel and LSTs only), and Ostend (5,000 tons).
2. Harry Crerar (1888–1965) was a hydroelectric engineer. Called up in 1914, he rose to the rank of lieutenant colonel during World War I and never left the army until his retirement in 1946. During World War II, he was chief of the Canadian General Staff (1940–41) and commanded the Canadian 2nd Infantry Division (1941–42), Canadian I Corps (1942–44), and Canadian 1st Army (1944–46). Politically astute and an excellent staff officer, Crerar was a mediocre field commander, and Montgomery had little confidence in him.
3. Simonds (1903–74) was a much more capable commander than was Crerar. He was commander of the 1st Field Regiment, Royal Canadian Horse Artillery, in 1940. Four years later, he was commanding an army. He served as chief of the Canadian General Staff from 1951 to 1955.
4. Wilmot, *Struggle for Europe*, 56.
5. Kurt Eberding was born in Reppline, Silesia, in 1895 and joined the army as a *Fahnenjunker* at the end of August 1914. He was commissioned in the infantry in 1915, served in *Jäger* battalions during World War I, and then served in the *Freikorps*. He joined the *Reichswehr* in 1920 and spent the rest of his career in infantry units. He was commander of the II Battalion of the 53rd Infantry Regiment when World War II began. He served in Poland and the Western Campaign of 1940; then he assumed command of the 53rd, which he led on the Russian Front (November 1941–August 1943). He led the 38th Infantry Division in the southern sector of the Eastern Front from August 25, 1943, until it was disbanded because of heavy casualties in November. He was promoted to major general on September 1, 1943, but was without an assignment until July 5, 1944, when he was given command of the 64th Infantry Division. A POW until August 1947, he resided in Solingen (just south of the Ruhr) after he release. He died in 1978.
6. Wilhelm Daser (1884–1968) was born in Germersheim and attended cadet schools in Bavaria. He joined the army as a *Faehnrich* in the 15th Bavarian Infantry Regiment in 1905. He fought in World War I, where he distinguished himself, and ended the war commanding a regiment at the age of thirty with the relatively low rank of major. He served in infantry units in the *Reichswehr* era and retired as a lieutenant colonel in 1931. He was recalled to active duty in late 1933 as a territorial officer and was promoted to colonel (E) in 1937. He

did not achieve full active-duty status until 1941. He nevertheless commanded the 388th Infantry Regiment (1939–September 1941) on the Eastern Front. Daser, however, developed heart trouble and had to be relieved. When he returned to active duty, he commanded the 251st Replacement Regiment (January–July 1942). He then directed a series of field administrative area commands until early 1944, when he became commander of the 165th Reserve Division. He assumed command of the 70th Infantry Division on May 15, 1944, and was promoted to lieutenant general on August 1. He resided in Ingofstadt, Bavaria, after the war.

Bibliography

Blumenson, Martin. *Breakout and Pursuit.* Washington, DC: Office of the Chief of Military History, Department of the Army, 1961.

———. "Recovery of France." In Vincent J. Esposito, ed., *A Concise History of World War II.* New York: Praeger, 1964.

Blumenson, Martin, and the editors of Time-Life Books. *Liberation.* Alexandria, Va.: Time-Life Books, 1978.

Blumentritt, Guenther. *Von Rundstedt.* London: Odhams Press, 1952.

Brandenberger, Erich. "Seventh Army (1 Sep 1944-25 Jan 1945)." Foreign Military Studies MS # 447.

Breuer, William B. *Hitler's Fortress Cherbourg: The Conquest of a Bastion.* New York: Stein and Day, 1984.

Brownlow, Donald Grey. *Panzer Baron: The Military Exploits of General Hasso von Manteuffel.* North Quincy, Mass.: Christopher Publishing House, 1975.

Chandler, Alfred D., Jr., ed. *The Papers of Dwight D. Eisenhower.* 5 vols. Baltimore: Johns Hopkins Press, 1970.

Chandler, David G., and James L. Collins, eds. *The D-Day Encyclopedia.* New York: Simon & Schuster, 1994.

Cole, Hugh M. *The Lorraine Campaign.* Washington, DC: Historical Division, Department of the Army, 1950.

Cooper, Matthew. *The German Army, 1933–1945: Its Political and Military Failure.* London: Macdonald and Jane's, 1978.

Eisenhower, John S. D. *The Bitter Woods.* New York: Putnam, 1969.

Esposito, Vincent J., ed. *A Concise History of World War II.* New York: Praeger, 1964.

Foster, Tony. *Meeting of Generals.* Toronto: Lorevan Publishing, 1986.

Fuerbringer, Herbert. *9. SS-Panzer-Division "Hohenstaufen".* Heimdal, Germany: Editions Heimdal, 1984.

Fuller, J. F. C. *The Second World War, 1939–1945: A Strategical and Tactical History.* 3 vols. New York: Duell, Sloan and Pearce, 1949.

Gavin, James M. *Airborne Warfare.* Washington, DC: Infantry Journal Press, 1947.

Goralski, Robert. *World War II Almanac, 1931–1945: A Political and Military Record.* New York: Putnam, 1981.

Guderian, Heinz. *Panzer Leader.* London: M. Joseph, 1952.

Guderian, Heinz Günther. *From Normandy to the Ruhr with the 116th Panzer Division in World War II.* Bedford, PA: Aberjona Press, 2001.

Guingand, Francis de. *Operation Victory.* New York: Scribner's Sons, 1947.

Harrison, Gordon A. *Cross-Channel Attack.* Washington, DC: Office of the Chief of Military History, Department of the Army, 1951.

Hart, B. H. Liddell. *The Second World War.* New York: Putnam, 1970.

Haupt, Werner. *Das Buch der Panzertruppe, 1916–1945*. Friedberg, Germany: Podzun-Pallas, 1989.

Hildebrand, Hans H., and Ernst Henriot. *Deutschlands Admirale, 1849–1945*. 3 vols. Osnabrück, Germany: Biblio, 1988–96.

Horrocks, Sir Brian. *A Full Life*. London: L. Cooper, 1974.

Irving, David. *The Rise and Fall of the Luftwaffe: The Life of Luftwaffe Marshall Erhard Milch*. London: Weidenfeld & Nicolson, 1973.

———. *The War Path: Hitler's Germany, 1933–1939*. New York: Viking Press, 1979.

Jacobsen, H. A., and J. Rohwer, eds. *Decisive Battles of World War II: The German View*. New York: Putnam, 1965.

Keegan, John. *Six Armies in Normandy: From D-Day to the Liberation of Paris*. New York: Penguin Books, 1982.

Keilig, Wolf. *Die Generale des Heeres*. Friedberg, Germany: Podzun-Pallas-Verlag, 1983.

Kemp, Anthony. *The Unknown Battle, Metz, 1944*. New York: Stein and Day, 1981.

Kraetschmer, Ernst-Guenther. *Die Ritterkreuztraeger der Waffen-SS*. Preussisch Oldendorf, Germany: KW Schutz, 1982.

MacDonald, Charles B. *The Battle of the Huertgen Forest*. New York: Modern Literary Editions Publishing Co., 1963.

———. *The Mighty Endeavor: American Armed Forces in the European Theater in World War II*. New York: Oxford University Press, 1969.

———. *The Siegfried Line Campaign*. Washington, DC: Office of the Chief of Military History, Department of the Army, 1963.

Mason, David. *Breakout: The Drive to the Seine*. New York: Ballantine Books, 1969.

Mehner, Kurt, ed. *Die Geheimen Tagesberichte der deutschen Wehrmachtfuehrung im Zweiten Weltkrieg, 1939–1945*. 12 vols. Osnabrück, Germany: Biblio Verlag, 1984–95.

Mellenthin, F. W. von. *Panzer Battles: A Study of the Employment of Armor in the Second World War*. Norman, OK: University of Oklahamo Press, 1956.

Meyer, Kurt. *Grenadiers*. Mechanicsburg, PA: Stackpole Books, 2005.

Milward, Alan S. *The German Economy at War*. London: University of London, Athlone Press, 1965.

Mitcham, Samuel W. *Desert Fox in Normandy*. Westport, CT: Praeger, 1997.

———. *German Order of Battle*. 3 vols. Mechanicsburg, PA: Stackpole Books, 2007.

Montgomery, Bernard Law, The Viscount of Alamein. *Normandy to the Baltic*. Boston: Houghton Mifflin, 1948.

Moulton, J. L. *The Battle for Antwerp: The Liberation of the City and the Opening of the Scheldt*. London: I. Allan, 1978.

Nafziger, George F. *The German Order of Battle*. 2 vols. London: Greenhill Books, 1999.

Powell, Geoffrey. *The Devil's Birthday: The Bridges to Arnhem, 1944*. London: Buchan & Enright, 1984.

Preradovich, Nikolaus von. *Die Generale der Waffen-SS*. Berg am See, Germany: Vowinckel-Verlag, 1985.

Ritgen, Helmut. *Die Geschichte der Panzer-Lehr-Division im Westen, 1944–1945*. Stuttgart, Germany: Motorbuch-Verlag, 1979.

Ryan, Cornelius. *A Bridge Too Far*. New York: Simon and Schuster, 1974.

Schneider, Jost W. *Verleihung Genehmigt!* Winder McConnell, ed. and trans. San Jose, CA: R. James Bender Publishing, 1977.

Schulz, Andreas. *Die Generale der Waffen-SS und der Polizei*. 3 vols. Bissendorf, Germany: Biblio Verlag, 2003.

Seaton, Albert. *The Fall of Fortress Europe, 1943–1945.* New York: Holmes and Meier Publishers, 1981.

———. *The German Army, 1933–45.* New York: New American Library, 1985.

Shulman, Milton. *Defeat in the West.* New York: Dutton, 1948.

Speidel, Hans. *Invasion 1944: Rommel and the Normandy Campaign.* Chicago: Regnery, 1950.

Stauffenberg, Theodor-Friedrich von. Papers.

Stoves, Rolf. *Die Gepanzerten und motorisierten deutschen Grossverbaende: Divisionen und selbständige Brigaden, 1935–1945.* Friedberg, Germany: Podzun-Pallas-Verlag, 1986.

Tessin, Georg. *Verbaende und Truppen des deutschen Wehrmacht und Waffen-SS im Zweiten Weltkrieg, 1939–1945.* 17 vols. Frankfurt am Main, Germany: Mittler, 1966–2002.

Toland, John. *Adolf Hitler.* Garden City, NY: Doubleday, 1976.

War Office, Great Britain. *The Trials of German Major War Criminals.* 42 vols. 1978.

Westphal, Siegfried. *The German Army in the West.* London: Cassell, 1951.

Whiting, Charles. *The Battle of the Hurtgen Forest: The Untold Story of a Disastrous Campaign.* New York: Orion Books, 1989.

———. *Bloody Aachen.* New York: Stein and Day, 1976.

———. *'44: In Combat from Normandy to the Ardennes.* New York: Stein and Day, 1984.

———. *Ghost Front: The Ardennes before the Battle of the Bulge.* Cambridge, Mass.: Da Capo, 2002.

———. *Siegfried: The Nazis' Last Stand.* New York: Stein and Day, 1982.

Wilmot, Chester. *The Struggle for Europe.* New York: Harper, 1952.

Yerger, Mark. *Waffen-SS Commanders: The Army, Corps, and Divisional Leaders of a Legend.* 2 vols. Atglen, PA: Schiffer, 1997–99.

Zweng, Christian, ed. *Die Dienstlaufbahnen der Offiziere des Generalstabes des deutschen Heeres, 1935–1945.* 3 vols. Osnabrück, Germany: Biblio, 1995–98.

Index

Stackpole Military History Series

Real battles. Real soldiers. Real stories.

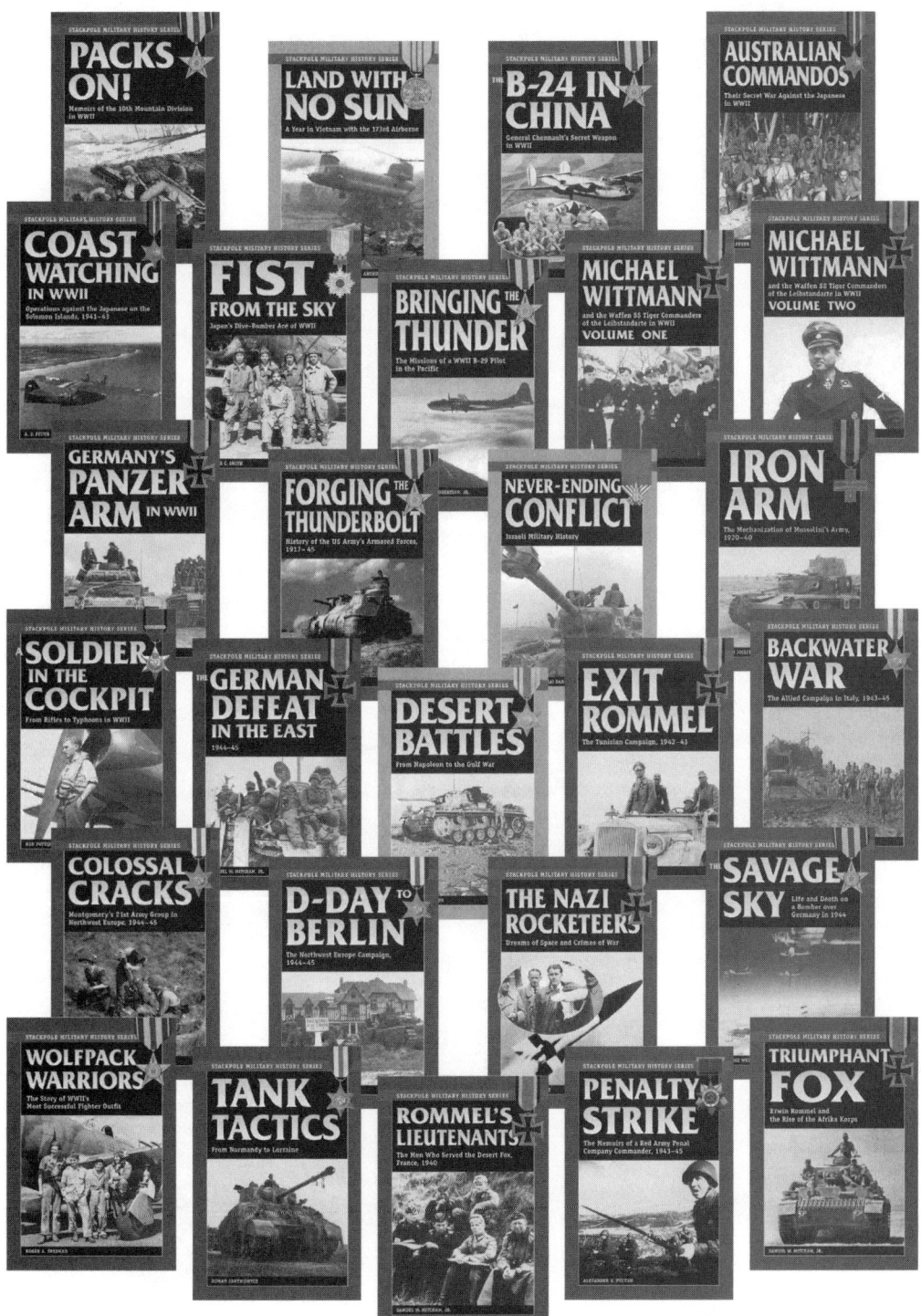

Stackpole Military History Series

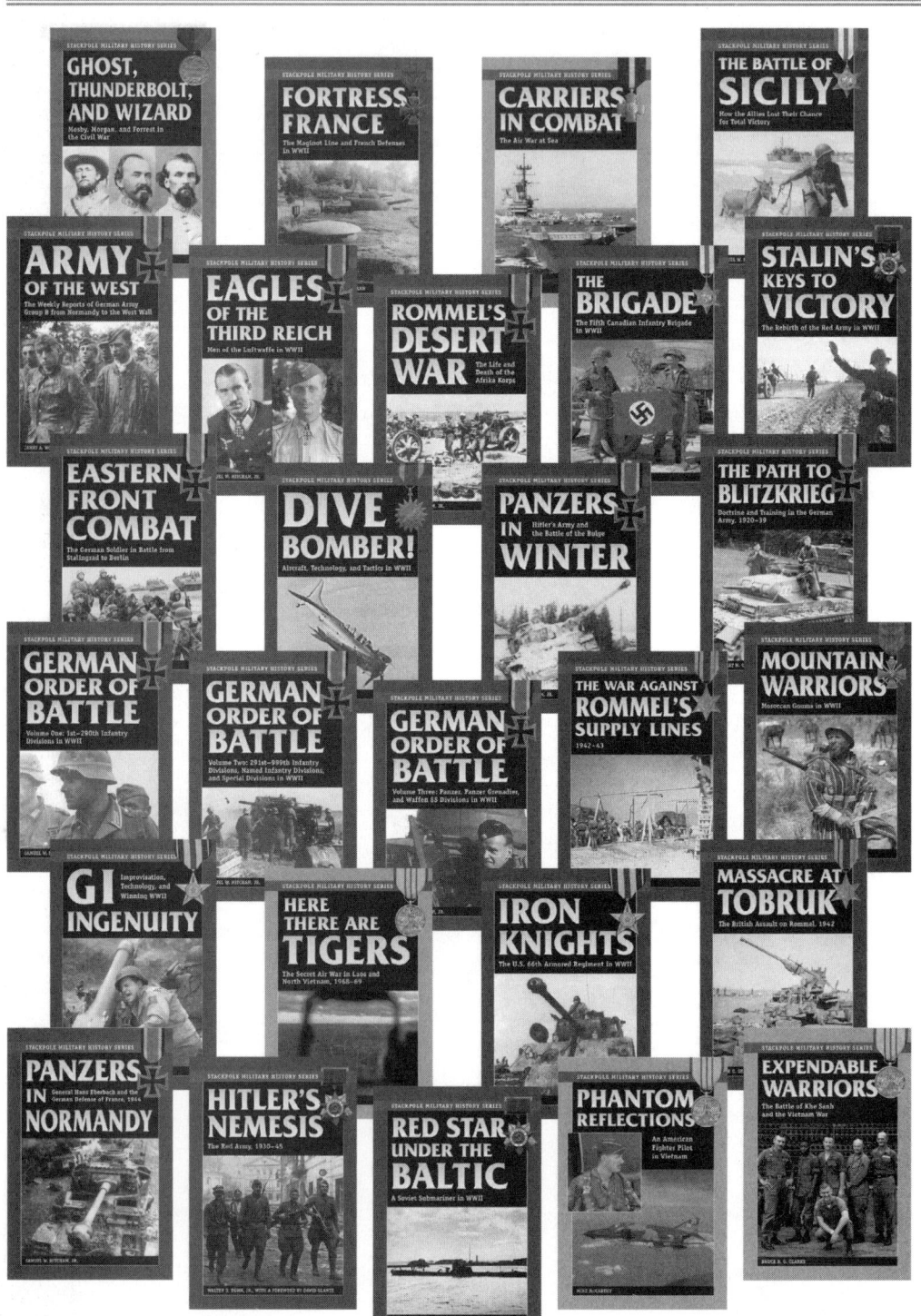

Real battles. Real soldiers. Real stories.

Stackpole Military History Series

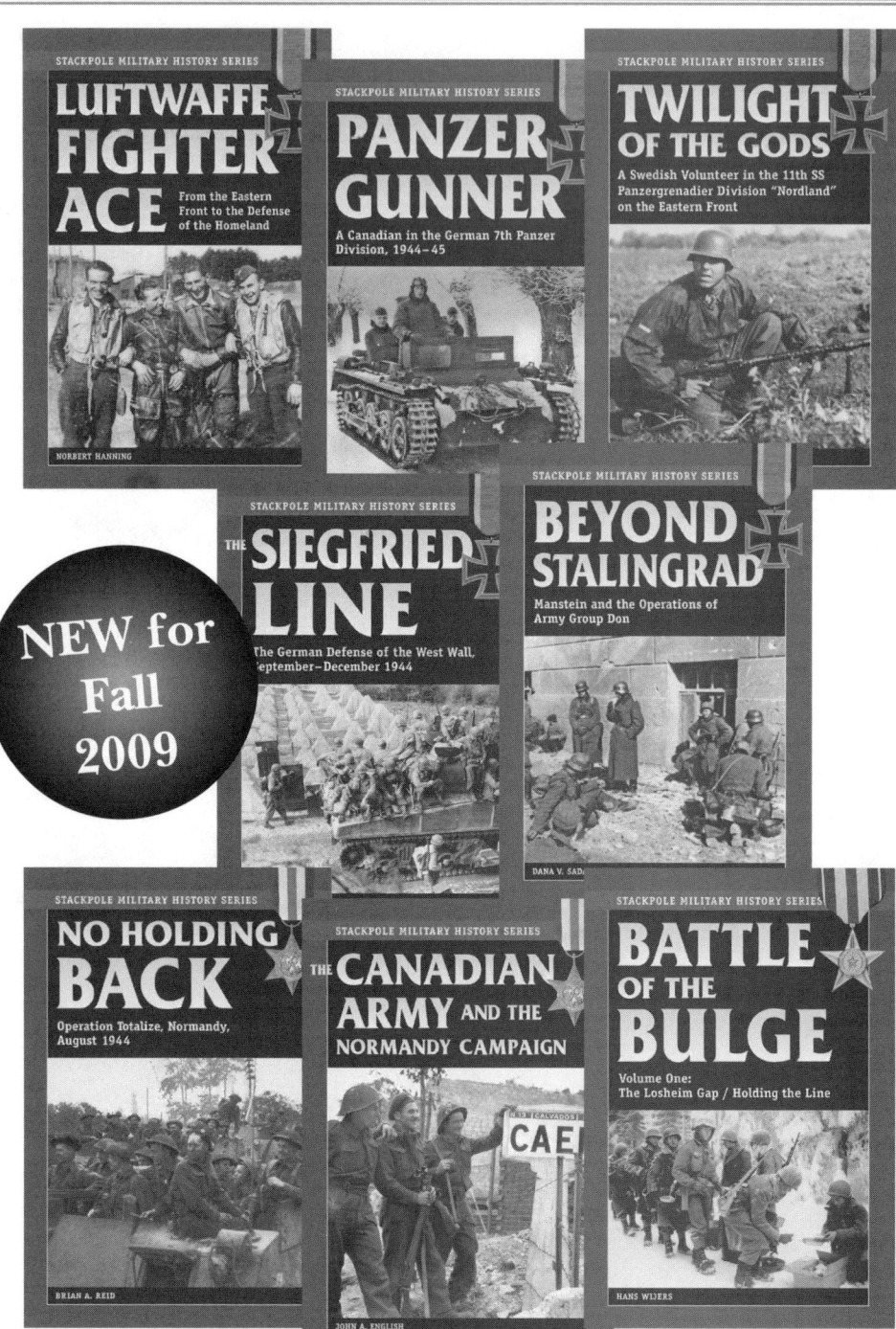

STACKPOLE MILITARY HISTORY SERIES

LUFTWAFFE FIGHTER ACE
From the Eastern Front to the Defense of the Homeland

NORBERT HANNING

STACKPOLE MILITARY HISTORY SERIES

PANZER GUNNER
A Canadian in the German 7th Panzer Division, 1944–45

STACKPOLE MILITARY HISTORY SERIES

TWILIGHT OF THE GODS
A Swedish Volunteer in the 11th SS Panzergrenadier Division "Nordland" on the Eastern Front

NEW for Fall 2009

STACKPOLE MILITARY HISTORY SERIES

THE SIEGFRIED LINE
The German Defense of the West Wall, September–December 1944

STACKPOLE MILITARY HISTORY SERIES

BEYOND STALINGRAD
Manstein and the Operations of Army Group Don

DANA V. SADA

STACKPOLE MILITARY HISTORY SERIES

NO HOLDING BACK
Operation Totalize, Normandy, August 1944

BRIAN A. REID

STACKPOLE MILITARY HISTORY SERIES

THE CANADIAN ARMY AND THE NORMANDY CAMPAIGN

JOHN A. ENGLISH

STACKPOLE MILITARY HISTORY SERIES

BATTLE OF THE BULGE
Volume One: The Losheim Gap / Holding the Line

HANS WIJERS

Real battles. Real soldiers. Real stories.

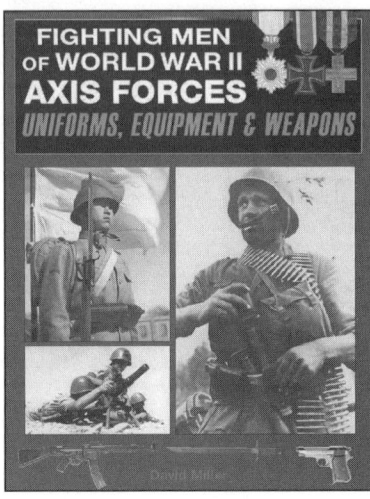
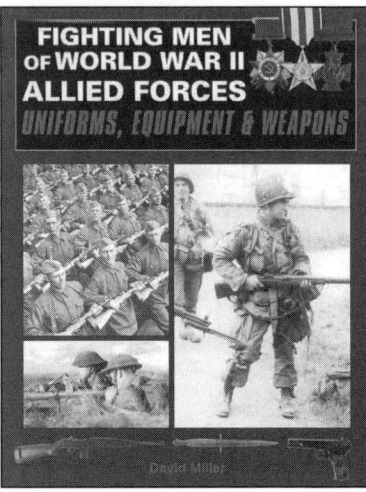